D0422798

The Market System

The Institution for Social and Policy Studies at Yale University

The Yale ISPS Series

# The Market System

*What It Is, How It Works,*
*and What To Make of It*

CHARLES E. LINDBLOM

Yale University Press   New Haven & London

Copyright © 2001 by Yale University.
All rights reserved.
This book may not be reproduced, in whole or in part, including illustrations, in any form (beyond that copying permitted by Sections 107 and 108 of the U.S. Copyright Law and except by reviewers for the public press), without written permission from the publishers.

Designed by James J. Johnson and set in Trump type by The Composing Room of Michigan, Inc.
Printed in the United States of America by R. R. Donnelley & Sons, Harrisonburg, Virginia.

*Library of Congress Cataloging-in-Publication Data*

Lindblom, Charles Edward, 1917–
The market system: what it is, how it works, and what to make of it / Charles E. Lindblom.
p. cm. — (Yale ISPS series)
Includes bibliographical references and index.
ISBN 0-300-08752-7 (alk. paper)
1. Capitalism. I. Title. II. Series.

HB501.L512    2001
330.12′2—dc21                                      00-043865

A catalogue record for this book is available from the British Library.

The paper in this book meets the guidelines for permanence and durability of the Committee on Production Guidelines for Book Longevity of the Council on Library Resources.

10  9  8  7  6  5  4  3  2  1

# Contents

# Acknowledgments

To explain and analyze the market system in such a way as to interest and satisfy a wide audience, I asked a number of people, young and old, well read and not, patient and less so, pro market and anti, to read the manuscript and give me their advice. I am grateful to them all—from those who read a chapter or two to those who consented to read the entire manuscript with sustained care. In acknowledging their contributions, I would like to single out several of them for their unusual and/or continuing help but cannot do so without falling into invidious distinctions wherever I might draw a line between the short and the long list. To all contributors, my thanks both for their efforts and for what I learned from them.

They are: Susan Rose-Ackerman, Michael Barzelay, Hans Blokland, David K. Cohen, John Covell, Robert A. Dahl, Susan Friedman, Laura Gilbert, Ronald L. Jepperson, Ira Katznelson, Alvin K. Klevorick, Steven W. Lindblom, Eric N. Lindblom, Richard R. Nelson, Bruce Nichols, Merton J. Peck, Howard R. Sacks, Ian Shapiro, Christopher D. Timmins, James Tobin, Shaoguang Wang, Edward J. Woodhouse, Ross Zucker, and the late William N. Parker.

For many helpful discussions, my thanks to Robert E. Lane.

For secretarial work, I happily acknowledge the intelligent and spirited help of Pamela A. Lamonaca and Pamela A. Greene, as well as the support of the Yale Institution for Social and Policy Studies, especially Donald Green and Barbara Dozier.

# Market System Ascendant

The massive social changes with which the twentieth century gave way to the twenty-first have written the preface to this book. Much of the world began an unexpected transformation. Communist systems are abandoning central planning of their economies and struggling to establish the market system in its place. China freed its farmers to produce and sell for profit rather than under instruction from the state. It began moving industry out from under the system of state-prescribed targets and quotas. Less buoyant, Russians try to swim in the same tide, both their Berlin Wall and their economy having come down in ruins.

Much earlier, the democratic world had been surprised to see the democratic socialists of Western Europe abandon their traditional ideological hostility to the market system. After World War II, they no longer pressed to abolish it. Instead socialist parties in France, Italy, and Britain advocated a new kind of market system, with state-owned rather than private market enterprises. But not for long. They began to turn to the familiar capitalist private corporation while they pursued their socialist aspirations through income redistribution and the social programs of the welfare state. And so, like the British Labour Party today, they talk not of state-owned enterprises but a "third way"—a way not yet well defined but in any case embracing the market system.

Meanwhile, nonsocialists, both liberal and conservative, have taken a renewed interest in the market system, resist-

ing both government regulation of business and social welfare programs. Much of their change of heart seems motivated by what they see as failures of the state: bureaucratic
lethargy, for example, or excesses of partisanship. Some of
it, however, arises out of the case now often made for the
market system—as, for example, in the drive toward a common market for Europe, in globalization, and in exploiting
the opportunities of the "New Economy."

Despite this great current of change, transition of communist systems to the market system may never be complete. Some nations of the former USSR—perhaps Russia itself—may return to old ways rather than continue to suffer
the hardships of transition. Many Russians see their embryonic market system as a cousin to gangsterism, so exploitative has become their transitional system—whatever it
might be called. Russia today reveals some of the worst aspects of the market system. The end of the story has yet to
be written.

What a beginning to a century! These great changes and
failures ask for a book neither to celebrate nor deplore but to
understand the market system, around which the dramas
revolve.

One can study economics for many years without understanding the market system. I graduated from college without understanding it. If my instructors understood it, they
did not take the trouble to explain its structure. They
taught about trees rather than forest, about inflation, monopoly, and international trade. They somehow failed to
present the overarching structure of social organization
called the market system. You perhaps have seen a picture
full of diverting detail that only on careful examination

abruptly reveals a face or other object that had been hidden in all the detail. That was my problem: detail was abundant, but for years I could not find the face.

For at least 150 years many societies have been trapped in an ill-tempered debate about market systems. Now we have an opportunity to think about these systems with a new dispassion and clarity. Market ideologues have learned that there is little to fear from communism. They can come away from their ideological barricades and talk sense about the market and its problems. On their side, socialist ideologues have realized that aspiring for a better society is not enough. They have to face the complexities of constructing one.

Even so, it will not be easy to think straight about the market. Mainstream economics still stumbles because the market's dazzling benefits half blind it to the defects. On the other hand, many critics perceive the benefits only through the smoke of their burning disapprobation. An often tight-lipped rigidity persists, even in the most scholarly discourse. One does not find much intellectual interchange on the market system between economists, most of whom admire it, and those scholars of history, literature, and philosophy who, like the sociologist-philosopher Jürgen Habermas, judge its consequences for values like freedom, rationality, and morality.

One's understanding of the market system is sometimes impeded by a sense of mystery or magic about how it works. Adam Smith acknowledged as much when he wrote, more than two hundred years ago, that market activities are coordinated by a "hidden hand." In our time, the full account must describe the workings of both the hidden hand and the many visible hands.

## What Is This Market System?

We need first to draw a distinction between market system and market. Although not all societies embrace or contain a market system, all existing societies make use of markets. Walking down a street in either Maoist China or the USSR, a visitor would have seen markets for haircuts, bicycle repair, and consumer commodities. An observant visitor would soon also have found markets (perhaps more black than legal) for raw materials and machines. Whenever people frequently pay other people to do something—sing a song or dig coal—those interchanges constitute markets. Yet despite the commonalty of such interchanges in Maoist China and the Soviet Union, these societies were not called market systems, because a market system exists only when markets proliferate and link with each other in a particular way. Just as a basket of parts does not make a computer until they are assembled or used in a particular way, so an assortment of markets does not make a market system until they are employed in a particular way—specifically to organize or coordinate many of the activities of a society.

The market system organizes or coordinates activities not through governmental planning but through the mutual interactions of buyers and sellers. To establish a market system it is not enough that people buy and sell. Also required is that their purchases and sales, not central authorities, coordinate the society. This gives us a definition of the market system sufficient for our immediate purposes: it is a system of societywide coordination of human activities not by central command but by mutual interactions in the form of transactions.

I find it useful to contrast the market system with another method of organization, though only small scale: the household. In premarket households, paternal or other authority coordinated the activities of members of the household to try to provide the necessities and pleasures of life. The household was organized to produce for its own use whatever was needed or wanted. It coordinated child rearing, housekeeping, and cultivation of the soil. Householders might only now and then reach beyond the household for some assistance—perhaps musicians for a wedding—or for a commodity they could not provide for themselves. They might only rarely see a coin. The market system appeared only when these households began to attempt production for sales rather than for household use—that is, when they became deeply engaged in producing for distant others rather than simply for family. Only then arose such large-scale and detailed social coordination as market systems provide.

Market systems did not wholly displace the production-for-use household. The household remains a bedrock of the contemporary market system, continuing to organize much of child rearing, food preparation, and maintenance of the home. What, then, changes with the rise of the market system? Typically, the household allocates one or more members of the family to go outside the household with production for sale—he becomes a cobbler, making shoes to sell—so that the household can obtain objects and assistance that it cannot produce on its own.

If not just a household but a whole society is to be coordinated, then in a wider social process the participants have to be assigned to the many tasks that need doing. Tools and machinery have to be made available to those who can use them. Farmers need to feed not only themselves but those engaged in industry. Hypothetically, this can all be arranged through central command, but in historical fact, it has been largely arranged by buying and selling.

Three kinds of markets are the most familiar: labor markets, agricultural markets, and markets for services and goods that industry provides to consumers. Two less obvious kinds of markets are no less necessary for a market system. One is markets for intermediate services and goods produced for other producers—for example, computer chips sold to enterprises that assemble computers from purchased parts. The other is markets for capital, specifically markets for loans, securities, and other kinds of investments. In these two kinds of markets the major participants are no longer ordinary people but entrepreneurs, enterprises, and financial institutions.

The rise of market-system coordination of the production of services and goods for sale outside the household was slow and uneven, but by about 1800, England qualified as a market system (some historians put it earlier), and Western Europe and North America followed.

Drawing people out of the household into a wider coordination was, however, an idea antedating the market system. The usual formula for doing so was central coordination. Ancient Egypt's rulers drew labor from each household in order to put it to work on irrigation projects, defense of the realm, and construction of temples and pyramids. Although royal coordination of a vast labor force declined in subsequent centuries, the idea of societywide central coordination did not. It was still alive more than three thousand years later, in the mid-nineteenth century, in the desire of communists and some socialists to organize society by central direction. At their most ambitious, they envisaged doing away with money, prices, and markets, all considered obstructions to rational and humane social organization. Because some utopians still aspire to it, the idea deserves a name. I shall call it physical planning.

A new idea of central planning arose in a late nine-teenth- and early twentieth-century reaction against the market system: convert the great structure of trade with money and prices into a centrally coordinated system. The new planners first came to power in Russia, through the Russian Revolution, and later in China, with a few small countries following in imitation. They were not twentieth-century Pharaohs or advocates of physical planning. They were more sophisticated planners proposing to make use of money and prices and even markets—but not of the whole market system, which they abhorred—as instruments of their central control. It is of course such a system that fueled the great twentieth-century communist challenge to the market system.

## Dimensions of Market System

Like the state, the market system is a method of controlling and coordinating people's behavior. If you call on a team of gardeners to do some weeding, you, not the state, exercise the control that brings them into coordination with you. They turn up and do the job. You did not coerce, compel, or even command them, but you succeeded in getting them to do what you want by paying them. When a hundred workers predictably appear at the gate of a factory every morning at 8, their appearance is not commanded by an agency of the state. They are there because they are controlled and coordinated by promise of money payments.

Can it really be true that the apparent disorder of buying and selling accomplishes anything so profound as control and social coordination? Everyone can see that the state accomplishes some coordination of the whole national society, but it is harder to see that the market system also does so—in fact organizes both nation and globe. But is it not true that people are either coordinated by the state or are left to do as they wish, all going their own way, as in the market? That is a colossal misperception. In market systems people do not go their own way; they are tied together and turned this way or that through market interactions. If they were in fact left to go their own way they would not achieve the prodigious feats of production that characterize market systems. That market participants see themselves as making free and voluntary choices does not deny that they are controlled by purchases and sales.

The market system is not, however, Adam Smith's laissez-faire, not a market system tied to a minimal state. In our time it is a governed market system, heavily burdened or ornamented with what old-fashioned free marketers decry as "interferences." In these systems, the state is the largest buyer: it has a long shopping list, including a military force, highways, and the services of police officers and bureaucrats. It is a mammoth supplier as well, although in providing many of its services—elementary education, as an example—it usually gives away the "product" rather than sells it. Rather than let supply and demand set prices, it often does so itself: keeping agricultural prices high to aid farmers, or holding agricultural prices down to curb distress among the urban poor. It forbids some kinds of sales: most nations now prohibit slavery. It taxes, not simply to raise revenue but to curb some industries, like tobacco. One way or another it subsidizes most industries, almost all of which hold their hands out. It is a gigantic borrower and a frequent lender. It engages in sales promotion abroad to enlarge overseas markets for its entrepreneurs. It collects enormous funds to disperse through social welfare programs. And it is a powerfully active manager of supplies of money and credit both through its controls over banking and its own fiscal policy.

Some of these governmental activities are necessary to make a market system flourish. Some are at least helpful, some are wasteful. Some represent nothing better than raids on the public purse. However evaluated, they are part of the story of how market systems work.

Although buying and selling may be natural to human-kind, market systems are not. They have in fact arisen only recently in history. Also not natural are the complexities of corporate law, the abstract shares in ownership called stocks and bonds, the rituals of collective bargaining. Nei-ther natural nor God given, market systems are also not all alike. And just as today's differ from those of fifty years ago, they differ from those the future will bring.

One can imagine a market system in which all enter-prises, or at least all the large ones, are state owned and op-erated as market enterprises. They are market enterprises because their outputs and inputs are decided by market buying and selling rather than by governmental command. One can also imagine a co-op market system in which all enterprises are owned by their customers. Another possibil-ity is ownership and operation by employees. But the now ascendant market system is of course the one that Karl Marx called capitalism, now more often called the private enterprise system. That is the kind of market system that will get most of our attention, but not to the exclusion of other kinds of market systems and of interesting market-state hybrids.

Movement today to the market system intertwines with

another great recent movement—from dictatorship to democracy. The Soviet Union expired in the pursuit of both. But the two movements differ: China's masters push toward market system but not democracy. And many countries with market systems have yet to attempt democracy or, like Mexico, only now reluctantly are doing so. If you applaud the movement to the market system as necessarily democratic, you are at least premature and possibly plain wrong: both China and Russia may carry market systems into and through the twenty-first century without democracy. In ostensibly democratic societies, market skeptics sometimes fear that the market system may bring an end to democracy. One of their fears is that big corporations already exercise powers inconsistent with democracy; and that multinational corporations overwhelm small nation-states. Again, we can begin by trying to get the facts straight, difficult as it is to unravel the many connections between market and democracy.

## What We Don't Know

Market advocates say that Western experience has now conclusively shown that the market system can make a society wealthy. They also say that it is clear that it also protects personal freedom—market societies do not degenerate into such impositions as the forced labor camps of the USSR. Market successes prove, they might add, the obsolescence of tired old attacks on the market. So, they say, we now all understand the system. They believe that we need technical studies by economists to maintain its health—doctors for the body economic—but that we adequately understand the elementary anatomy and physiology of the market system.

Yet it might be that technology and industrialization rather than the market system deserve credit for making societies wealthy. And don't some countries with market systems—Indonesia, among others—trample on the very freedoms that market systems are alleged to strengthen? Or must we confess that many nation-states are troubled about just what place to give to market system—the Japanese government, for example, first heavily indulging and then backing off from its heavy state participation in market investment decisions? Most market societies also seem troubled by the task of combining market system with welfare state. They are also uncertain about market regulations to protect the environment. In some, an especially troubling question has arisen: Can market employment be made available for all able-bodied adults, or does the market combined with high technology now begin to render the least skilled workers redundant, in effect exiling them from the market system, to be supported by state welfare programs?

Issues like these pose a great deal more than technical problems that require only the professional skills of economic doctors. They are great issues of liberty and equality and of individualism and community, as well as more tangible issues, like conflict between growth and environmental protection. If one can hope for at least modestly intelligent choices on issues like these, they will come from a better understanding of what the market can or cannot do or, more precisely, what people can or cannot choose to do through their use of the market system. For example, if the market system in fact constitutes an irreducible source of income insecurity or extreme income inequality, that would set upper limits on the uses of tax and welfare policies to redistribute income.

Despite the growing consensus in favor of the market

system, it is of course possible that the millions of people who now endorse it are on the wrong track. Such consensus as exists is a political phenomenon, not a scientific demonstration. We cannot simply ignore the many highly informed dissenters who believe that experience with the market system has already shown, to anyone who cares to look dispassionately at the evidence, that it has put us all on the road to disaster.

They argue that it exhausts the world's resources and also threatens an environmental catastrophe through, among other possibilities, global warming. They also show that it has already created health-threatening urban environments while simultaneously drawing ever more people into the cities. Clearly, they can also show, it has not put an end to the inhumanity of acute poverty. And all these ills, they argue, it will bring to the newly marketized societies. That alternatives to the market system might do worse is not a good reason for failing to examine what the market system may do to its participants.

None of these and many other claims for or against the market system—all significant for our futures—is obviously true or obviously false. Is the market system efficient, as its advocates believe? Look at its prodigious output. Is it inefficient? Look at poverty and inadequate medical care. Do market societies spoil the environment and exhaust our resources? Yes, but so do all societies—perhaps we mistake the cause. Does the market system degrade personality and culture? On that point, what shall we count as evidence—persons who pursue money to the exclusion of any other values, or the institutions for science, education, and art that flourish in market societies? Is the market system ally or enemy of democracy? What we call democracy does not exist except in market societies; yet the influence of money in politics arouses suspicion that none of these societies are very democratic.

Revealed in this debate are a few overarching questions about the market system. What does the market system do for the market-oriented societies? What accomplishments and ills has it brought them? Is it likely to do the same for the countries now constructing market systems? What future does it offer? What different kinds of market systems are worth considering? In short, to what condition has it brought us, and to what condition can we now take it?

Talking about the future now seems to require a new vocabulary. Terms like information revolution, photonics, cellular entrepreneurial networks, and globalization suggest the dimensions of the world's rush to a technologically sophisticated future. It looks as though information has become the basic resource, displacing in part the traditional trio of labor, land, and capital. How are these highly mobile new resources of information or knowledge to be organized or coordinated, not only nationally but globally? Almost no one proposes to use only the central authority of each of the nation-states. Nor have I heard many voices advocating the creation of a world state to coordinate the new technologies of information and knowledge. What I do hear is that the new forces will "open up vast new markets," that markets are "spreading around the globe," and that "information technology is accelerating the rate of change in market societies." All the more reason to understand the market system as, for good or bad, the big globalizer. It is the major institutional instrument for undercutting the autonomy of individual nation-states and for quickening the restless movement of labor and capital over the face of the earth.

Although dispute on the market system is endless, we are going to establish some key facts about it. It can coordinate human behavior or activity with a range and a precision beyond that of any other system, institution, or social process. But it is a harsh and often cruel coordinator. It is both an ally and enemy of personal freedom—ally because it opens up a range of choice for each participant, but enemy because it closes off some major choices that a free people could otherwise make. It destroys many mammoth historical inequalities and then introduces inequalities of its own. It achieves extraordinary efficiency because it permits participants to make precise and calculated choices. But it is grossly inefficient because of the choices it has closed off. Historically, it has supported democracy—there are no democratic nation-states except in market societies—but it has sabotaged important democratic features of ostensibly democratic states. It is also a rival to democracy because both market system and democracy allow people to exercise popular or mass control over elites in government and business. Its scope is much broader than often conceived to be; it can do more things than most people think it can. Yet, paradoxically, it does not operate in some arenas everywhere identified with it. We shall also find grounds for believing that no market system has yet been well supported by the state.

Do I have a central or overarching thesis in this book? Yes, if you want one; no, if you don't. Some common theses are not mine. I do not try to convince you that you should, taking everything into account, admire or deplore the market system. Nor do I suggest that the historical argument on the market system has come to an end with a victory for the market system. My thesis is that there are great unsettled issues about a place for the market system in the future of any society.

But what moves me to write is a desire to examine the market system as an extraordinary social process, just as one might, in wonder or even awe, examine an enormously complex machine or biological organism, whether benign or threatening. Although the market system is roughly familiar to all of us, not even economists wholly understand it; and I as an economist want to extend my own understanding as well as that of the reader. I can think of many purposes to which an improved understanding can be put, and the gain in understanding is itself a pleasure.

# How It Works

# Society's Coordination

Having presented the market system as a method of social coordination, I need now ask: What does social coordination (or organization) consist of? How is it accomplished? Coordination is a big concept. It will open the way to show the broad effects of the market system on society rather than confine its effects to that segment of society called the economy.

For the time being, let us rid ourselves of the idea of an economic system. Pretend that we have never heard of any such thing. Also drive out of our minds concepts usually used to explain the market system, like supply and demand, commodities, production and distribution. For a short time, forget them all. They would distract us from understanding the key relation between market system and social coordination or organization. Think society, not economy.

Imagine 20 million families scattered over an uninhabited territory as large as France. At first they do not constitute a society but are no more than an unorganized aggregate. Each family retreats into isolation, and some wage war on others. How might they become a society? Through practices that coordinate them. These are practices that create interchanges with each other for security and cooperation and, no less, for obtaining food and necessary objects, like tools.

If you and I agree to lunch together, we have accomplished a small coordination. A political party is a larger coordination, and 80 million people at peace with each other still larger. Some familiar coordination may not even be recognized as coordination: a parent's care of a child, for example. At the other extreme, coordination requires a conspicuous set of social mechanisms: the activities of legislators, teachers, and recordkeepers, for example.

Coordination ranges from tyrannical to democratic. My notion of a well-coordinated or organized society might envision a dominating elite—Plato's philosopher-kings or an aristocracy, for example. Yours might envision egalitarian institutions.

There are two functions of coordination. One is to curb injuries that otherwise people inflict on each other. That requires constraints on violence, theft, and interference with each other's movements. Let us call this coordination for social peacekeeping. The second purpose is more ambitious—to organize the giving and receiving of help. Almost everyone helps others, and everyone receives help from others, although not necessarily from precisely those to whom one has given it. Call it coordination for cooperation.

For either kind of coordination—peacekeeping or cooperation—wholly voluntary initiatives alone will not do. Rather, both kinds of coordination succeed because people are subjected to controls. Law is of course a great coordinator, protecting, among other things, the privacy of my home from injuries of invasion of it. Custom also is a great coordinator: for example, it gives people a common language, hence many possibilities of cooperation. But the controls that induce coordinated behavior go far beyond these two.

Wanting to be tough-minded, we sometimes dismiss cooperation as aspiration rather than necessity. But social cooperation is not pie in the sky. In fact, nothing is more obvious than that cooperation, large scale as well as small scale, pervades every society. A human infant dies unless at least one adult steadfastly supports it in its early years. No one builds even a simple roadway without help—no more than one's own driveway, and that with help at least from whoever made the shovel. Only by cooperation—by helping others and being helped—can we curb epidemics, advance science, or enjoy the pleasures of play and friendship. And it takes cooperation among legislators, judges, and police officers to construct and administer rules for curbing injuries.

I think we fail to grasp the full significance of cooperation because the common meaning of the term is narrow. Cooperation, we often imagine, is a situation in which A helps B and B helps A, both doing so deliberately and knowingly. An example: you and I cooperate to move a heavy piece of furniture. With that restricted concept, we mistakenly overlook the larger kind of cooperation, fundamental to the existence of society. A helps B. B helps C, D, . . . or Z, perhaps also but not necessarily A. The help may be either intended or unintended, and it may be offered unknowingly, just as it may be received unknowingly. When you remove unsightly debris from your property, saving me the trouble of calling the police to compel its removal, you may not have known that you were benefiting me. Aggregates of people become societies and people survive and flourish because of this second kind of cooperation. It is the foundation of social life and at the core of the market system.

Although we often associate cooperation with a sense of community, no such sense is required for cooperation broadly defined, for often cooperators neither talk with nor even know each other. Or they may detest each other. Like two ambitious cabinet ministers who must cooperate if only to keep their positions, they may look malevolently on each other as rivals. Usually people link with each other only impersonally and at a distance, as in the cooperation of research meteorologists all over the world. The efforts of all, mostly strangers to one another, help to improve the accuracy of weather prediction. Nor is cooperation necessarily high minded. People usually cooperate not altruistically but because it serves their purposes or because they are compelled to do so. They also often cooperate without intending to, or without even becoming aware that they are actually engaged in cooperation. When I deliver empty bottles to a local recycling center, somebody trucks them away to a processing facility. Other steps follow. I may give not a moment's thought to the chain of cooperation in which I constitute a link.

To get a sense of the beyond-the-horizon scope of cooperation, it is revealing to try to calculate how many people cooperate in order to graduate a student from secondary school. (No need to ask how many have to love each other, know each other, or be aware of their roles.) Informally, parents and other family members do much of the necessary teaching, they themselves having been taught by their parents and other family members. We add to that number all the child's classroom teachers, from kindergarten through high school, and the teachers who trained them. Include classmates—they teach each other and, in so doing, draw on what they have been taught by their family members. We must include also those who build and maintain school buildings—a complete account would include everyone from ancestors to meter readers. The list runs not into hundreds or thousands but millions of cooperators.

Superficially, it looks as though people fight more than cooperate, as seems evident in controversies on public education, foreign policy, and taxes, for example. Yet each fight is evidence of cooperation. We fight over education and taxes only because we are cooperatively engaged in maintaining a public school system. The fight is about who is to be in charge of the cooperation, how it is to be carried out, who is to pay for it, and who is to benefit. Conflict over sharing the benefits can be sharp, persistent, and often bitter, which is as true for quarreling spouses as it is for communities competing for government funds.

I am inclined to think that many of us do not appreciate the accomplishments of social coordination either for peacekeeping or cooperation. We do not stop to consider that many millions of people are well enough coordinated to live at peace with each other, nor that cooperation has permitted humankind to create—with no end yet in sight—new means of gratifying many of its aspirations.

Instead, our attention is drawn to malcoordination, both the vast scope and severity of mutual injury—the human animal is still a killer—and the ills of grossly inefficient cooperation: ignorance, poverty, and malnutrition among them. Yet one would not want to minimize this malcoordination, for it is not simply an inefficiency but a continuing tragedy. It is therefore difficult to think straight about social coordination, both the great human accomplishment and the great failure.

## Coordination Without a Coordinator

A market system is a method of social coordination by mutual adjustment among participants rather than by a central coordinator. We need, therefore, to understand the possibilities of coordination without a coordinator. The idea of coordination through mutual adjustment comes as a novelty to many people, yet we are all constantly engaged in it.

Husbands and wives typically achieve coordination, for both peace and cooperation, by working things out through mutual adjustments to each other. Each adapts to the other's peculiarities and finds ways to influence the other. They may succeed in their coordination with no more than an occasional appeal to an overseeing mother-in-law. Civil servants constantly engage in give-and-take to work out their coordination, as do scientists, teachers in a school, politicians, and children on a playground.

Many people define coordination as the activities or accomplishment of a coordinator, a definition that blinds them to cooperation by mutual adjustment. They sometimes also fall into a comparable misperception: that coordinators by definition coordinate. Ostensible coordinators do not necessarily coordinate; they sometimes make a mess of things. Legend has it that the greatest central coordinator of them all flooded the earth to erase some creative mistakes. Many central coordinators have tried to bury theirs.

The distinction between central and mutually adjusting coordination can also be seen as the distinction between unilateral and multilateral control. Who exercises control— a central coordinator or many interacting participants? Both systems of coordination use the same tool kit of controls: talking things over, mutual back-scratching, paying someone to do as one wishes, issuing commands. (Clearly centralists have the power to command, but so also do many of the persons engaged in mutual adjustment.) Both systems also make use of less attractive controls—for example, threats: "Do it or else!" The difference is the unilateral-multilateral contrast.

You can unilaterally control and thus coordinate five of us as we work together to launch your boat. Or the six of us can achieve a nice coordination simply through multilaterally watching, responding to, and influencing each other. Or think of two dozen pedestrians on a city street corner facing a similar group across the street. How do they coordinate to avoid collision? A central coordinator on the sidelines could call out instructions to each on when and by what route to move through the oncoming others. Intolerably slow and clumsy—would anyone bother to listen? Without anyone's giving it a thought, however, everyone coordinates quickly and precisely through various mutual adjustments. Each person warily watches the eye and body movements of those nearest. To some, one defers. To others, one's movement signals a gentle threat. In a few seconds the two sets of walkers pass through each other without injury. Their coordination may or may not have been assisted by custom or rules, such as "keep right."

Mutual adjustment is not always small scale. Language provides an example of large-scale multilateral coordination. To say that 300 million people read, write, or speak Spanish means that they have come to agree on certain sounds and symbols—an enormous feat of coordination, indeed of cooperation. But no overarching authority—no person, no committee—could have designed the Spanish language, or Malay or any other tongue. Languages arise out of centuries of mutual adjustment in the use of sounds and symbols. They are only marginally influenced by attempts to impose central controls, such as that of the Academie Française, which seeks to protect the French language from impurities.

Morality is regulated through mutual adjustment on an even larger scale. Through moral rules, humankind has achieved a nearly worldwide coordination of a few dimensions of behavior: many people are presumably morally constrained, for example, from inflicting physical injury on others. These moral rules are not centrally designed and imposed but have emerged from mutual adjustment. An even

larger scale mutual adjustment? Biologists now tell us that
50 billion atoms coordinate to make each of your DNA
molecules, and 1,000 million million cells to make your
body. No central coordination; all through mutual adjustment.

The international political order of the past fifty years
stands as conspicuous evidence of the scope of mutual adjustment. During that time, mutual adjustment has averted
nuclear war or any orgy of destruction like that of the first
and second world wars. One might think that the United
Nations and NATO bring central coordination to bear, but
they lack the necessary unilateral authority to do so because
member nations are unwilling to grant it. They do, however,
facilitate mutual adjustment among nation-states.

The Internet may turn out to be the key technology for a
mammoth expansion of multilateral worldwide communication. It opens up possibilities of mutual adjustment that
are not yet even imaginable.

Participants in mutual adjustment of course differ
greatly in the capacities they bring to interactions. Pedestrians at a crowded intersection differ from each other in their
mutual influences: height, weight, fierceness of visage,
vigor of stride, and the like. A prime minister or CEO not
strong enough to practice unilateral control over colleagues
can nevertheless bring bigger guns to bear on them than any
one of them can respond with.

We all know that societies deliberately design some formal structures of mutual adjustment—the United Nations,
for example, or a nation's tripartite wage board. Much more
frequently, mutual adjustment arises inconspicuously,
without design. And participants in interchange often bring
their influence to bear more inadvertently than deliberately—they need not be aware of their parts in a vast coor-

dination. Their incentive to bring a new term like "on line" into use is their own convenience, not a desire to take responsibility for language planning.

Face-to-face or voice-to-voice interaction is not a requirement for mutual adjustment, frequent though it is. Global ethical codes, for example, have emerged from tacit agreements among people, most of whom never see each other. Coordination, say, of growth patterns of neighboring municipalities is often achieved by officials' taking account of one another's moves rather than negotiating.

All real-world coordinating systems are, of course, hybrids in which centrality and mutual adjustment depend on each other, neither being wholly absent. Many of the extraordinary mutual adjustments of American politics were set in motion by the design of the U. S. Constitution, with a constitutional convention playing a centralist role. That auto traffic moves on congested roadways is a joint accomplishment of centrally designed rules and endless mutual adjustments among drivers.

## Reluctant Recognition

Like all forms of coordination, mutual adjustment naturally is imperfect. Yet I think we have been misled by the nervous though greatly honored minds of Western political philosophy to underestimate it. An overriding concern seems to run through the history of thought: How can a society maintain order? Obviously by controls that induce people to behave in orderly ways. The philosophers writing about order lived in societies in which the controls believed necessary for order lay in the hands of elites who exercised them over their "inferiors." Perhaps the philosophers could not imagine controls exercised in any patterns other than

unilateral and hierarchical. Nor, considering their own favored positions in society, would they regard that as an attractive possibility. I suggest that, as a consequence, the
study of order or coordination became in large part a study
of how elites could unilaterally keep the masses under control and of how they could justify their doing so. Take as an
example from the first days of political philosophy Plato's
*Republic*, which, despite its monumental merits, makes a
suspect case for the justice of hierarchical or unilateral elite
rule over mass. Aristotle's very notion of order was hierarchical.

How severely philosophy and theology may have mis-
perceived the problem of order or coordination is revealed
in the history of disorder. The greatest disturbers of social
order have not been peasants, though they occasionally
have tried to revolt, but the holders of unilateral authority—the would-be central coordinators: among them, Alexander, the marauding Roman emperors, Genghis Khan, the
rapacious quarreling lords of medieval and Renaissance Europe, Napoleon, Lenin, and Hitler.

A few figures in the history of thought have found significant place for mutual adjustment. Not surprisingly,
they have given more thought to how a society can act in-
telligently than to how it can be made obedient. In the second century B.C., the historian Polybius claimed that the
merits of early Roman institutions were not attributable to
design from the top but to a continuing set of political interactions constituting successful trial and error. In 1748,
we find a fuller but still embryonic appreciation of mutual
adjustment in Montesquieu's *Spirit of the Laws*. In the almost two thousand years that separate these two, others of
like mind must lie buried in the history of philosophy, and

it is noteworthy that perhaps no one has searched hard to find them.

One might write a short history of thought in such a way as to bring coordination through mutual adjustment to front and center. With his *Principia* in 1687, Newton, "the greatest scientist that ever lived," would come first. He explains the physical world as a mechanism of mutual adjustment of heavenly bodies. He attributes nothing to central coordination, nothing to a central sovereign mind—in short, nothing to God except responsibility for setting celestial mutual adjustment in motion. Next, in 1859, would come Darwin with his *Origin of Species*. He explains the multiplicity of species, their patterns of change and evolution, and begins the explanation of life itself. Like Newton, he finds the explanation in mutual adjustment, in his case among living things. His monumental theory of evolution—about complex biological coordination without a coordinator—continues, like an icebreaker in Arctic waters, to open channels of thought that appreciate mutual adjustment. He finds no place for a central organizing mind or authority. If God the centralist exists, God is nevertheless not necessary to the explanation.

Then, in 1776, Adam Smith explains in *Wealth of Nations* the coordination of society as the accomplishment of mutual adjustment rather than of central competence of king or finance minister. He fails, however, to generalize his explanation of social order beyond market life. Finally, in about 1900 comes Freud, now out of fashion and not a match for the first three, but nonetheless a pivotal figure. Peering into human mind and behavior he realizes that each of us is internally an arena of mutual adjustment. We consist of conflicting impulses, perceptions, and volitions, and we are not governed by a unified sovereign intelligence.

## Merits of Mutual Adjustment

It appears that every society needs both central and mutually adjustive coordination, each in its place. Some of the merits of mutual adjustment make it indispensable; I mention only a few beyond those already apparent.

For limiting injury, rules and authority will in some circumstances do well, for their main message is simply "Thou shalt not!" But cooperation requires an allocation or assignment of a coordinated set of tasks. A society neither constructs a medical-care system nor clothes its people by giving orders to participants on what they must not do. To achieve positive cooperation, somehow society specifies each of a great number of tasks to be performed, as well as the circumstances in which each is to be performed and by whom. A medical-care system rests not simply on a set of prohibitions but on complex procedures to determine how physicians are to be trained and qualified, their responsibilities and conditions of work, and their rewards.

Moreover, the assignments have to be endlessly adapted. They are not once-and-for-all assignments but are tailored to changing needs, as for medical care, and to factors such as the caregivers' training, experience, and age. If, in addition, cooperating persons want to exercise a degree of free choice about how and when they participate, cooperation becomes all the more complex and lies even further beyond the reach of rules and authority.

Rules and authoritative instructions are often too clumsy. They can apply only to more static categories. For an extreme case, imagine members of a soccer team trying to cooperate to win a game simply by following prescribed rules and authoritative instructions shouted from the sidelines. In actual practice, players signal one another with movements and voices in a moving cooperation, their signals much more precise and fast-changing than those supplied by rules and authority. Cooperation among government officials, even though partially prescribed by rules and authority, also requires bilateral or multilateral interchange of signals, incentives, and threats, as in negotiations in multiparty systems to form a cabinet.

For most social cooperation—from family life to politics—societies consequently use complex processes of interaction rather than rules and authority. And just as rules and authority are clumsy, they are often also excessively compulsory. Interactive processes often make better use of information and intelligence than do rules and authority. In appropriate arenas, mutual adjustment provides unique advantages in coordination. It diffuses possibilities for bringing insights, information, and innovations into society, allowing information and ideas to enter the system at many points. Observe the flood of innovations, like wireless Internet, transforming computer communications worldwide. In a hierarchy, every centralist in the line of authority can veto any idea that comes up the ladder or from the outside, since it is the centralist's responsibility to decide yes or no. In mutual adjustment, there is no centralist gatekeeper.

Both the scope and efficacy of mutually adjustive coordination are underrated. Consider the possibility that it is more frequent than coordination by an ostensible coordinator, whether the coordination is of spouses, drivers, acrobats, or negotiators in a wage dispute. Although, like central coordination, it of course often fails, it is the workhorse of social coordination in society as a whole.

## Coordination in the Face of Scarcity

In the days before affluence multiplied the number of tourists swarming over Italy, it took little effort in coordination to accommodate those who wished to see the Michelangelo murals in the Sistine Chapel. Today this coordination requires regulated hours, tickets, and queues. *When there is not enough of a given benefit to satisfy everyone, coordination, whether for cooperation or peacekeeping, becomes difficult yet all the more necessary.* "Not enough" means that some go without and that almost no one is wholly satisfied. That is, some Vatican visitors will be rushed through the chapel while others will not even gain admittance. This is a major point about social coordination: when there is not enough of a benefit to go around, coordination imposes deprivation and consequently must cope with frustration, aggravated conflict, and sometimes rage.

For most objects and experiences to which people aspire, there is not enough to go around, whether the benefit is something intangible, like sightseeing opportunities in Rome, or something tangible, like bread. Not enough bread to go around? No, there is not. The shortage is disguised because society limits the number of people who ask for it: they must pay for it. Take away that constraint and the shortage would be obvious. Take away the legal rules that limit the kinds of disputes that can be taken to court, and a crippling shortage of judges would be apparent. Although some shortages are only too visible, most are obscured by constraining those who make requests or demands. Rules of eligibility—for example, entrance requirements for admission to college—are common constraints. Making people offer something in exchange is even more widespread a constraint. We become so accustomed to constraints that we forget that they exist only because of shortages and would not be necessary if there were enough to go around.

In fact, there is not enough to go around, not even in the wealthiest societies. Even those who seem to have everything are at least half aware that they could make use of more educational services for their children than even the best schools now provide and more medical services than any society yet offers, to say nothing of more personal services in the household, more chartered or owned aircraft, and more living space. For millions of less fortunate people all over the world, shortages are more obvious, and the world is far from able to bring these millions up to the level of the average Western European wage earner.

To denote the situation in which there is not enough to go around except by constraints on its availability, the common term is scarcity. It is a good term if we take care not to use it to mean a small amount of something or a few of something, which is one of its other meanings. And we must not use it to suggest niggardliness or to imply that nature is stingy. Scarcity does not mean a small amount but denotes a relation between aspiration and availability. Millions of square miles of fertile land are spread over the globe, but it nevertheless remains scarce—not enough to go around—because so many people aspire to cultivate it. Relatively few doorbell-ringing evangelists come to my neighborhood. But they are not scarce because so few householders want their ministrations. Opportunities to see the Sistine ceiling did not become scarce because the chapel shrank but because more people wanted to enter.

Finally, even if every member of society forswore further aspiration, maintaining his or her share of scarce things would require coordination. Without the sustaining patterns of coordination long ago established, a society would backslide. It would be reduced to living on the simplest of diets in the crudest of shelters without either clean water or schools or much of anything else. The benefits we have today derive from already practiced cooperation; to retain them, the cooperation must be continued.

# Market-System Coordination

The market system is a mammoth coordinator through mutual adjustment and is especially adapted to the difficulties of coordination in the face of scarcity. Many of us—even some economists—believe that the market system coordinates economic behavior and only economic behavior, as though there exists some identifiable area of behavior called economic, which is the only behavior that the market system can coordinate. That belief has to be abandoned. The fact is that the market system coordinates an enormous range of behavior, just what variety we do not yet know. Again, think society, not economy.

Although even Cro-Magnons traded with each other, probably using shells as money, we have seen from prehistory to the Industrial Revolution of the eighteenth century that buying and selling were for most people only adjunct methods of social coordination. Notwithstanding the development of trade routes in the ancient world, custom and political authority carried the burden of social coordination. Only in the last three centuries has much of it shifted to the market system. For a market system to become a mammoth coordinator, slavery had to give way to wage labor, and static feudal ties of worker to land had to be replaced by market transactions in labor and property. And the guilds' social control in the cities had to recede to allow freer buying and selling.

## Cooperation

We ask first how the market system achieves cooperation, looking only later at market peacekeeping. We need no theory or elaborate analysis—only a commonplace example or two—for this display of the capacity of the market to accomplish cooperation through mutual adjustment. Almost everyone who lives in a market system knows the elementary facts of market cooperation. The examples will, however, call attention to some aspects of it that are usually taken for granted, their significance often missed. My purpose here is not to construct an argument for the market system but simply to tag its attributes significant for market-system cooperation.

During the course of a morning, a number of people step into a Milan cafe for an espresso. They do not doubt that it will be available. What justifies their confidence? Making the coffee available rests on a great deal of cooperation, specifically, the assignment to many people of performances that together accomplish a feat beyond the capacity of any one person alone. It is accomplished by market transactions that assign and link both multiple performances and multiple chains of them. Farmers cooperate in growing and harvesting the coffee beans. Truck drivers or locomotive engineers transport the beans to a seaport on highways or railroads that have been constructed by many kinds of cooperating laborers. At the seaport, longshoremen and ships' crews join the chain. At a dock in Genoa, shipping the beans on to Milan calls again on performances from longshoremen, warehousers, and truckers. Somewhere along the chain, some people roast the beans, and others fabricate bags for carrying them. Think of other participating cooperators: insurers and inspectors, wholesalers and retailers. Not to be forgotten is the espresso machine and the chains of cooperation that constructed, delivered, and installed it. However great their distance from Milan, innumerable people play their roles in cooperation, and no less so than the surly or obliging waiter in the cafe. Remember the nursery rhyme, "This Is the House That Jack Built." (But do not idealize the process; sometimes trucks are hijacked, enterprises embezzled, or the offers of would-be cooperators rejected.)

Because we do not often pause to reflect on such chains or webs of performance, we might miss the details of market cooperation. Look inside a small segment of it. For the small performance of providing pencils to a pencil-chewing accountant in the Milan importer's office, a hundred people may directly engage in their assembly, another hundred in fabricating the erasers to be attached, a hundred in the construction of the building in which they perform their pencil-making tasks, a thousand easily in the generation and delivery of electric power, another thousand as easily in the fabrication of the metal wires for power transmission, and, finally, several thousand in digging, refining, smelting, and transporting the necessary ore. But there is no "finally." Perhaps a pencil maker was one of those who asked for a cup of coffee in the Milan cafe. Cooperation is not linear but multilateral.

None of the chains or webs connecting activities in Colombia with those in Milan can we dismiss as random, accidental, or coincidental. The cooperation shows a high degree of predictability. A coffee grower does not stand hopefully at the edge of a rural road waiting, as though for a visit from a rich uncle, for possible buyers to come for the coffee beans. Each grower depends on a buyer and is only infrequently disappointed.

Consider, for another example, some of the many connections in cooperation practiced in the manufacture of shoes. A Korean enterprise operating in Indonesia assembles the shoes with designs and materials specified by a firm in Oregon and with further design by a firm in Taiwan. Cattle raised, slaughtered, and skinned in Texas provide leather for the uppers. Hides go by rail freight from Texas to Los Angeles, then by ship or air to Pusan for tanning, then by air to Indonesia. Midsoles are made from petroleum-based chemicals, one of which is distilled and "cracked" from Saudi petroleum shipped in a tanker to a Korean refinery. Synthetic rubber manufactured in Taiwan with electricity from nuclear power plants provides the outer soles. A Japanese-made machine sews the corporate logo on the shoes. Shoes are stuffed with paper made from trees harvested in Sumatra, then packed in boxes from a paper mill in New Mexico and shipped across the Pacific to the United States in a supercontainer ship. Each of these cooperating enterprises links with hundreds of close-at-hand cooperating suppliers and employees and with thousands or millions of more distant suppliers, like those who provide the fuels that smelt the ore necessary for the nuclear powerlines. (Again, to appreciate the scope and detail of the cooperation is not to idealize it. A common complaint about the shoe industry is that it grossly underpays its overseas laborers for their contribution to the cooperation.)

Even those performances and objects that appear to be locally supplied require long chains of cooperative performances. If you call on a carpenter to replace a rotting fence post, he can do the job only because of the earlier cooperation of those who made his shovel and hammer. And of course they in turn were dependent on all those who provided them metals, a power supply, and so on.

Take special note, too, of the enormous constructions provided to make available a cup of coffee, shoe, or new fence post. Mines, ships, factories, locomotives, and generators are all part of the cooperation. Not until land and labor are supplemented by such human-made resources—capital is the common term for them—do societies break out of their thousands of years of poverty. That accomplishment requires two noteworthy special tasks of social coordination to create capital.

The first is a diversion of a large allocation of labor and natural resources from producing directly for ultimate users to producing things that themselves produce. It is a diversion, say, from producing wheat to producing tractors. The second is the rise and proliferation of highly specialized participants. A scribe sitting at a table, pen in hand, is replaced by a printing press or copy machine. The copying processes now call for manufacturers of presses, parts suppliers, maintenance mechanics, transport services, instructors—a long list of specialized role players.

Significant in all this is not the lifeless coffee bean or shoe but a web of human performances, a weaving together of human effort. A market system is a pattern of cooperative human behavior, not simply a bag of beans on the move. To understand market cooperation one has to keep the eye on that behavior, not on objects like shoes or cups of coffee. Although the performances often culminate in an object, often they do not. Physicians, gardeners, and teachers, for example, play their roles in cooperation through the help their performances directly give to others; they do not simply offer objects to those who call on them for assistance. In advanced industrial societies less than half the working population is engaged in producing objects; most instead produce performances. And when market activity does result in objects, it is human performance that accomplishes that result.

The term marketplace is, incidentally, almost always a misnomer. The market system is not a place but a web, not a location but a set of coordinated performances. Some interactions connected with each other in a market system occur in definite locations—a farmers' market or a stock exchange—that can be called marketplaces. But many markets are placeless, their interacting participants widely separated. They are better represented by telephone connections or Internet communications than by any place.

Although the market system organizes cooperation, I would not call that its purpose. The market system does not exist "for" cooperation, or for any of the other purposes often attributed to it. It is not "for" satisfaction of want or for capital accumulation or for elite exploitation of the masses, three diverse purposes often assigned to it. People, not social processes, pursue purposes, as do some animals and organizations. But market systems do not, though of course participants in them do. It is a mindless and purposeless market system that accomplishes the great tasks of social cooperation. And, again, it organizes cooperation that serves all kinds of individual purposes; it is not limited to facilitating a category of purposes called economic.

The proposition that the market system arranges social cooperation goes down hard with people who have long identified the market with competition, even with dog-eat-dog ferocity. True, market systems embrace many arenas of competition. But every participant in the market system links cooperatively with millions of others while competing with relatively few. In the coffee example, shippers are linked cooperatively with countless other participants in the market system, but each competes with a relatively small number of other shippers. Shippers also compete with other employers looking for employees or with shippers of tea (since final customers can shift from coffee to tea or vice versa). Yet the scope of their competition does not at all approach the scope of their cooperation.

Indeed, in our time the market system has become a global coordinator of cooperative performances of at least 2 billion people. No other method of social cooperation matches the market system in scope and detail. We are often disposed to give first place to the state as an organizer of cooperation. But no government has ever organized so many people in such an articulated and detailed assignment of performances as displayed in the coffee and shoe examples, which lock many millions of people into specified cooperating roles. Moreover, there exists a global market system but no world state. Even within one country the market system organizes a detailed cooperation—millions of assignments to precisely defined roles—that state or government has rarely attempted and never accomplished.

View the market system as number one, without peer, in a class by itself. It is the world's broadest and most detailed organizer of social cooperation—with the longest arm and the most dexterous fingers. Whether one regards it as a great boon to humankind or suspects that the long arm and dexterous fingers are those of a monster, the market system is an extraordinary organizer of cooperation.

I am not claiming that the market system provides an optimal result or equilibrium in market mutual adjustment. We have already noted that people differ in what patterns they are willing to call coordinated—you may want a high degree of equality in outcomes, and I not. Or you may think that some values—resource conservation, for example—are neglected in the coordination achieved. Nevertheless, I think that no one can deny that specific assignments for countless participants are coordinated to bring coffee to a Milan cafe or shoes to people all over the world. Questions about the quality of the coordination can wait.

All the cooperation described requires a great deal of help from the state. The state establishes liberties, property rights, and obligations of contract without which people cannot buy and sell. It makes great efforts, not always highly successful, to curb hijacking and pirating. It builds docks, canals, highways, and railroads. It maintains a monetary system, hence it is drawn into the regulation of banks and the issuing of credit. To encourage enterprises not to allow risk to sap their energies, it often promises to share losses if they occur. It also commonly offers businesses the privilege of declaring bankruptcy to escape creditors. It sends armies abroad to open up markets. It joins with other states, as in the World Trade Organization, to establish and administer rules for international trade. The prospect of sales might be thought to be a sufficient inducement to energize market activity, but no market system can survive without governmental aid. And governments offer aid not merely to keep the market system alive but to stimulate growth. If the market system is a dance, the state provides the dance floor and the orchestra.

The state is in constant attendance on the market system, as can be seen in any nation's frequent moves to cope with ever-changing situations. To deal with the Asian financial disturbances of the late 1990s, the government of Taiwan floated the currency and imposed restrictions on acquisition of foreign exchange by Taiwanese businesses. It induced financial enterprises to use funds to support the stock market, it provided money to facilitate the purchase of houses, and it pressured banks to extend enterprise loans. It took a number of measures to increase the profitability of banks, reduce the stock market transaction tax, and create new tax incentives for high-tech industries. Month by month, governments maintain scrutiny and an ever-changing set of policies toward the market system.

## Peacekeeping

Does the market's contribution to peaceful order—to curbing injury—match the cooperation it accomplishes? That is not an easy question to answer because many people find the question itself puzzling. Market systems, they will say, typically flourish in peaceful societies. Consequently, there remains no peacekeeping task for the market system to perform, even if it had a potential for such a function. That is a persuasive line of argument—until one asks how these peaceful market societies came to be peaceful.

The plain fact is that a collection of people can escape descending into violent conflict over who gets what (land, slaves, high office, recognition, or whatever) only by developing social processes for answering these questions peaceably. That being so, when we see a society at peace internally we cannot infer that its members lack the aspirations that might bring them into conflict. We infer instead that appropriate processes have been worked out to resolve their many conflicts. One of these processes is the market system. It does not simply flourish in peaceful societies; it helps to make those societies peaceful. Almost three centuries ago Montesquieu captured the idea in his concept of *doux commerce*. Again a caution: the market system makes societies peaceful, but that is not necessarily efficient, equitable, or humane.

One claim for the market system as peacekeeper runs like this: People fight with each other when they are dissatisfied with their lots in life. But higher income—and especially growing income—reduce frustration, conflict, and consequent mutual injury, making possible a peaceful and stable political order. Market systems give rise to high incomes and growth, as they have in fact historically in Western Europe and North America and now conspicuously in Asia. Q. E. D. The market system makes for social peace.

Although the argument may be correct, it falls short of asserting that the market system itself provides social mechanisms for reducing mutual injury. It says instead that citizens will be disposed to keep the peace because they are well enough off in market societies to be willing to obey the laws laid down by the state to curb mutual injury. The state is the peacekeeper.

The market system itself produces patterns of behavior that themselves reduce mutual injury and keep peace in the society, quite aside from inducing people to obey the law. With a little indirection, we can see how.

Prospects of mutual injury and social disorder call for ways to protect each person or family from incursions by others. For social peace, each person or family needs a defended little island of autonomy. If that were all there is to it, the defenses erected by custom and law might be sufficient to keep the peace. Through these defenses citizens could establish rights or entitlements to be enjoyed by each person, not to be interfered with by others. That would seem to leave no role for a market system as peacekeeper. Indeed, under these conditions the idea of the market as a contributor to social peace might strike us as strained or bizarre.

But people want more than static defense against incursions. They are at least mildly ambitious for new satisfactions of many kinds. They struggle with each other for more, a struggle made all the more intense because there is not enough to go around. They want to enlarge their claims (again, not claims labeled economic but claims of any and all kinds), especially their claims for shares in the benefits of cooperation (and, again, not economic cooperation but cooperation of any and all kinds)—a bigger share of whatever pies are cut. Much of what they win is at the expense of others. Without a peacekeeping mechanism they would inflict many injuries on one another. And the peacekeeping mechanism consequently has to cope not merely with the static defense of established positions but with the intricacies and ever-changing character of conflict and injury as people struggle for more in the face of scarcity.

In that struggle, each person's ambitions constantly change during the course of life. Say one wants to acquire in early adulthood a place to live, possibly a spouse, and a circle of friends. As the years pass, one strives for a better place to live, a widened circle of friends, and then, as a septuagenarian, for the care with which some societies slowly escort their members to the grave. Even from month to month or week to week one moves from one aspiration to another, and often back again. One needs to acquire a supply of food today, but then not again for a week or so. Or perhaps an unanticipated need for medical care arises. Hence, for peacekeeping, every society needs a system for settling such endless questions as who does which job, who holds which position, or how much food and of what kinds is to be allocated to each person or family? Leg of lamb every day or only once a week or month, and to which persons? How often does a new jacket go to any person who desires it? What kind of jacket? The market system is just such a peacekeeping mechanism.

We tend to take this for granted, rarely pausing to reflect on the potential for violence in the struggle over potentially conflicting claims and the significance of the market system in substituting peaceful exchange for a more violent allocation.

Conventional economics looks on from a different angle. It tells us that scarcity poses an efficiency problem. If there is not enough to go around, then a society must find some method to weigh its alternatives. If more autos can be made available only by taking labor and materials away from other lines of production, like kitchen appliances, then somehow people or officials have to decide whether constructing more autos is worth reducing the supply of kitchen appliances.

This conventional line of analysis is correct. We shall in fact explore later how the market system provides the—or one—required method for efficient choice. But here I am observing that a more fundamental problem created by scarcity is that of potential violence. The first requirement posed by scarcity is not efficient choice but rather a method for allocating conflicting claims to desired scarce performances and objects so that people do not assault and kill each other in pursuit of them. The market system is such a method.

It is here useful to think of the market system as though it were a political process—not governmental yet nevertheless fundamentally political. Societies are poised at the rim of disorder because of ever-changing conflicting aspirations for countless scarce objects and performances. To this explosive situation the market system brings a solution. It limits every person's claims to a sum of money obtainable by that person's offer of something of value on the market: a rule—look at it as a political rule—of quid pro quo. Up to the limit of that sum, each person can then make whatever specific claims—for shoes, travel, or fame—for which the funds are sufficient. A potential for war of all against all is converted into a peaceful process—a political accomplishment of extraordinary sweep and efficacy.

The procedure is supported both by law and popular acquiescence. Even when they protest it as inequitable, most participants continue by and large to live by it. They do not push their individual claims much beyond what the rule of quid pro quo permits, thereby avoiding injuries that would otherwise be inflicted in a violent struggle.

The market system has played a much larger role in peacekeeping than it has been credited with in history. The sociologist Barrington Moore suggests that men of overweening ambition long pursued riches and power through violence: Alexander, Caesar, Attila, and the warring lords of Western Europe and early twentieth-century China. Not until late in history did ambitious men turn instead to the market to attain great wealth and power: the Fuggers, the Rothschilds, and the American robber barons, and now Soros and Gates. The anthropologist Leopold Pospisil tells a parallel story. Papuans in New Guinea, he found, are of two strategies for acquisition: highlanders raid each other, and lowlanders trade with each other. The alternatives are sometimes sharply presented: either get what one wants by taking it from another, or get it by an offer of a quid pro quo. One is a formula for violence, the other for peace.

Perhaps the dominance in our minds of the quid pro quo

rule is so overwhelming, so taken for granted, acquiescence to it so automatic and unthinking, that we hardly take note that every transaction that establishes a claim is an implicit waiver of other potentially troublesome claims.

Some of the conflicts apparently resolved by the market system surface again in the form of governmental policy questions about taxes, pensions, and affirmative action. Problems also arise when people violate the rule of quid pro quo by stealing rather than buying—not simply through street crime but in embezzlement and other fraud. Nor does the market system cope well with the inextinguishable smoldering fire of class conflict. And market resolution of conflicting claims is tightly tied to an inequitable historical distribution of property claims, as well as to the distribution of skills among people. Both ties produce a highly inegalitarian outcome. Nonetheless, the market constitutes a prodigious mechanism for keeping the social peace.

The market system is of course not the only possibility for keeping peace. Conflicting claims can be resolved by law, administrative authority, and other institutions. Even in predominantly market societies many conflicts are so resolved, ranging from conflicting claims to children by separated parents to claims for office by competing candidates. Significantly, for all the power of the state, communist systems could not cope with conflicting claims to objects, performances, and jobs without making use of consumer and labor markets. The rules and authority of the state, they found, were not enough.

## For Both Cooperation and Peacekeeping

Some attributes of market-system coordination, for both cooperation and peacekeeping, are worth special note.

*Diffusion of participation and control.* The market system is remarkable—unique, I think one can say—in its extreme diffusion of participation and control. Among the billions of persons coordinated by the market system, all share in control over it. Although entrepreneurs are far more influential participants, they are not the only ones who exercise control. You and I and every buyer also do so. So does everyone who offers a performance for a wage or fee. One "votes" through one's spending, thus creating a massive controlling influence. Market "voting" has a far higher rate of participation than can ever be achieved in democratic balloting. Among those coordinated no one is inactive or a passive nonparticipant; there are no nonvoters.

*Simplicity of decision problems.* Although entrepreneurial problems, especially in a big corporation, may appear daunting, they are small when compared with the problems of efficient choice when faced by central planners. Market transactions resolve questions over the distribution of income, the rate of investment, and the allocation of the labor force, yet no decision maker has to face such problems. A corporate executive does not have to decide how to best allocate steel for society but only whether the enterprise should buy it, sell it, or make it. And in coping with such choices with the benefit of efficiency prices, the executive can measure, make estimates, and obtain feedback.

*Coordination of conflicting sets of preferences.* Market-system coordination is remarkable in solving a mammoth problem posed by a discrepancy between two always present desired patterns of coordination. Imagine a society whose rulers or voters wish to put 40 percent of the workforce into heavy industry, like steel and automobiles, but no more than 20 percent want to work in heavy industry. How to reconcile the two patterns? Conscript the necessary

labor, or try to get by with a reduced heavy-industry program? The market system achieves a reconciliation so quietly that most of us are unaware of either the problem or its
solution.

If people want more than they are getting of the products
of heavy industry, they of course will buy more and, it follows, buy less of other products. That shift will open up
new jobs in heavy industry and reduce them in other fields.
At the same time, the enlarged demands for heavy-industry
products are likely to raise their selling prices and thus reduce the necessary shift of production and employees to
heavy industry. Hence the two patterns of preference both
move to meet each other. Although everyone knows that
workers move in this way, we do not often stop to appreciate that their movements, together with shifts in purchases, achieve a reconciliation of two conflicting patterns
of preference.

Some peoples' personal circumstances compel them to
hang on to an existing job—they cannot move. But to move
even large numbers of people from one industry to another
does not require that the new jobs attract all the employees,
only the number sufficient to accomplish the reconciliation.

*Adaptability.* Despite the detail or precision of assignment of millions of roles and claims in market coordination, roles and claims are not fixed but are highly flexible. If
coffee drinking becomes more popular, systematic adjustments by all linked cooperating participants then follow:
more beans grown, more coffee shipped, more ships provided, even more pencils manufactured. The past three
decades have seen rapid changes in roles to produce and
make use of computers. The speed of change in market coordination escapes the rigidity of many other social patterns.

*Black and gray markets.* For various reasons, people or their rulers forbid some kinds of market transactions: for example, in infants, sometimes in bodily organs, or in scarce concert tickets bought up and resold by scalpers. Or transactions are taxed or otherwise restricted—some governments, for example, heavily tax the importation of automobiles. Participants may then move to illegal transactions, intermixing black markets with legal ones. Anyone who has cheated on an income tax return may be a participant in an illegal market.

In communist systems, illegal transactions are common. Consumers create networks of favors and reciprocal obligations in order to obtain objects and performances not available through legally established channels. Managers of enterprises find that the planning system cannot be counted on to provide them with necessary inputs, which they then arrange to obtain by illegal transactions with other enterprises. Planners understand that these illegal transactions are necessary to make the system work, and they look the other way rather than suppress them. Not quite black, these are gray markets.

Black and gray markets account for a significant share of market activity all over the world, though their magnitude is difficult to estimate. They are found both in market systems and in communist systems, sometimes obstructing and sometimes facilitating coordination.

# Bones Beneath Flesh

The market system is not a place or a thing or even a collection of things. It is a set of activities of distinctive pattern. Certain customs and rules are required to make a market system, and to the degree that they are observed, a market system exists. Think of them as constituting the skeleton of the market system.

To identify these customs and rules is to throw various lights on the market system. They illuminate, for example, how it could have come into being and why participants play the roles they do. The lights also reveal the tight connections of the market system with liberty and property, and they place money and entrepreneurship in the system.

Let's start from scratch, building the skeleton one bone at a time.

1. Custom and law grant broad (but not equal) control to participants over the disposition of their own time and energy—in others words, legal *liberty*—in the pursuit of aspirations or claims of any kinds. *You are free, for example, to put your energies into building a house.*

In that statement there is hardly a hint of cooperation, only of possible mutual injury and the consequent need for peacekeeping. Nor is there yet a hint of market interactions. Nevertheless, broad personal freedom (of scope and limits to be discussed later) is a building bone or building block. Without it—peasants under feudal obligations were without it—a market system is impossible.

2. To broad rights to control one's own time and energy we add a parallel set of broad rights to control useful things. They are ordinarily known as *property* rights—customs and laws that enforce distribution of rights to make use of, offer, or deny to others such objects, including land, that people find useful in pursuing any aspirations. *To build a house, you possess—specifically, exercise control over—a piece of land, some building materials, a hammer and saw.*

The required rights do not have to be precisely the bundle of rights that in existing market systems goes by the name of private property. In particular, these rights may diverge from the great inequality of existing property rights. "Private property" is a term that raises people's temperatures when they move, as they often do, to the defense or the attack. Whether, however, existing property rights are applauded or deplored, some broad set of rights to control useful things is a necessity. Together with liberty it will set mutual adjustment into motion as people use their freedom and assets to pursue their aspirations.

These two rights, liberty and property, seem like perverse foundations for a system of broad social coordination, for they guarantee that, except for specific prohibitions, people can do as they wish. Yet coordination would seem to require that people do not simply do as they wish but instead bend to the requirements of cooperation and peacekeeping. All the more interesting, then, are the ways in which the two rights support cooperation and peacekeeping.

3. The third custom and rule necessary to a market system: quid pro quo. Aside from persuasion, the only permissible way to obtain desired performances or objects from another person, unless they are given as gifts, is through

contingent offers of benefit to the other. This rule immediately displays the possibilities of cooperation, and peaceful cooperation at that. One can neither threaten nor steal nor ask the state to use its powers to take or to compel another's cooperation. Interchange takes the form of a quid pro quo. *You can obtain your neighbors' help on your house or induce them to build it for you by offering them contingent benefits.*

The three customs and rules create a widespread process of mutual adjustment in which each participant explores innumerable possibilities of benefit for both self and other, thus innumerable opportunities for cooperating and reducing conflict. You can offer objects or your help—a performance—to induce others to teach your children or provide you with food or entertainment. You can cast about to obtain a variety of benefits offered in response to your offers. There is no prescribed list of options, no prescribed channel. You can search in any direction in pursuit of any aspirations with as much energy as you care to throw into the search.

There remains, however, a constraint on your opportunities to pursue your aspirations or claims. So far as our rules provide, you are limited to bartering. You have to find someone who can provide what you want. You want a massage—can you find someone who has the skill? That requires a *coincidence.* And if you find such a person, you are still blocked unless the masseur wants what you can offer. Will the masseur accept some vegetables from your garden? That requires a *second coincidence.*

Even so, barter is an advance over a kind of loose coordination common in many earlier societies, like the Kwakiutl, in which gifts obligate the recipient to make a reciprocal gift. Since the receiver decides how and when to reciprocate and can delay, such a custom of reciprocal gift-giving—unlike barter—offers little opportunity to use an offer of benefits to obtain a specified benefit in exchange.

The first step in solving the double-coincidence obstruction to coordination is a fourth rule or custom.

4. Some object of value that everyone is pleased to have enters into exchanges. Whether seashells, gold, or paper certificates, it is *money*. With money, the need for coincidence drops from two to only one—the second coincidence is no longer necessary. Although you still have to find someone who can offer you what you want, you do not now have to find one who wants a particular service or object that you can offer, for you offer not a particular service or object but the universally desired object. *To induce a carpenter or metalworker to help with your house, you do not have to find those who want your performance or objects. Any carpenter or hardware supplier will accept money as a sufficient inducement to give you the help you want*

5. With the use of money comes a shift of participants' activities from household use to performances and objects for *sale*. Instead of persisting in traditional household efforts together with peripheral barter or sales of surpluses, participants now let sales opportunities determine what they do. *You decide not to build a house but instead look for a line of activity that will increase or maximize your money income. Then you use the money income for various purposes, including buying a house.*

The shift to production for sale now eliminates the need for the first coincidence, which is that each person finds others who have what he or she is willing to buy. Can one find such others? With activity now aimed at sales, the society is full of people motivated to anticipate and satisfy my desires by offering whatever I stand ready to buy.

The market would be a pitifully poor social coordinator if it were, as it is sometimes naively conceived to be, a set of interactions in which people exchange surpluses of things they happen to find themselves able to offer. The market system is not a gigantic continuing flea market; indeed, it is not fairly characterized as an exchange system. Market relations do not begin with exchanges of performances and objects somehow "there" to be exchanged. Market relations determine what is to be made or done—and brought to exchange.

6. The search for sales opportunities gives rise to *intermediaries*. Would-be sellers find opportunities to sell objects and performances not only to people who directly want their goods, but to others who are also engaged in selling. They find it possible to sell trucks to persons selling kitchen appliances. Or they sell parts to the manufacturers of the appliances. Or parts to the manufacturers of other parts. Or electric power to any and all manufacturers. Or financial and accounting services to them. It is thanks to chains and webs of these intermediaries that the cafe operator and the coffee grower can cooperate to provide a cup of coffee to a customer. The intermediates provide the shipping, warehousing, processing, and other performances that forge the links between grower and cafe. Separated from and ignorant of each other as grower and cafe are, they could not otherwise be linked together. Thus *the house you buy drew for its construction on innumerable performances and objects coordinated through transactions to which you were not party.*

7. Some participants become specialized in intermediary roles, specifically in creating new intermediate links and in organizing combinations of labor, land, and capital

either for an intermediate link or for end objects and performances. To say the same thing less precisely but in a more familiar way, some participants create enterprises, and they are called entrepreneurs.

Entrepreneurs take advantage of the possibilities of roundaboutness. They offer not just hardware to users but create factories and office buildings, machines, equipment, parts, and other inputs for making hardware. In so doing they create enormous productive capital that accounts for much of the great increase in output that has accompanied the rise of market systems. To Marx this cumulation of capital was the core process of the market system, warranting the name capitalism.

When the entrepreneur who makes hardware counts on other entrepreneurs to build a factory and on still others for necessary machinery, each of these entrepreneurs counts on other entrepreneurs in turn. Long chains or large webs are thus constructed, and coordination of them becomes intricate and enormously far ranging.

Not ordinary people but entrepreneurs are the most frequent participants in market systems. They make careers of activities that move and transform labor and other inputs into called-for objects and performances. They are the moving spirits in the market system, the participants who make not only the most frequent but the most consequential decisions.

8. Many entrepreneurs operate on a scale that transforms their roles. They create collectives that can do what individual entrepreneurs cannot. They do this through the common practice of assembling spending power—that is, by borrowing through offers of interest or dividends. That enables them to organize larger feats of coordination than

are otherwise possible. *Thus, the construction of your house made use of electric power and materials that could have been provided only by a collective like Morgan Building Materials with capacities beyond those of an individual market participant.* The familiar dominant legal form of these collectives in our time is the corporation, odd as it may seem to call the corporation a collective.

These, then, are the bones of the market system: liberty, property, the quid pro quo, money, activity for sale, intermediaries, entrepreneurs, and collectives. Again the market dance waits for the state to provide the floor and the orchestra. Even the ordinary market participant counts on the state for safety on the way to the supermarket, but the dependence of entrepreneurs on state aid might be called desperate. Their initiatives put them at high risk of great loss; hence, as noted, they will move only timidly or not at all without a variety of state aids.

## The "Chaos" of the Market?

When we reflect on the millions of people who cooperate to deliver a cup of coffee from Colombia to Milan or on the claim that no institution, not even the state, matches the market in capacity to organize cooperation, we might wonder why we still hear from time to time the phrase "the chaos of the market." Chaos it is not. What might people mean by such a charge? To some people it means only that markets often look chaotic. An early morning wholesale produce market looks messy. Trading in many stock exchanges—a turbulence of gestures and cries—sometimes looks more like a street demonstration than an organized

interchange. I grant the superficial appearance of disorder
in some markets. Despite this appearance, all the noise
and movement are part of a precise, fast-moving coordination. To supply a city with fresh produce constitutes an
impressive feat of coordination, yet the accomplishment
is a daily one in early morning fruit and vegetable markets
all over the world.

Others see more than a superficial appearance of disorder. Through recorded history and folk memories, we are repeatedly reminded of the depression of the 1930s in which
many millions of people all over the world were exiled from
the system by losing their jobs—a descent toward chaos for
them. In some nations that descent engulfed a third of the
population, even if most people in every society continued
to find orderly life, work, and social interchange. One might
fear that it could happen again. Perhaps. But more than a
half century has gone by without a repetition of such a catastrophe. Societies have greatly improved their knowledge
of how to stabilize the market system through, among
other possibilities, governmental expenditure and management of the supply of money and credit.

Still, like all social institutions large and small, the market system in its normal operations fails us—falters in its
coordination—on some counts. Every few years it falls
into that abnormality called recession—small depressions
dwarfed by that of the 1930s, yet still damaging. So frequently does it fall into recession that we might as well call
those abnormalities normal. They impose hardship on millions of people. But neither recessions nor any of the other
defects of the market system warrant the careless assertion
that the market system produces chaos. In our time the
greatest threat of worldwide disorganization of the market

system may lie in reckless banking and incompetent governmental regulation of financial markets. Feeding on itself and growing, disorder might spread from one country to another, as it did from Indonesia in 1997 to other Asian economies, Brazil, and Russia. Even for that, however, "chaos" is hyperbole.

# Enterprise and Corporation

In market-system coordination, everyone gets into the act. Among those coordinated there are no inactive or passive nonparticipants. Yet, as I have said, entrepreneurs and enterprises, the largest of which are corporations, are the kingpins. What are the powers of these market participants? How are they controlled? I think we can do better than such popular formulations as that corporations today rule the world (they do and they don't), that enterprises are governed by irresponsible rapacious executives (often the case but of less significance than might first appear), that, for good or bad, corporations have displaced the market system (a wild exaggeration), or that they can be trusted to govern themselves (power corrupts).

Entrepreneurs and corporations are typically the immediate or, as I shall say, the proximate decision makers on what cooperation is to be attempted and by what means. Proximate decisions have to be made on converting objects and performances (like steel) into other wanted objects and performances (like file cabinets, painted and delivered). In the immediate situation, people in the mass do not—and cannot—make such decisions. Entrepreneurs, who do make them, are of course governed by their anticipations of mass response—they cannot survive if customers do not buy. Still, the proximate decision is theirs: on what pesticides are to be made available to farmers, say, or whether to manufacture quiet cement mixers. Look at the long chains of interactions that connect inputs at one end to performances and objects desired at the other end—from coffee grower to cafe. You and I wait passively at one end of a chain and are absent from the thousands of interactions between enterprises that construct the chain that finally reaches us.

Just as enterprises are the most frequent participants in the market system, so also are they, except for some governments, the biggest. On one side of many a transaction stands an individual person; on the other side a corporate collective. As a jurist put it, "elephants dancing among the chickens." There is not even a rough similarity of influence between Nestlé or Unilever, on one hand, and one of their customers or employees on the other. General Motors, among the world's largest corporations, has hundreds of thousands of employees. The transactions that put the performances of each employee at GM's disposal in return for a wage do not look at all like the transaction between a village blacksmith and a hired helper. Indeed, these corporate collectives are often the size of a nation rather than of a person. Each of the world's largest corporations, if measured by sales, produces more than the gross national product of many a nation. Of the one hundred largest organized entities in the world, only a half are nations, the other half corporations.

A single enterprise is often itself a collection of enterprises reaching into many markets. Bertelsmann, anchored in Germany, contains 375 companies in 30 countries, including book publishers, bookstores, radio and television stations, printing plants, makers of tapes and records, magazine publishers (more than a hundred), and paper manufacturers. And there are networks of legally independent enterprises like the six *keiretsu* conspicuous in Japan, each conglomerate built on overlapping stock ownership. In all market systems, looser combinations of enterprises rest on "relations of reciprocity, altruism, friendship, reputation, and collaboration as principles of governance."

Corporations not only proximately control a society's flow of the performances and objects that you and I want but also control great cumulations of whatever it takes to make them available: land and capital, and a labor force. Custom and law permit corporations to acquire massive funds with which to buy or hire these resources. Through bank loans, issued stocks or bonds, and other forms of credit, corporations control aggregates of capital that they could not own outright with their own wealth and income.

The state often steps in to curb corporate market power, another reminder that the market system is always mixed with other social institutions and processes. In our time, the market system is heavily and constantly regulated. Whether the state will curb the corporation's market power depends on the political system, in which the corporation is a steady and powerful participant. In many circumstances the outcome turns out to be state support rather than a curb on corporate market power, as when the state imposes import restrictions to protect the monopoly powers of a domestic corporation.

As everyone knows, whether they think about it or not, entrepreneurs and enterprises, especially corporations, exercise political power beyond the capacity of ordinary citizens. Their power in government not only broadly distorts democracy, it also enables them to extract from the state a variety of benefits, often at great cost to everyone else: for example, financial bailouts that protect executives, stockholders, lenders, and creditors from losses deriving from mismanagement. Common as such extractions are all over the globe, they are unlikely to reach the magnitude of the American bailout in the 1980s of the savings-and-loan banks, a rescue that has been estimated to cost taxpayers more than $200 billion. But I set aside business political power until Chapter 17. Here I want to examine market power, as well as its political determinants.

The executives of all but the smallest enterprises constitute, as proximate decision makers, a key group of movers and shakers in market societies. Their services to society are conspicuous, great, and indispensable, yet, because of their great power, troubling. In these respects executives are like government officials. In their functions the two groups are parallel but not identical. They share responsibility for proximate decisions over society's greatest tasks or achievements in social coordination. It is a characteristic of market societies that many of these tasks are turned over to the proximate control of market executives.

In market societies some major decisions—for example, on taxes or whether to drop bombs—are in the proximate hands of government executives. In the hands of market executives are no less important proximate decisions on how labor is to be allocated to the society's many industries, or what industries are to be established, or how income shares are to be distributed. In democratic societies the two groups differ in how they are controlled, the governmental group by ballot and political agitation, the market group by customers who can refuse to buy. They do not differ, however, in importance or magnitude of task. The greatest tasks are divided between them, and both sets of tasks are indispensable.

## Elites and Mass

Following respected precedents, I shall call members of the two groups elites, in contrast to everyone else, whom I shall call mass. In doing so I should like to strip the words of their frequent nuances—as when "elite" implies aristocratic superiority or sophistication in taste. Nor are elites necessarily conspiratorial and exploitative, even if they often are; nor are masses necessarily ignorant and unruly, even if they often are.

An old and continuing social problem is how to maintain mass control over elites. By democratic standards, mass or popular political control through the ballot is always a partial failure. Failures in control of market elites seem roughly parallel to failures in control of governmental elites. That is what monopoly amounts to. The word denotes many of the familiar ways that market elites evade or weaken mass control over them. Advertising is of course one, including misrepresentation of product. Driving competitors out of business is another. With patents, governments bestow monopoly powers on market elites. Governments also come to their aid with import quotas, tariffs, licensing laws, and other inventive restrictions on the range of competition. All of these practices limit the power of a customer, which he can exercise only if he can refuse to buy.

In politics, popular control over elites is a general requirement for democracy and often defines democracy. Yet it calls for at least occasional exceptions. Some issues under some circumstances, most of us believe, are better left in the hands of the government elites. Similarly, monopoly has its place. Monopoly prices, as in the pharmaceutical industry, which rests on patents, provide funds for research and innovation. Whether patents offer more protection and income than is desirable for that purpose is, however, much disputed.

Monopoly is not, however, a broad enough concept to

encompass all the major obstructions to mass or popular control over market elites. Often more dangerous to human welfare are other failures in popular or customer control. In market systems, buyers control only the most conspicuous features of what market elites offer. You and I choose the shape and softness we desire in a mattress. But we have only weak or no market control at all, aside from an occasional boycott, over elite decisions on many of the attributes of the mattress not visible to us—its flammability, for example. An even greater failure in customer control lies in buyer ignorance of, hence impotence on, decisions regarding the location of enterprises, on their working conditions, and on what potentially dangerous chemical or other ingredients they use or discharge as waste. Ranging aggressively over the earth in our time, corporations like Hitachi or Texas Industries transform land, air, water, and human habitation, often destructively, relatively free from popular customer control exercised through the market system. Some of these impacts are controlled through government regulation, although mass often fails to control the government elites who do the regulating.

I am aware that many people do not care about these impacts and make roughly the same case as just noted for monopoly. They trust that the impacts are only local and small. Or they claim an offsetting advantage of weak customer control—it allows enterprises great breadth of autonomy and stimulates their ambitions. Corporate independence, even corporate irresponsibility, they would say, accounts for the high outputs of market systems. Problem or not—we return to it in Chapter 11—weakness of popular control over market elites is a fact.

But again, in all systems, not only market systems, elites do in large part escape mass control, a proposition widely subscribed to by political analysts, and a hundred years ago dubbed the "iron law" by Robert Michels. Both market and democratic governmental elites often claim to be "servants of the people." But they are too big and powerful to be servants and no more likely to behave as servants than would a giant in your household. Often they respond to an aggregate of preferences—that is, to election returns or sales reports—but they do not much respond to any of us as individuals. And the aggregate of preferences they often mold or manipulate rather than simply accept. They listen closely to each other, but to mass they listen less than they talk. For mass to instruct them to do anything is usually impossible. Instead, at best, mass waits for their decisions and only then, if it learns about them and does not like them, can sometimes negate them by refusing to reelect the elite or to buy from them. Cyclists could not persuade British motorcycle firms to install self starters, but they could and did shift to Japanese cycles, leaving the British industry in ruins.

How can one characterize in some summary way the power of market elites and the power of mass to control them? Some of my American colleagues tell me that they live in a democracy; others say they do not. Both groups are correct, for one group's criteria for democracy are satisfied by American institutions while the other group's more demanding criteria are not. Does the market system provide a tolerable or unacceptable degree of mass control over market elites? It depends on criteria, and there exists no standard set.

## The Two Elites Contrasted

I do not know of any better way to move toward a summary statement than to pursue a few steps further a comparison of the powers of governmental and market elites. To a significant degree both elites reveal a hostility to mass control. They often believe that they know best what mass should have. More than that, members of both elites enjoy special powers, opportunities, wealth, positions of prestige, and deference that mass demands slowly erode. Elites resist the erosion. Have they ever not done so?

Elites usually deny their hostility to popular control, and in fact they do not always recognize it in themselves. The lords and bishops of sixteenth-century Western Europe convinced themselves that their controls over the peasantry benefited rather than exploited them. They maintained this in the face of gross deprivation of the peasantry in contrast to their own wealth and privileges. In England, eighteenth- and nineteenth-century upper-class citizens hostile to the Chartists and to other advocates of democratic movements defended inequality and poverty as necessary to English society. Charles Dickens's portraits in fiction of deprivation and misery did not sway them to the contrary. Although contemporary elites do not try to justify these earlier positions, now often denounced as inhumane, they defend today's elite positions: hostility to organized labor, defense of inequalities of wealth, and attacks on the welfare state. They publicly defend their positions again not as advantageous to elites but as for the common good.

The hostility of market elites to mass is, however, directed far less at customers than at employees. The historical record is one of dogged, harsh, and often bloody entrepreneurial resistance to employee demands for better pay and working conditions, protection against arbitrary managerial authority, and—sometimes—employee participation in management. Market elites are vulnerable to challenge when employees cite the practice of democracy out-side the workplace as a reason for bringing it inside as well.

Yet in market systems employer power over wages is greatly limited. In both union and nonunion employment, competition drives wages up inexorably as new opportuni-ties for profit, especially those created by capital accumula-tion and new technologies, make employees increasingly valuable to entrepreneurs. The powers of even the most hostile entrepreneurs are curbed by that competition. Slowly, fitfully, and with occasional relapses, as in the '90s, wages rise in all market systems. In market systems workers are now wealthy when compared with their grandfathers.

For many employees, that is not enough. The conse-quent never-ending struggle of workers for more control over market elites—and the wages they pay—is no minor attribute of market systems. In their cold war, employers and employees persist even where and when they put vio-lence behind them.

In their relation not to their employees but to their cus-tomers, market elites differ significantly from governmen-tal elites in their relations to citizens. Historically, govern-mental elites have resisted mass or popular electoral control so successfully that most of the world's people have not yet established democratic governments. Even where demo-cratic government exists, political elites often twist and turn to weaken it: for example, trying to "buy" political of-fice, as did Helmut Kohl, as head of Germany's Christian Democratic Union, and Joseph Kennedy, in winning the American presidency for his son. In contrast, market elites have less reason to resist mass control achieved through market purchases. For what the market elites derive as benefits from the market system depends greatly on their providing, not denying, buyers what they want.

There are great exceptions to that benign proposition. "I owe the public nothing," attributed, perhaps mistakenly, to the great financier J. P. Morgan, expresses a historical hostility of market elite to mass. When enterprises can establish some degree of monopolistic control over their markets—a common possibility—they are motivated to raise prices. Earnings go up; what people get goes down. Also at the expense of their customers, enterprises, especially large bureaucratic ones, often offer executives a variety of routes to enrichment, from embezzlement to esoteric financial ploys that divert funds from the enterprise to private purses, as in the debacle of the American savings-and-loan industry.

Advertising appears to be clear evidence that market elites want to manipulate mass rather than simply respond to the preferences signaled by purchases. Yet one wonders why an enterprise would not prefer to sell people whatever they want, not spending greatly, as enterprises do, to influence their preferences. Perhaps the most compelling explanation of sales promotion is that investment and long lead times are necessary to provide people with what they want. Once an enterprise sets out to satisfy potential customers, it intends to be sure that they do not then change their minds, a situation reminiscent of early portrait photographers, who fastened the subject's head in a metal clamp not to imprison the subject but so that a movement would not spoil the picture. The executives at Braun, as an example, are capable of a variety of entrepreneurial responses to mass needs; but, having geared up heavily to produce shavers and other appliances, they struggle to induce consumers to buy—and buy more of—what they have prepared themselves to sell. That would also explain why, in advance of investment, market elites often spend on research into buyer preferences.

I have observed that in the market system, some kinds of elite decisions—on enterprise location, working conditions, use of chemicals, and disposal of waste—largely escape control by buyers. We can now generalize that observation. With your spending you can specify that you want a particular accomplished *output*—say, a cellular phone. But you can exercise almost no market power over the production process. On these decisions, not on what is to be made but where and how, buyers' controls are almost nonexistent.

Political voting is strikingly different. One usually casts a vote for a process—or for an intention—rather than for an accomplished output. Voter or representative in legislature or parliament votes an instruction to government officials to try to reduce inflation or curb crime, the result of which remains in doubt. One often votes for a hoped-for change, for a candidate who takes a position, or for a party with a pledge, but rarely for an accomplished result or output.

This distinction between control over result and control over process may soften in the future. The Internet opens up new possibilities for boycott or for other collective action among buyers who may be stimulated to take a stronger interest in process. The Internet of course also strengthens buyer control over results when buyers use their new voices to protest or applaud the design or quality of products and services offered them and use their new ears to pick up information on purchases they contemplate.

Some further useful contrasts between voting with ballots and voting with money have to be approached with care. They are only rough comparisons, a little like comparing a shovel and a rake. Both tools break the soil and for that reason can be compared, but their functions differ, and there is little point in faulting a rake because it is not useful for deep digging. Similarly, balloting and market voting are forms of mass control of elites. But ballots have the function of resolving conflict or, more precisely, of deciding who wins and who loses. The results of balloting impose losses on those outvoted. But when you vote with your money for a cellular phone, no one may lose. Although conflict arises on who gets what share of the product of social cooperation, when you come to the market to cast your money vote for the phone, your share has already been decided by decisions on wages, interest, and dividends. Your money vote simply expresses your choice of the particular form—the phone— in which you want to claim some of your already decided share.

Still, the differences between the two methods of voting are illuminating. In a market system a customer's vote gives the market elite relatively precise direction: one can vote, say, for a touring bicycle, 23-inch frame of bonded carbon fiber tubes, and 21-speed wide-range gearing. Political voters cannot match that specificity, even though they can vote for an individual candidate or party. One of the many imprecisions of balloting is that the voter must choose a candidate or party that takes a position on each of many issues, only some of which the voter intends to endorse. The winning party or candidate does not know whether it won a voter's ballot because the voter wants a tax program offered by the party or candidate or because the voter wants to endorse the candidate or party on some other issue.

Another precision in market voting: When you cast a money vote, you simultaneously pay. Your vote specifies precisely the temperature of your desire, taking into account the cost of trying to satisfy it. In balloting, you cannot be equivalently rational. Political voting is a more clumsy all-or-none. You do not know what your vote is going to cost you. Some people will have to pay taxes, but who, when, and how much you will pay you do not know and cannot specify in your vote.

In the market system, moreover, voters do not merely signal or inform the elite; they compel it. The enterprise whose executives do not respond to consumer signals goes broke. Conversely, the political vote does not in any comparable degree compel the political elite. A winning candidate or party has difficulty reading the signals, trying to understand what the vote pattern says on each issue. That in itself typically denies the political vote any significant compelling power on any issue. But even if elites know clearly what voters want on any issue, the compulsion to respond is weak, often to the point of vanishing. Did my constituents make it clear to me that they want a tax cut? Yes, but they may have forgotten about the issue by the time of the next election. Or they will vote for me again even if I disappoint them on a tax cut if I gratify them on some other issues. Or it will be easy for me to posture in favor of a tax cut, then blame the failure to achieve it on others.

In democratic theory, it is a point of pride that political voting usually assigns one vote to each adult, not at all like the gross inequality of market voting. The pride is misplaced, however—although the claim is true, it is misleading. To influence an election, obviously your spending can multiply the power of your single vote, as presumably every campaign contributor at least half realizes. Market inequality, it is increasingly obvious, translates into inequalities in popular control over government.

The economist Joseph Schumpeter, among others before

and since, eloquently argued more than fifty years ago that political voting on issues demands too much of voters. Because it demands, so he wrote, more thought and information than the voter can manage, political voting cannot serve effectively as a control over governmental policies in the way that market voting does over entrepreneurial policies. The political voter confronts such complex problems as how to cope with ethnic conflict, a problem without obvious solution. As Schumpeter saw it, even a complex choice among life insurance policies is easier than a choice of policies to reduce ethnic conflict.

It is an important contrast. It points to another as well, as Schumpeter saw. Mass control over governmental elites would on some counts be improved if mass chose not among alternative policies but chose instead, as it usually does, among alternative elites. Let the elites choose the policies; leave mass the function of turning out any government elite that disappoints. In effect, voters give up a method of specific control for which they lack the competence in order to practice a looser control for which their competence may suffice.

Such a strategic choice is not possible for buyers. In a market system, there is little room for escape from the necessity to cast market votes through one's purchases—and to cast them frequently and endlessly. If you do not vote, you get nothing.

There is no question that entrepreneurs and their enterprises are powerful participants in the market system, many thousands of them each dwarfing the ordinary individual participant. As disproportionately strong and key participants making the major proximate decisions, they are like their brother governmental elites. Popular control over them, as through voting by spending, imposes a strong

and sometimes overwhelming constraint on some market-
elite powers. But it is a wholly inadequate constraint on
others. Popular control of market elites is on several points
stronger than popular control over governmental elites, although the latter is itself far from ideal.

## Islands of Command in a Market Sea

Elite and mass power aside, the place in the market system
of the collective enterprise, especially the large corporation,
is not quite what it is often taken to be. For that reason it is
all the more interesting to examine further. A common understanding is that the enterprise, especially the corporate
enterprise, is the key institution of the market system, indeed the quintessence of it. While not at all challenging
that interpretation, I would, however, point out that it is
also internally a nonmarket or even antimarket institution,
though lodged within a market system. It is a way of achieving coordination of some activities through managerial
command rather than through market interactions. To that
extent—and it is a great extent—corporate coordination is
a rival to rather than an instrument of market-system coordination.

Think of a clothing enterprise in need of a variety of col-
ors for the cloth it uses. It might arrange to buy already dyed
cloth from various suppliers. Or it might buy cloth and then
turn it over to dyers who on contract color it in their own
enterprises. Or it might opt for a cheaper, faster, or more
controllable process if it were to organize the dyeing under
its own managerial supervision. If it chooses to dye its own
cloth, it has displaced the market system for coordination
of the dyeing process and in its place has carved out a small
arena for coordination under its own authority. It has cre-

ated an island of authority or central planning in a market-system sea.

Every collective enterprise obviously coordinates some of its inputs and participants by its own command, at least managing most or all of its workforce. Vast national and global coordination through market transactions succeeds in assembling for Hindustan Motors, for example, a labor force, equipment, and inputs of many kinds. Yet the task of coordination is not completed until, within the enterprise, all the inputs are further coordinated to produce an intended output. This further coordination can to some degree be accomplished by market transactions within the enterprise. Hindustan could pay workers for each output while charging them for use of equipment and other inputs, leaving to each worker the decision on where and how to proceed. But with few exceptions, it will instead pay workers simply to accept managerial authority—that is, to do their tasks as a coordinating management directs. As an employee might perceive it, market coordination stops at the door of the enterprise; on the other side of the door, authoritative command awaits. A market transaction brings an employee to and through the door; then command takes over.

In any society coordination first requires large-scale coordination to assemble workers and inputs in an enterprise, and then smaller-scale coordination within each enterprise. In market systems, market transactions largely accomplish the first requirement; but central command broadly displaces the market system for the second.

In recent decades, highly centralized authority within the enterprise has appeared to be on a decline. At the same time, innovative forms of mutual adjustment have been on the rise, with decisions being made by work groups instead of by foremen, for example, and horizontal communication taking the place of some of the older vertical communications (from management down to lower levels). These reforms represent decentralization of management, but they do not necessarily include moves within the enterprise from management coordination to market-system coordination.

Many corporations have greatly stirred themselves to make just that move as well: that is, to shrink their arenas of command, whether decentralized or not, and make more use of the market system internally within the enterprise. Like every corporation, Lufthansa—one of many examples—faces the problem of how best to coordinate its various divisions. Dissatisfied with its internal coordination by command, in 1995 it transformed several of its divisions—cargo, maintenance, and data processing—into separate corporations to be coordinated by sales to and purchases from the parent company and its other divisions.

Yet coordination by command is inescapable in some arenas. Gathered around a patient prepared for surgery, a surgical team cannot coordinate through market transactions between members. The team's collective success requires a managing surgeon or a delicate nonmarket mutual adjustment among the members. So ordinary a task as loading a freight car or running an assembly line requires elements of managerial coordination that market transactions cannot adequately accomplish.

When one enterprise tries to minimize its internal tasks of coordination through command by turning to the market system, it may shift only those tasks to another enterprise, making coordination by command that enterprise's problem. For example, concerned with high costs and the various difficulties of managing a labor force, Benneton, the

Italian clothing company, contracts with many small enterprises for some of its needs: embroidery and pressing,
among others. While that reduces the size of Benneton's internal command system, it does not necessarily shrink the
place of coordination by command in clothing and supporting enterprises. It has simply transferred to the contractors
the task of managing the workforce, which is now their
problem, not Benneton's.

In these several ways, the collective enterprise in the
market system creates islands of command coordination in
a sea of market mutual adjustment. The structure of every
collective enterprise is the result of entrepreneurial decisions on the size and shape of the island. If Volkswagen buys
windshields and tires from other enterprises, then it will be
a smaller enterprise from one that coordinates their production itself. The very existence of a collective enterprise or
corporation represents an entrepreneur's choice of command over market system for some range of activities. Factories and other collective enterprises, consequently, are
markers of—one might say monuments to—market inadequacy, paradoxical as that may seem. The more the coordination by corporate management, the less by the market
system. The corporation is indeed an alternative to the
market system. We can imagine, for example, the shoe
manufacturer of Chapter 3 deciding to bring under its own
management the tanning operations that it now buys in international markets.

That is not the whole story of why entrepreneurs create
corporate islands of command in a market sea. Entrepreneurs also seek the special privileges given by the state to
corporate investors. By law, investors are freed from responsibility to repay debts incurred by an enterprise. Although
they may find their stock shares worthless if the enterprise

fails, that is the limit of their liability. Governments have granted this and other privileges, like interlocking of governing boards in order to improve the prospects of corporations. Governmental motives to help are mixed: they range from a predatory desire of officials to enrich themselves to statesmanlike intentions to stimulate desirable investments. One suspects that the grants of privilege have far exceeded expectation. In any case, they have made enormous enterprises attractive to investors and entrepreneurs. Researchers of corporate history are greatly divided on the relative importance of the factors that explain the growth of large corporations. The dispute is especially severe between those who find efficiency to be predominant and those who find monopolistic aggrandizement together with corporate political influence to be predominant. Whatever one thinks on that issue, enterprises do grow; and internally they require management beyond what the market system can provide. One can think of the world of corporations as a world of planned systems, coordinated with one another not by a plan but by the market system.

## Forms of Ownership

For at least one hundred years, the great issue in how to control the enterprise was private versus government ownership. Socialists believed in government ownership, and that belief defined socialists. Socialists also wanted government-owned enterprises to be taken out of the market system to operate under a hierarchy of political controls—democratic socialists specifying, of course, that the controls be democratic. Market controls, many socialists thought, were not controls at all but a confusion of self-interests. Slowly they learned that the market is indeed a system of controls, in some respects highly functional. They also learned that private enterprises did not necessarily gain— and often lost—in efficiency when taken over by government as owner and operator. Their passion for government ownership and operation gradually fell off. Even if government enterprises might be made superior to private, socialists began to believe that they would not be much superior. The path to a better system would have to run in another direction: through the welfare state and reduction of excessive inequalities in wealth and income, as well as in education, status, and opportunity.

As a consequence, a number of societies have privatized a number of the industries that were socialized after World War II. And they have moved beyond grand debate over broad programs, such as to nationalize (or privatize) all large corporations, to debate over proposals specific to a single industry or enterprise.

In the meantime, during the noisy debate over private versus public enterprise, market societies quietly developed a variety of forms of ownership and enterprise. One was the enterprise owned and managed by its own employees or some category of them. Although such enterprises are infrequent in industry, they are common among service enterprises: law, accounting, medical care, trucking, and taxi services, among many others. In Sweden, for example, worker cooperatives account for all taxi services and, as in Israel, 50 percent of trucking.

Another form of ownership is the agricultural cooperative engaged in buying and then marketing—and sometimes processing—its member-owners' products. Milk co-ops, for example, also manufacture cheese. In Western European nations, the co-op share of agricultural marketing is often about 50 percent.

Retail enterprises owned by their customers are common but usually marginal, accounting for less than 5 percent of retail sales in Britain, less in Germany, and less than 1 percent in the United States. Enterprises are often also jointly owned by other enterprises that want the products of the joint enterprise. They account, for example, for 80 percent of the U.S. hardware market. Associated Press is such a jointly owned enterprise. Farm enterprises commonly establish such jointly owned enterprises to provide them with seeds, fertilizer, and equipment.

Not very common the world over are nonprofit enterprises, owned neither by investors nor by customers nor by employees—not owned at all, yet nevertheless with legal standing and an authorized controlling governing board. In the United States, however, they account for a large share, sometimes more than half, of such human services as hospital care and higher education.

Often bitter questions about private property and its unequal distribution continue to be debated. For all but a few dissenters, personal private property rights—your rights to "your" clothing, for example—are not much disputed. But who should own an enterprise is indeed disputed. It is a question not about personal property rights but about control over productive assets—the rights to control the use of such assets as land, buildings, and machinery, and then claim their earnings.

The common corporate form of organization separates ownership of assets from actual control over them. Formal ownership—which means possession of stock certificates—leaves most stockholders passive and powerless. The control of the assets of the conventional corporation lies in the hands of a small number of executives chosen by members of a de facto self-perpetuating governing board or by an executive team. Those in control usually own shares of stock, but often those shares are issued to them as payment or bonus for their performance, clear evidence that the ownership followed rather than preceded their assumption of control of the enterprise and was not a prerequisite to it.

In today's world the relation between formal ownership and actual control has become even more complex. Hence the question: Who actually exercises control over the corporation—its executives or its stockholders? A variety of answers is possible. An answer for Germany, for example, is "not necessarily either," for the great German banks that supply corporations with credit have taken, as a condition of making loans, a strong hand in corporate management. An answer increasingly true for the United States is again "not necessarily either," but for a different reason. American managers of huge investment funds claim a share of control of the corporations in which they invest.

I make this point about the various connections and disconnections between ownership and control not to lament either, nor to express any regret for the powerlessness of most stockholders or owners. Instead, I make it to suggest that it no longer so much matters who formally owns a corporation as how its executives operate: by what rules, for what objectives, subject to what incentives, with what rewards, and to whom responsible. One can imagine a society's designing packages of controls, each unique to a category of enterprises, the society no longer to be characterized by any terms as simpleminded, as, say "the private enterprise system."

There may be, however, one basic critical distinction between two kinds of corporations. Some corporations have easy access to governmental funds that bail them out when they run into difficulties. Others do not. Many, perhaps most, state-owned enterprises fall into the first group, as do some conventional corporations. They are notorious for calling on public funds to save themselves and their employees from the consequences of their own managerial errors. China is burdened with sick enterprises kept alive by governmental funds for fear of the unemployment that would follow if each had to stand on its own feet. In the other category, do not look for industries that are never bailed out—there are none. But there are many enterprises for which bailout is infrequent or even rare, not easy to win, and uncertain. Some state-owned corporations and many conventional corporations fall into this category. The significance of the first category, about which more is to be said later, is worth some speculation at this juncture. For the existence and persistence of ostensibly private enterprises in the first category undermine the common distinction between the market-oriented enterprise and the centrally planned one.

One last reminder. Enterprise outputs and prices are proximately decided by human beings, often in tough negotiations with each other; they do not simply emerge from "market forces." Such forces do indeed both push and constrain. But what are they? When an enterprise sets a price or negotiates a wage with a union, the influences that bear on it, although often conceived of as abstract "market forces," are, if spelled out, in fact the activities of all other market participants. This is to recognize once more that the market system is a system of human behavior, not wholly understandable in any other terms.

# Maximum Reach

What is the maximum domain, scope, or reach of the market system? At this maximum, which of a society's tasks or processes can be coordinated by the market system? In recent times, proposals have abounded to organize through the market system various activities earlier assumed to be beyond market scope—the operation of prisons is an example. Whether it makes sense to try to expand or constrict the market system depends on an understanding of what it can and cannot do. Can it, for example, organize collective efforts or only individual efforts?

Clearly it is possible to coordinate the disposal of orphaned infants by permitting market transactions like those for heifers. But many societies choose not to do so—choose not to push the market system to its fullest use. Thus we distinguish between maximum market domain and chosen market domain. Let us explore its maximum domain in this chapter, its chosen domain in the next.

Those who live in a market system form a realistic rough estimate of its maximum domain, yet conflicting images trouble their estimates. On the one hand, they often see the market system as pervading all aspects of life. "Everything for sale," as in a recent book title: votes, legislative favors, love, loyalty, and, according to some fundraising evangelists, divine intervention to bring health and wealth. On the other hand, they see the market system as limited to one of several distinctive major segments of society, politics embracing another, church and religion an-

other, family another, and so on. These views are not confused but perceptive. The market system indeed pervades
all aspects of life. Congregations hire pastors and build
buildings. Artists buy instruction and sell their performances. This reality notwithstanding, we can separate aspects of society. Individual, family, church, and state all buy
and sell in the market system and are in that sense part of it;
but we find it not too difficult to distinguish each segment
from the others and each from the market system in which
each participates.

## Domain Misperceived

Yet scope remains elusive. Even if we distinguish between
market system and church or between market system and
state, we find it difficult to say—and most of us do not even
try—just what activities do or do not fall within the scope
of the market system. One common proposition is that the
market system coordinates the economy, but not the whole
society. That is a mistake, and a good way to begin the
analysis of market-system scope is to see why.

What in fact do people pursue through their market activities? Food and shelter, of course. But also entertainment, novelty and adventure, power, prestige, love, privacy,
sociability, and companionship. Indeed, it appears that the
entire range of human aspiration is pursued both inside and
outside of market activities. *There exists no set of purposes
that is distinctly market,* and the scope of the market system has nothing to do with the character of the purposes
people pursue in it. On this point, we get a clear implication
that market-system scope is far broader than it is sometimes said to be.

To understand the market system's scope one has to rid

one's mind of the idea that there exists a defined set of human activities, such as go by the name of economic, to which the market system is limited. The scope of the market system is far broader than such an idea suggests. And that is why, back in Chapter 2, I sounded the note: think society, not economy.

A common set of distinctions sets economy against polity and contrasts both of them with society. I find this threefold distinction more often obstructive than useful. For one thing, the polity—the political system—is the dominant participant in the market system, as a rule maker and as a price maker (buyer and seller). Whatever "economy" might turn out to mean, polity and economy are fused. As for a distinction between economy and society, the latter consists of many processes by which a mere aggregate of people is coordinated into an interacting people curbing injury to each other and cooperating. But that is precisely what market systems broadly—both nationally and globally—accomplish: coordination for social peace and cooperation. For our purposes, we do not need the tripartite distinction. Again, the scope of the market system is far broader than it is often said to be.

Let's get rid of some further misconceptions on scope. A frequent opinion is that the market system's scope is the organization or coordination of a society's material or materialistic pursuits. Some people incorrectly take this to mean the pursuit of objects—things that have weight and volume. Market domain is much broader than that. In advanced industrial systems, commodities—that is, objects or things—account for fewer market sales than do services—that is, performances rather than objects, ranging from concerts to repairs.

Even when people buy a material object, they do so in

pursuit of nonmaterial ends or objectives. They buy clothing for, among other reasons, social conformity. They buy food for, among other reasons, taste. In any case the very idea of end or purpose seems to imply an intangible—ends and purposes by definition usually refer to states of mind, not objects.

One might think, however, that to pursue a nonmaterial objective like social conformity or a pleasant taste one must always first acquire a material object or thing—a shirt or a lobster. Market or not, almost everything we do of course requires objects: tools, materials, and the like. But market life is not distinctive or conspicuous in this respect. Even a prayer meeting usually requires chairs and hymnals, perhaps a candle. Play requires toys.

It is careless to suggest that market activity consists of fabricating objects or things. Although fabrication is a part of market life, producing theatrical performances or restructuring a corporation is also market activity. And the provision of Colombian coffee to a Milan cafe is overwhelmingly an accomplishment of a long chain of performances, a process going far beyond the fabrication of objects.

To many people, "material" or "materialistic" refers not exclusively to physical objects but to any purpose or end, however intangible, pursued through money and market. According to that meaning, buying a concert ticket is a material or materialistic pursuit. If that is so, then an aspiration to seek nirvana through the paid-for advice of a guru becomes a material aspiration. Although it is a curious departure from the literal meaning of "material," such an interpretation does not help us at all. It simply declares that market activities, whatever they may be, are by definition to be called material. That leaves us without a clue as to what activities can and cannot be organized through the market system.

One has to jettison other similar misconceptions. The market system coordinates the pursuit of wealth? That is too narrow, for it also coordinates the pursuit of performances. Does it at least include coordination of the pursuit of wealth? Here thinking often goes wrong. By definition, wealth consists of those things that can be owned and sold in the market as distinct from things, however valuable, that cannot. Furnaces heat buildings, as does the sun. Furnaces can be and are owned; the sun cannot be and is not. Consequently, furnaces are wealth; the sun is not. But we do not know which kinds of performances and objects can be owned and sold, which not; all we know is that if a thing can be brought into the market, whatever it is, we will call it wealth. We have gone in a circle. Instead of saying that the market system coordinates the pursuit of wealth (as well as of performances), we should correctly say that, if it can coordinate the pursuit of an object, we shall call that object wealth.

We might be tempted to think that the market organizes work. Not play. Not prayer. Not scientific discovery. Not reading, walking, singing, dreaming, or inventing. The market system is only the world of work. For some purposes, such an interpretation will do. For most purposes, however, including ours, it is too loose. Moses worked to lead his people to the Promised Land, Leonardo to paint the Mona Lisa, and Einstein to create relativity theory. But most of us would think it demeaning, as well as false, to classify their work as market activity rather than, respectively, as political, artistic, and scientific. Do I work in my garden? Do I ever work at parenting? Does the pope ever work? Yes, yes, and yes; but none of these efforts counts as market activity.

Another circular interpretation is that market activity consists of activities involving commodities and services. It does, but the statement is empty, again a tautology. What is a commodity? It is a thing or object that is bought and sold in the market, distinguished from other objects that are not. An heirloom teapot is not usually a commodity but can become one if offered for sale. My kidney is not a commodity unless offered in a market for human parts. What is a service? It is in this context—that is, when linked in the phrase "commodities and services"—a performance that is bought and sold in the market, distinguished from those that are not. Your helpful advice to a friend is not, in this context, a service unless you charge for it. But we still need to know which kinds of objects and what kinds of performances can and cannot be coordinated through the market. All that this interpretation tells us is that whichever objects and performances enter into the market system, they will be called commodities and services.

## Maximum Domain

A satisfactory answer to the scope question lies in the preceding three chapters and needs only to be made explicit. We again discard the concept of the economy as unneeded and obstructively implying too narrow a scope. We begin with a recognition that, at its maximum, the market system can coordinate the provision of any and all performances and objects that can be bought and sold. It is not limited to any subcategory of that category. We then go on to specify what it is about some objects and performances that makes it possible for them but not others to be bought and sold.

Clearly the qualifying performances and objects constitute an enormous category. It includes ideas, inventions, artistry, promises, consultations, and energies of all kinds. It also includes the movement among persons and enterprises of every object you can think of—found objects, hand-crafted objects, pieces of land, tools, buildings, buried ore, mechanical devices. It includes the pursuit of life—through reproductive services now for sale—and the pursuit of death—through assisted suicide, recently for sale.

Although the category includes tag sales and my sale of a used car, the characteristic and by far most significant buying and selling is that in which entrepreneurs engage when they buy inputs and sell outputs in production intended to be sold. Their transactions do not, however, fill the market-system domain.

Again, market domain is not defined by the character of participants' objectives. Nor, of course, is it defined by the ethical merit of its transactions. The market system makes room not only for the most conventional enterprises and transactions but also for the new Russian mafia just as it made room for nineteenth-century robber barons. Any aspirations or objectives, from wealth to piety, can be pursued in the market system if the pursuit calls for buying and selling.

Just which kinds of performances and objects can be bought and sold? Those that satisfy each of three conditions. Obvious as the conditions are, they are nevertheless significant in underscoring the immense range or reach of the market system. Objects and performances can be bought and sold—to become goods and services—if

- they are subject to contingent human control,
- they are scarce,
- and they can be obtained without compulsion by voluntary reciprocating offers of benefits.

Let us look at each.

*Contingent control.* No one can offer the sun, magnificently uncontrollable, for sale. But urban rights to sunlight—including rights to obstruct, by high-rise construction, a neighbor's access to direct sunlight—are for sale in some societies. To offer a performance or object for sale obviously requires that human beings can physically offer or deny it. This control has to be like a valve or gate—it must be precise enough so that the performance or object can be offered to another person contingent on that person's responding with a specified price. To take an example of the contrary, rarely, if ever, is genuine deep affection offered for sale; although human beings can generate it, they do not control it well enough to turn it on in order to induce an offer of a price. Hence the market system deals instead in simulated affection, which is supplied contingent on reciprocal response. People who can afford to do so sometimes spend heavily to obtain marks of affection rather than affection itself, as well as to gain evidences or marks of prestige, like honorary degrees or medals.

*Scarcity.* It is pointless to offer a performance or object in hope of a reciprocal benefit if what is offered is not scarce. "Scarce," it will be remembered, does not mean in small amount; it means that there is not enough to go round unless desires are somehow constrained. If a performance or object is not scarce, offering it will induce no response. Air transport and opticians' skills are scarce. So also is power—or beauty—of some kinds, fame, or a reputation for integrity or rapacity. If available without constraint—if everyone has all of each that he wants—no one would offer any for sale, and no one would buy.

Scarcities are not God given. In some hunting and gathering societies, land is not scarce. But aggressive members of the community or invaders, like the Europeans who invaded American Indian territory, made land scarce by enforcing exclusive rights over it.

What objects and performances are not scarce? An endless variety: in our day, for example, most of the poems that have been written, innumerable inventions, sand in the Sahara (but not in a sandbox), rainfall (in some areas), an obsolete computer, and conspicuously incompetent professors. Until and unless they become scarce they are all beyond the coordinating reach of the market system, except for the professor guaranteed a salary by tenure even if now without skills. Note also that not excluded from the market system are some widely deplored performances—the services of an arsonist, for example. You and I may not want them, but some people do. Since arsonists are scarce, those who want their services have to enter the market to hire them.

*Voluntarism.* Because market coordination proceeds through voluntary offers of benefit, the market does not coordinate when coordination requires systematic compulsion. This is a great restriction on market domain. Coordination often requires that people be compelled; they cannot always be sufficiently moved by an offer of benefit. To induce many millions of young people to join the army often requires compulsion, for pay and perquisites may not be enough. To build a highway or a shopping mall often requires that landowners reluctant to sell their land be compelled by the state to surrender it. To finance many collective projects—from building a new jail to a new school system—requires the compulsion of taxes. And of course many proposals for redistribution of income and wealth require taxation or some other form of compulsion—you cannot be paid to give up some of your income or wealth.

Compulsion is not wholly absent from market systems.

Some forms of monopoly compel, as do many relations between employer and employee. But the distinctive market-system method of inducing a response—of achieving coordination—is to offer a benefit in return for a voluntary response.

The frequent need for compulsion limits market domain more than is immediately apparent. Market activity, we know, requires a foundation in custom and law that market activity itself cannot provide. It requires at least a compulsory protection of both liberty and rights to assets without which no one can offer performances and objects in exchange. Similarly, other rules derived from both custom and law—rules of contract or fair trade, for example—cannot themselves be made effective by market interactions but instead require compulsion. International trade also requires special legal foundations through agreement among states, ranging from the 1944 agreements of Bretton Woods to emerging international rules on capital movements. And the state itself cannot be created by market relations—we cannot create a government simply by buying one. Among other reasons, the "consent of the governed" is never universal; some citizens have to be compelled.

## What About Collective Pursuits?

To an on-off control switch, scarcity, and voluntarism, should we add a fourth defining element of market-system domain—that the market system organizes only individualistic ventures? Critics often say that market systems permit participants to pursue only individualistic ends, not collective projects. We can all selfishly pursue a larger apartment or new clothes for our children, but we cannot pursue collective goals like crime reduction or environmental protection through the market because they require the powers of the state to compel cooperation.

For some collective projects the argument is correct. Suppose an irrigation project is undertaken. Barring a happy unanimity—an unlikely possibility—there will be those who oppose the project or do not want to pay for it. But because the project requires compulsion by the state, dissidents will have to be taxed.

Not all collective efforts require compulsion. Consequently, the market is not limited to the accomplishment of individualistic objectives. Societies pursue many collective goals, such as economic growth or a high rate of literacy, through the market system. They are achieved as a by-product of individual goal-seeking by participants who are not necessarily even aware of the achievement. In recent years an upgrading of occupational competencies—for sheet metal workers and translators no less than for computer programmers—has often been declared an urgent national goal for a country seeking to compete internationally. Yet often more is done to achieve upgrading through the market system, specifically through on-the-job training, than through governmental programs. Some of the greatest collective achievements of Western societies have been of this kind—high standards of living among them. Perhaps even freedom, a great collective goal, is more an inadvertent outcome of market interchanges than of its deliberate pursuit.

Market systems also coordinate many collective projects that are less than societywide, projects that proceed through an agreeing group. Colombian coffee growers have established the National Coffee Fund to build schools. Groups of householders sometimes buy land, buy a fence to control access, and hire a private police force to guard the entrances. They have by their purchases shifted some of the task of coordination from the authority of the state to their own collective market efforts.

But then comes the notorious free rider. A number of persons wish to join in obtaining a service or good that the market can provide except for one obstacle. The obstacle is that performance or object is of a kind that cannot be restricted to those who pay but will be available as well to those who do not pay. Even if all the residents of an urban area are willing to pay for a tree-planting program, the project is likely to fail if many of them, knowing that they can enjoy the trees even if they fail to pay their share, refuse to pay. Payments have to be compelled, as through taxes. The market system does not work.

In short, what is decisive for whether the market system can or cannot accomplish a collective project is not that it is or is not collective but that it does or does not require compulsion.

So we are left with our three requirements for admitting an object or performance into the market system: it must be subject to an on-off switch, it must be scarce, and it must respond voluntarily to offers of benefit. Within these limits the maximum scope of the market system remains enormous. And, once again, you will not gain any insight into market-system scope by postulating something called the economy, which then defines its scope. Think society, not economy.

A cloud in the sky does not enter into the market system. But if it can be seeded to produce rain (the on-off switch), if more farmers want its rains than can be accommodated (its waters are scarce), and if technicians in airplanes are willing to seed the cloud in return for benefits, seeding the cloud becomes part of market-system activity. A mound of unwanted ore does not enter into the market system. To bring it into the market system, uses for it have to be discovered—enough uses to make it scarce. Even so, it does not become a market commodity unless persons are found who will extract and transport it not by command but by offer of money. Make a list of as many objects as you can think of in a minute—or in an hour, if you have that much time to give it. Then check all those items on your list that are or could be bought and sold. You will see that the market's maximum scope is vast; market-system activity permeates our lives.

Finally, I turn to a terminological question that helps us understand market-system scope. Suppose that the state, rather than command its citizens to make their goods and services available to the state for constructing a new highway, instead buys, hires, or rents them from willing citizens. Do we say, as I am inclined to say, that the venture is market-system coordinated? Some economists, thinking of a theoretical model of a pure market system, would say that market systems by definition respond only to individual choices of goods and services. They would say that state purchases (or renting and hiring) go beyond the market system and should be characterized as a hybrid form of state and market system.

The terminological issue is unimportant. The distinction between the two paths open to the state, however, is a very great one. In the real world, the state is a frequent buyer, not just a commander of its citizens. A large part of state activity is market activity, and that buying and selling accomplish great feats of social coordination that could not be accomplished if only individuals bought and sold. On this score the state is not a rival to the market system but rather greatly extends its scope.

# Chosen Domain

Wisely or foolishly, societies—more specifically those masses or elites that make policy—choose not to use the market system as fully as they might. They turn instead to other methods of coordination, or they mix the market system with the others. Public education in most societies is not organized by market demand, although teachers are recruited through the market system. Many societies also try to keep child labor—or narcotics or judicial decisions—out of the market system. Why do societies curb the use of the market system? It is not hard to find good reasons, and some poor reasons as well.

One reason is ideological or philosophical hostility, such as Lenin and his associates brought to the new Soviet Union and Mao to China. Lying behind ideology are, however, a set of specific objections to the market system. Almost everyone acknowledges the validity of most of them. I shall not, however, evaluate them. I want simply to display the variety of objections to the market system that account for its less than maximum scope.

Many people believe that, regardless of output, the market *process* itself is sometimes undesirable—even unethical or immoral. Blood donors, many people believe, should give their blood, not sell it. Many people shrink from engaging in financial transactions with friends or family members. Some people fear that social solidarity is undercut by the very process of buying and selling. At least a few eccentrics will not protect themselves by buying insurance, fearing that doing so would reveal to God their lack of faith in divine care. And if many people enjoy shopping, some detest it so much that they will make do without some of the services and goods that the market offers. Some people—perhaps most of us—enjoy some performances and objects only if they are given to us; the pleasure is spoiled if we have to buy them. We love to get something for "free." And research studies report that some people find no pleasure in voluntary work when they are paid for it. A great historical example of society turning against the very process of buying and selling is the Council of Trent's prohibition in 1562 of the selling of indulgences; societies still struggle with whether prostitution and drugs should be legalized. Most people now find the idea of a market in slaves abhorrent. For similar reasons, some societies long ago decided to curb the hiring of children to labor in mines and factories.

Many people doubt the competence or motives of individual choice and want to establish a deliberating collective authority over some decisions. They are now engaged in debating, for example, whether the body parts of deceased human beings can be marketed or should instead be allocated by a collective authority. Many societies prefer collective decisions on environmental protection to individual or corporate market decisions—they want the state, not the corporation, to control emissions of industrial wastes. For good reason, people do not trust sellers to be wholly truthful about their products and therefore favor governmental regulation of food and drugs.

To many, market inequality is unacceptable. Most societies want at least an early elementary education for children, regardless of parental ability to buy it: hence taxes and compulsory education rather than a market. Some medical services, especially those that reduce epidemics, are distributed freely rather than sold, for fear that market distribution would not be wide enough. To deal with wartime scarcity, many societies rationed essential commodities rather than let low-income families be frozen out.

For many people, the market is too harsh. They want employers to be restricted in their rights to discharge employees, or they may want the state to bail out an enterprise on point of failing. Saving jobs in enterprises that can no longer survive without government subsidies is a worldwide phenomenon, prominent in Italy, India, and China.

In perhaps most societies, "upper classes" think that both philanthropy and government subsidies are necessary to raise the provision of the fine arts above what the "lower classes" would otherwise be willing to pay for in the market. Were the arts left wholly to the market system, orchestral and operatic classical music might vanish from concert halls.

All societies forbid some of the market interactions through which a person might construct inadmissible control, outside the market system, over others. For example, they do not permit individuals to use the market, except under great restriction, to recruit, equip, and organize private armies. Exceptions are small private armed forces that enterprises use for security of their premises, neighborhood security services, and the private "armies" that enterprises have sometimes used to break strikes. Some societies prohibit market purchase of firearms.

Many societies also restrict some market interactions that concentrate control of communications in private hands or in too few private hands. They also want to keep government officials at a distance from market forces. If litigants could buy favorable decisions from a judge, as they can in what we call corrupt judicial systems, one of the pur-

poses for which societies establish a judiciary—dispassion-
ate adjudication—is undercut.

Societies sometimes reduce the domain of the market
system not because compulsion is necessary but because it
is cheaper. Although we can imagine each of millions of
householders paying neighbors to remove their unsightly
and unsanitary trash, it would be cheaper simply to use
municipal ordinances to compel their removal. Similarly,
wealthy people can buy a good deal of privacy—building se-
cure living quarters and fences, hiring their own guards—
but they will often find it cheaper simply to use the law to
lay down and enforce rights to privacy. For all its rhetorical
celebration of liberty, a society may draft rather than hire
its army simply because it is cheaper to do so.

A large category of circumstances in which societies
want to prohibit or constrain market coordination—one
that includes some of the reasons already listed—consists
of transactions that produce significant spillover effects,
that is, consequences for persons not party to the transaction (see Chapter 11). If, for example, the market transactions of business enterprises pollute air or water—or if I create nuisances for my neighbors—the state will often step in
to overrule or modify market coordination.

A strikingly different objection to the market system is
harbored by political elites in authoritarian systems. They
fear a connection between the market system and the political power of citizens, for they see that market systems disperse power or control over the society. They would rather
exercise the controls themselves, as indicated in persistent
Soviet party and governmental refusals to disperse control
through markets following announced intentions to do so.
In democracies, rulers sometimes, for reasons that may include their own enrichment, prefer to maintain some con-

trol of the volume and allocation of new industrial investment rather than give it wholly to entrepreneurs.

Finally, however loud their commitment to the market system, entrepreneurs are highly motivated to seek—and win—a great variety of state protections for their own markets, protections that sometimes strengthen the market system but often restrict it. Italy, for example, has been operating under a complex licensing and regulatory system that has protected small, especially family, businesses from market rigors. Permits are required in order to establish a business and for each of various categories of products to be sold. Hours of work and scheduling of midday closings and vacations have also been governmentally controlled. More conspicuous protective dikes in any market system are tariffs and other curbs on imports, as well as outright subsidies to the petroleum, mining, and agriculture industries—for that matter, to many dozens of industries. They all have the effect of weakening the ordinary market direction of production, justified or not by their contribution to strengthening entrepreneurial initiatives. Taken together, they often represent a widespread slapdash introduction of central planning, a shunting aside of the conventional market system less by central direction than by central misdirection. And they narrow the range of market choice for both sellers and buyers.

Almost all these reasons for curbing the market are in principle good reasons. But they do not specify a correct choice between market system and alternatives; they only alert us to circumstances in which the choice is worth thinking about. Whether, for example, blood or body parts should be bought and sold is a question that has no right answer. The appropriate answer depends on such factors as what people value, their attitudes toward risk, and their confidence in what they believe they know. It also depends on the suitability of alternative coordinating processes.

## Alternatives

I take note once more that the state is the greatest participant in market systems. It is a buyer of such things as public buildings, bridges, and armaments—a very long list. Among its many purchases, it hires soldiers, astronauts, nurses, police officers, gardeners, and people in every other occupation one might think of. And of course both the corporation and the family or household participate in the market system.

Obvious as the market participation of these three institutions is, each is also an alternative to the market system. The state can hire an army or, not making use of the labor market, simply command its young people to enlist. A corporation can buy its electric power or produce its own. A household can patronize a barber or, setting aside the market system, do its haircutting at home. To the three I add a less familiar fourth alternative—civil society, amorphous as the concept is. The society's choice of domain for the market system depends on its estimate of the capacities of each of these four alternatives.

The state tends to overshadow the other alternatives. Because the market system cannot administer the compulsion necessary for social order, it is the state, foremost, that does so. And because the market system cannot establish itself, it is of course the state that does so, through, inter alia, laws on liberty and property. To be sure, custom also often serves this purpose, but never sufficiently.

The household is a nonmarket coordinator surrounded by market coordination. Within a nuclear family, members ordinarily do not sell and buy each other's performances or objects, although I have known husbands to tip their wives for a good dinner, very likely more demeaning than rewarding. Parents only peripherally pay children to do chores; in some societies they rent out their children. On the whole, children are coordinated by parental authority rather than market system. Between spouses too, the allocation of responsibilities is decided less by a market transaction than by various forms of inegalitarian mutual adjustment within a framework of moral rules.

Not infrequently, observers of the market system minimize the household as a social coordinator. True, the household cannot achieve the nationwide or global coordination that the market achieves. Yet in many societies in which women have chosen not to make their labor available to the market or have not been permitted to do so, nonmarket family labor of women and children, together with the part-time work in the home of the male spouse, add up to more than the total of labor coordinated through the market system. Even with two wage earners, contemporary families still coordinate a great amount of family labor—the family remains a prodigious social coordinator. Despite long-voiced speculation on possible societies without families, and despite some exploratory moves in that direction, as in the Israeli kibbutzim, the family's role in social coordination remains, for the time being, well established and a very great restriction on the scope of the market system.

Indeed, the market system is better described as a coordinator of collectivities called households than as a coordinator of individuals. It is as an agent of such a collectivity that a wage earner enters into the market to earn an income to be distributed within the household. And it is as an agent of it that some members of the household purchase goods and services to be distributed among its members.

The collective enterprise, especially the big corporation, is the third alternative to the market system. While enterprises extend the market system's domain in several dimensions, they restrict it in others. For enterprises constitute, as we have said, islands of nonmarket or managerial coordination in a market milieu. Where once a dozen smaller enterprises may have constituted, through their market interchanges with suppliers and customers, an important part of the steel industry, many of their market activities may have been brought under the authoritative direction of the single corporation that displaced those market interchanges.

Although the state is the principal instrument of systematic compulsion required to achieve social coordination, both enterprise and family are also instruments of compulsion. Enterprises are, among other things, systems for inducing people, in return for wages, to accept the compulsions of their employers. Enterprise compulsions are limited; obviously an employee can leave an enterprise more easily than a citizen or taxpayer can emigrate. Family compulsions are notorious.

A substantial and perhaps increasing share of the task of social coordination is borne by the fourth alternative: civil society. For some people who use the term, it denotes coordinating collectivities other than enterprises and governmental organizations. These collectivities, remarkably diverse in structure and objective, seem to resist efforts to be categorized as nonprofits. Among them are political parties, lobbying organizations, charities, clubs, research laboratories, and museums.

These entities may operate largely outside the market system—for example, a reading club whose members meet monthly for discussion. On the other hand, they, especially the larger ones, may make substantial use of the market to recruit staff and to assemble other inputs necessary for their activities—for example, a political party. Many make use of the market system for labor and other inputs. They may not sell anything; or, if they do, they may not maximize the quid for the quo they offer. At an extreme are some conventional business enterprises selling in the market but disguised as nonprofit enterprises to escape taxes on their income or to create an image of benevolence rather than profit seeking. Some motor clubs offering maps, travel information, insurance, and other products appear to be of this type.

For some people, civil society means more than organizations. Its activities also include acts of friendship or compassion, favors and return of favors, and other forms of personal cooperation neither compelled by the state nor organized by buying and selling. These are enormously important and ubiquitous forms of social cooperation and sociability. Some interpreters of civil society attach the greatest importance to those interchanges, believing that through them each of us forms and endlessly reconsiders our values, life purposes, and, for the shorter term perhaps, our recreation and politics. We are each a creation of these interchanges, beginning with parental influences over us.

In a variety of informal small-group interactions, as in family life, people curb mutual injury and help one another, whether out of affection or helpful impulse or habit. They look after other people's children, come to the aid of friends, enter into interchanges pleasant in themselves. People often seek in small-group interchanges an area of social interchange in which the market rule of quid pro quo can be forbidden.

In these personal relationships, peace and cooperation

require neither the heavy hand of compulsion nor the kind of explicit quid pro quo benefits that people offer each other in the market. Although in these interchanges people pursue many of the same aspirations as in their market activity, here markets are unnecessary and in some cases would obstruct aspirations. If I want a genuine friendship, for example, the friendship relation would be destroyed if I paid for it. In these relationships there are often rewards on both sides but no specific contingent quid pro quo. From the activities of civil society, including play and adventure, people draw immediate satisfaction from experience. This differs from the means-end pattern of using resources to achieve satisfaction that characterizes life in market systems. Of course, we often use the market system to obtain necessary equipment or to bring us to a location where we will enjoy play or adventure. But once equipped and located, we can for a time stop our buying and selling.

Two final comments on scope or domain of the market system. The first is that social interchange and institutions cannot be partitioned into mutually exclusive domains. If we observe a group of people engaged in building a church with paid labor and bought materials, we can quickly identify the activity as within the market domain. But their purpose is to facilitate worship, thus the activity falls within the domain of religion. We might also look at the project, depending on the architecture, as an artistic effort or accomplishment, thus no less within the domain of the arts than in the market domain. We cannot partition social life into mutually exclusive territories.

The second comment: The idea of a society in which the market system alone is society's coordinator is obviously nonsense and is fortunately only rarely espoused. Most of us well understand the need for state, family, enterprise, and the various arrangements of civil society. There exists in some societies, however, conspicuously in the United States, a related idea—that government is best that governs least, a proposition usually attached to an unspoken corollary: that market system is best that coordinates most. Yet a market system of maximum domain would by most people be considered inhumane. And a "least" government would not only leave debris to gather in the streets but would allow the spread of deadly epidemics. Determining the domain for market, state, family, enterprise, and civil society—for each of them—is a serious task for every society, not to be disposed of by all-too-common dogma.

# What To Make of It

# Quid Pro Quo

The market system works well enough to induce societies—East and West, North and South—to make increasing use of it. Its great accomplishments lead many of its enthusiasts to overlook the dark side apparent to its critics. Yet who can deny that most market systems, among them the most wealthy, leave great numbers of people in poverty? Or that they blight many lives and destroy many communities?

In this group of chapters I want to examine selected attributes of the market system that are especially pertinent to anyone's evaluations of it. Is the market system efficient? Does it support personal liberty? Does market life degrade culture and personality? No one can say conclusively, but we can find empirical attributes of the market system that bear on the answers.

With that preface, I single out what might be judged to be the market's core empirical attribute, one that bears on all evaluations of it. It is the market system's operating rule, set by both custom and law, that you take out according to what you put in: a quid for every quo.

If you have grown up in a market society you may find it difficult, as I do, to imagine a society's operating without the rule. So let us make an effort to view this rule as it might be perceived by someone not shaped by the customary beliefs of market societies.

Imagine an interplanetary visitor. Full of questions ever since his arrival on Earth a few days ago, he has already displayed an annoying preference for short answers. He wants facts, not theory. The physical world, both natural and human-made, that he sees about him looks much like what he sees at home, so he tells us—meadows, forests, and buildings of many kinds. Our social arrangements he finds less familiar.

Seeing some signs of affluence, he asks who builds our houses. We explain that very few people build their own; almost everyone has the construction done by others. "And is everyone supplied with living quarters?" No. We tell him about the homeless. He seems taken aback.

"Food?" he asks. "Do people grow what they need?" No, we tell him. People earn money and then spend the money to claim food—or housing, or whatever they want. He asks, "Is everyone provided with—does everyone have a claim on—food?" No, some not. "Then how do they live?" We explain that sometimes someone or a charitable organization takes pity on them and gives them some food. Sometimes the government helps them. Sometimes they die.

Apparently he does not like what he is hearing. "You are well dressed," he says. "And you have schools for your children, I would suppose. Autos, I see around us. A variety of recreations?" Yes, we assure him that we have all of these. "All of you can claim them?" Again we explain: not everyone. "But don't you feel some obligation to meet at least the minimum needs of everyone?" No. Such an obligation, one of us says, would rest on government. "Does your government recognize such an obligation?" No; only in a limited and disputed way. Although it frequently comes to the rescue of needy persons, it does not do so generously, and most people think that taking government aid in these circumstances is demeaning.

"So, then, some of you have your various needs met and

some do not? Why not all of you? And whose needs are met and whose are not?" We try again to explain. If you can't obtain something you want by doing it or making it yourself, the only permitted way to get help from others is to offer the others something they might want—your labor, your money, or other assets—to induce them to help you. Our visitor silently thinks about what we have said. "What if they do not have anything to offer?" Too bad, we reply; they would be out of luck—unless some charity saves them.

He finds this hard to believe and wonders whether he has misunderstood. "You must have some kind of arrangements to make sure that everyone has something to offer— valuable enough so that everyone can get what they need?" We stumble with our answers. We tell him that everyone's liberty is legally protected, so that means that everyone can at least offer labor for wages. "But," he asks, "what if someone can't earn as much wage as the family needs?" That causes problems, we concede, especially for the unskilled. "Do you then make sure the unskilled are trained?" No, they have no claim on anyone for training—unless, of course, they can offer their labor to get it. The visitor snaps at us: "A circularity, is it not?" He then recovers and apologizes.

We explain to him that one can offer more than labor. One can offer objects or assets: land, buildings, equipment, and the like. Our society recognizes the right to hold, exercise control over, and use assets—a set of rights we call private property. "That sounds better," he says. "And you have arrangements to distribute assets so that everyone has enough of them to get what his family needs by renting, lending, or selling them?" No, we confess, we do not. Many people have assets only in the form of food and clothing; they own no additional assets to offer to earn money. "How would a person acquire such assets?" We silently reflect on that question. . . . Two ways, one of us suggests. One can offer one's labor to induce another to offer an asset. Or one can use whatever assets are in hand to obtain more through exchange of them. The visitor's face begins to color. "Are you—how do you say it?—putting me on?" He walks away.

Apparently his curiosity overcomes his anger. He walks back to us with another question. "Do you mean to tell me that in your society, other than a claim to liberty to work for wages and to hold and use assets if you can get any, no one has any claim on anyone else, on government, or on society other than what one can claim by offering something in return? Not even modest claims recognized just because every person is a human being and member of society? No claims derived from compassion or sympathy? No claims derived from a desire to reduce suffering? You and you and you who seem to have what you want"—his forefinger stabbing at my chest—"you accept no such humane claims? You call yourselves human beings?" And this time he does not wait for an answer but stalks off.

Just as well for his composure that he leaves. For he has so far not uncovered another custom and rule in our society that would heighten his indignation. A person often fails to establish an effective claim even while making an offer of great service or benefit to others. For one can make a claim effective only by offering a benefit that can be offered for a price. If, say, Bill Gates's mother herself made some contribution to society, as seems undeniable, by rearing her remarkable son, her contribution won her no claim; the market awarded her nothing. In response to benefits conferred on others by the good neighbor, the alert and active citizen, the supportive friend, the devoted and enlightened parent, the market offers no quo at all.

I see the visitor the next day in a small group. He tells us that his society goes through intermittent disorganization—every ten years or so a spasm, lasting from a few months to a few years, of reduced production and employment. We have the same problem, we tell him. But it soon becomes clear that his problem differs from ours. He learns from us that when people in our society lose their jobs they lose their income. "For us," he says, "that depends on how and why they lose their jobs." We explain that in our society it does not matter how and why. Our rule is no job, no income. That disturbs him. "You don't take away their income if something goes wrong with the system and people lose their jobs through no fault of their own?" Well, yes, we do, one of us replies.

In the parable, I have not fairly represented contemporary earthly societies because I underplay such claims as pensions for the elderly, family allowances, and unemployment compensation. But to establish such claims societies have had to turn away from the market system to other processes. The market system itself is as harsh as the visitor finds it. Market interactions provide nothing to you or me except what we can get by making a market offer. That you and I might have rights or claims simply because we are human beings or members of society, or because we are formed by society, or because we play our roles in society as we have learned to play them is irrelevant to what claims we can make through the market system.

## Defenses of the Rule

In our day, perhaps most people would not defend the rule of quid pro quo unless it were supplemented by other rules and procedures, such as those of the welfare state. Some people nevertheless defend the rule as itself sufficient without such supplements as pensions and unemployment compensation. Although they offer several defenses, all are flawed; and the flaws represent misunderstandings of the market system worth our attention.

The rule is efficient, it is claimed, because if you can take out only an equivalent of what you put in, you will strive to make a greater contribution. Reasonable as it sounds, this defense claims too much. The rule does not at all encourage—does not reward—many kinds of contributions. It rewards market contributions only, not parental contributions to child rearing and not great political leadership, to mention only two of many possible examples. As an incentive system, it is incomplete, narrow. It distorts incentives by rewarding some kinds of activities but not others, however great their value.

As for market contributions, the rule may motivate them or retard them, depending on circumstances. Because the rule reduces some people to the weakness of disease and the demoralization of poverty, incentives to make a market contribution are often dulled or extinguished rather than stimulated. For people not near such an extreme, reducing rewards for contributions, as through taxation, sometimes stirs them into greater market efforts rather than discourages them. Historically, the rise of the welfare state, with its loosening of the quid pro quo tie, has not reduced work effort; in fact, it has probably raised it, a probability strengthened by the welfare state's contributions to health and education. Research shows that nations with high taxes, which reduce taxpayer income and finance governmental benefits, thus reducing the tightness of the quid pro quo, do not lag in productivity or capital growth. There is no correlation between a tight quid pro quo and high output. Although incentives require some connection between contribution and reward, no one has sufficient grounds for believing that the tighter the connection the stronger the incentive.

It is quite possible that incentives would be strengthened if a society followed the rule only to allocate supplemental claims to shares in the society's cooperatively produced output. It might grant outright some minimum, or floor, claims to income, with everyone being equally entitled because all qualify as human beings and members of the society. Only above those claims, then, would additional claims be made through market quid pro quo. The welfare state has been traveling such a road: floor benefits through public choice, additional benefits through market choice.

If the rule is to be justified on grounds of ethics, rather than efficiency, it will have to be for reasons other than those commonly advanced.

1. Sometimes the rule is defended as a self-evident ethical principle—you should take out from social cooperation only according to what you put into it. But the claim goes awry. People who have been reared in market systems often lack a capacity to perceive that there is nothing self-evident in it. Most societies in history in fact acknowledge a variety of claims to shares on grounds other than the quid pro quo: some based on birth and ancestry, some on good conduct, some on prowess of one kind or another, some on the mere fact of membership in the social group, or some in simple acknowledgment of human status. The rule is not self evident or universal.

The fact is that every generation makes use of and otherwise disposes of a mountain of inherited productive capital equipment: improved land, buildings, machinery, and other capital goods produced by earlier generations. How that inheritance should be distributed to and used by the current generation—and who should have legal authority over it—are difficult questions for which no one answer is obvious. The "take out what you put in" rule will not do, for earlier generations did most of the putting in. How to distribute what they put in cannot be decided by the rule taken as an ethical proposition.

Nor can the rule be defended as natural, since many earlier societies operated by other rules no less natural than the quid pro quo. And even if it were natural, so also are hate, violence, and cruelty—perhaps slavery as well. All are curbed because they are unethical, however natural they may be.

2. The market quid pro quo rule acknowledges no ethical value—no human merit or contribution to society worth rewarding—other than the capacity to offer the kinds of objects and performances that can be sold in markets. The rule recognizes the contribution of a Tata but not a Bohr; or of a psychotherapist but not of a sometimes equally helpful friend. It does not recognize any claims on behalf of a spouse who stays home to raise a family. I know of no ethical principle that defends distributing the benefits of social life only in response to market contributions, in disregard of all other contributions.

3. Even if market contributions were the only ones to justify a claim to a share of the benefits of social cooperation, awarding benefits to match what one can sell in the market is ethically questionable. Your market contribution may be either greater or less than the value of what you offer for sale.

Consider: you provide interior decorating services for

£35 per hour. Ten years ago, you provided the same services to the same number of people at a much lower price, even adjusting for inflation. Now that you are paid more than before, can we say that your contribution to market cooperation has risen? We might say that, although you make the same contribution, people now value that contribution more than before. But not necessarily. Perhaps all that has changed is the distribution of wealth and income, with the result that some people who earlier valued your services no less than they do now are now able to spend more on them, thus raising the price you can charge. Generalized, that conclusion means that because what the market pays anyone depends on the existing distribution of wealth and income, we cannot estimate a person's market contribution (to say nothing of other contributions) by looking at what one is paid.

Look at the discrepancy in another way. To obtain his great share of society's income and wealth, John D. Rockefeller needed a market for oil, a technology for oil extraction and refining, railroads, and capital markets. Bill Gates needed a market for computer software, an educated population, a telephone system, and capital markets, among other things. Take any one component away and the whole accomplishment fails. What any individual can accomplish in market cooperation depends on the skills, capacities, and placement of the others and thus on the degree and quality of organization of the whole system. Given such interdependence, that one's market contribution (again, to say nothing of one's other contributions) can be or should be measured by what one can sell is at least highly disputable. The market value of what one can sell at a price is neither the obvious measure nor the only measure of it.

For yet another reason, one's market contribution diverges from what one sells or earns in the market. An apartment house provides an unmistakable benefit for or contribution to society—living quarters. But does the owner, as distinct from the building, make any contribution? If the law were to transfer ownership from me to you, you as the new owner would, by conventional thinking, then be called the contributor. Yet nothing has changed except the transfer of rights to claim rent. In this kind of case, whether one is conventionally credited with making a contribution of assets depends not on one's actual contribution—that is, not on anything one does—but only on who holds property rights over assets offered in the market. Again the ethical argument that markets allocate claims in response to market contribution is shattered.

## Consequences of the Rule

If common ethical justifications of the rule of market quid pro quo fail, some specific empirical consequences of the rule, if it were not modified by nonmarket rules and procedures, threaten any ethical justification that might be erected.

The first, of course, is that in practical application the rule would leave millions of people on the globe destitute unless charity or nonmarket processes like the welfare state came to their rescue. Applied to infants, the rule would guarantee that none would reach adulthood; the world would lie depopulated in one generation. But we do not apply it to infants or even older children not yet capable of making a sufficient contribution. They have not yet inherited any assets to offer in exchange. Nor are they yet sufficiently trained. Yet these same incapacities afflict many millions of adults to whom the market nevertheless applies the rule: adults with an insufficient biological inheritance of brain and brawn, or with inadequate or no assets at all to offer in exchange, or with inadequate training.

Second, in tying each person's claims to what that person can sell, all claims are tied to accidents of birth and history. In great part, inheritance decides what you or I can offer in the market: first, a biological inheritance of cognitive ability and muscular skills; second, a social inheritance of early education and assets; and, third, an inheritance of a place in a society that possesses a supply, large or small, of assets and skills that determine the possibilities of social cooperation. With little inherited ability, poor early rearing, and paucity of inherited assets, you would clearly be destined to a meager share in the benefits of market cooperation. You would also be destined to a meager portion if you were born into an unproductive society that lacks assets and skills.

Third, the market quid quo pro rule entails insecurity of income and status, even if these risks are reduced by insurance. Employed today, one may lose one's job tomorrow, shortly then lose one's savings, home, and even status in the community. Business fluctuation, recession, and depression evict people from their jobs and cut off their claims to income from their labor. Illness and temporary disability put a stop on one's market claims, and old age often promises a termination of all market claims. Some people of course have the funds with which to buy insurance against some of these losses. Yet so intolerable is this state of affairs for most people that, beginning with Germany in the 1880s, industrial societies have departed from the rule by granting nonmarket claims through such systems as old-age pensions, unemployment compensation, workers' compensation, and subsidized medical care. Even much earlier, some nations offered at least stingy forms of relief, as in Elizabethan England. They thus have acknowledged, although they have not yet successfully countered, the unacceptable consequences of the rule.

Fourth, the rule plainly distributes income and wealth unequally. In the United States, 1 percent of the people own roughly a third of the nation's wealth. In Latin America as a whole, the top 10 percent receive 40 percent of the national income, the bottom 30 percent receive less than 8 percent. For some observers, that fact alone leads them to an adverse judgment about the market. Others grant a defect but count on such nonmarket programs as old-age pensions and the other programs just mentioned to achieve satisfactory reductions of inequalities. And still others defend existing market inequalities. They acknowledge poverty as a problem because it represents an extreme of inequality, but they do not think that inequality short of poverty constitutes a problem.

Within nations, a slow historical movement away from severe old inequalities appears to respond to two intertwined sources: one, an ethical tradition—in the West, the Greek-Judeo-Christian tradition—and, the other, democratic politics. The movement is of course always stubbornly resisted, mainly by those who fear losing their large shares.

One can play down market inequality as a blight on the grounds that nonmarket systems reveal a history of even greater inequality or that communist systems, for all their ideology of equality, continue to practice severe inequality. But that does not deny the magnitude of market inequality. Nor does the impossibility of complete or exact equality justify such existing inequality as follows from the rule of quid pro quo.

# What Efficiency Requires

Despite what we have said about the rule of quid pro quo, all over the world a pattern of market-system success seems clear. Although some market societies—Paraguay, for example—leave most people in poverty, the highest standards of living for masses of people are found only in the market societies. To Adam Smith the market system accounted for the "wealth of nations." His explanation, once derided in some circles, seems confirmed by the collapse of communist systems, whose central direction of economic life increasingly lagged behind the market systems in output and standard of living. In the third world too, nations on the market path grow faster than those not. China's moves toward the market system appear to have set a world record for speed of growth. If either per capita output—often measured as per capita gross domestic product—or some other measure of standard of living is taken as an indicator, the market system is impressive. That is not surprising, considering that it is, as we have seen, the most embracing and precise system of enormously large-scale cooperation that humankind has ever invented or stumbled into.

Is that all that needs to be said about efficiency? No, for many questions remain. Does the market system simply pile up output, or does it make efficient choices among possible outputs? Beyond manageable questions like that lie harder ones, such as: Can production be called efficient if it is achieved, as some people believe, by exhausting the earth's resources or by environmental degradation? And still harder questions: Is a market system efficient whether it is efficient in making people happy or, say, perversely efficient in elite exploitation of the population?

Let us begin with the usual or conventional efficiency problem—efficiency in producing goods and services.

## The Core Efficiency Problem

Just as you cannot appreciate the accomplishment of climbing Everest unless you know that it is a bitterly cold ascent in oxygen-thin air, you cannot understand the distinctive attributes of the market system bearing on efficiency without first understanding the obstacles to it. Just what are they?

By the laws of thermodynamics, input and output are always equal. In that sense, all physical transformations are consequently equally efficient, all at 100 percent. Electric power that goes into a factory comes out not only in the form of a desired product but in heat discharged into the atmosphere and in waste products hauled away.

The relevant concept of efficiency, however, is the ratio of valued outputs to valued inputs. Forget the 100 percent relation between all the outputs (both usable heat and heat lost up the flue) and all the inputs (both oil and air) that heat your living quarters. Relevant efficiency means a high ratio of valuable usable heat to the valuable oil input.

It is not necessarily inefficient to use a ton of some input to produce a pound of output. It depends on how that ton and that pound are valued. Physical properties of goods and services tell us nothing about efficiency—there is no way to infer efficient choice from those properties. No set of choices can be called correct, right, or efficient except by reference to how they are valued.

Suppose that, either through markets or through central command, a society assigns valued inputs—labor, parts, machinery, and so on—to the manufacture of rubber boots. Production will be inefficient if the workers do not work hard enough or if they are badly organized. But if output is raised through incentives and better organization—more of the same valued output is derived from the same valued input—we see a clear gain in efficiency. Call this technological efficiency.

But the society may be manufacturing the wrong output—that is, output not valued or not greatly valued. Consumers, or their rulers, would rather have more electric hair dryers than more boots. Or, either through central planning or the market system, the society may assign to the factory kinds and amounts of labor, machinery, or parts that would be more productive of value if manufacturing gardening tools instead. The choice of efficient outputs and inputs is a great and difficult challenge for any kind of society. It requires appropriate choices of outputs and inputs in each enterprise in the chain that connects inputs—like coffee beans to a cup of coffee served in a cafe. It also requires an efficient selection of enterprises—a trucking company where needed in the chain, or an insurance company where needed. Call this allocative efficiency.

Through their market choices wealthy societies have shifted their energies out of farming and heavy industry into travel, insurance, and financial services. Their allocations will continue to change. In developing countries, poor people spend some of their new income on bicycles. Then, as their incomes rise further, they reallocate their spending from bicycles to motor scooters. And entrepreneurs endlessly make choices between labor and machines, as well as move capital investment from Oslo to South Korea. The allocation process never stops, but most of us are hardly aware of it.

In any society, however, this allocation process can go badly. Poor choices can hurt people far more than can gaudy inefficiencies, like bribery, or the failures of technological efficiency. Poor allocative choice in the form of wrong products, wrong inputs, and wrong choices on maintenance and technological innovation brought an end to Soviet and Maoist communism. In the Great Depression of the 1930s in the Western societies the allocative choice process broke down in another way. It failed to allocate to any activity at all much of the human energy that was available—in short, people were unemployed. Today the world may need an efficient allocative process less to raise its income than to protect past gains against decline. For every generation lives on the wealth of past successes, all vulnerable to erosion.

Now consider a complication. Here we have an output of steel that is highly valued by planning officials in a society but not so highly valued either by the citizens of that society, or by you as an observer. Or here we have an allocation of steel that is highly valued by those in the market who buy it, but not highly valued by a team of development economists hired to advise the government on the nation's development strategies. Whether an allocation is efficient depends, then, on who is doing the evaluations, or on whose evaluations count. Consequently, there is no one allocation that is efficient—it all depends.

Despite differences in evaluations, efficiency matters greatly to almost everyone, even though what one person or group applauds as efficient, another person or group may deplore as inefficient.

Allocative efficiency, no matter who judges it or whose

values count, requires, among other things, a detailed allocation of participants to each of countless specialized occupations and jobs. Social scientists follow Adam Smith and the sociologist Émile Durkheim in finding specialization of roles—that is, division of labor—to be a fundamental source of efficiency. But sometimes they forget to say, perhaps because they regard it as obvious, that specializations are efficient only if adapted to human wants and to each other. A specialization in lens-grinding is not efficient if no one makes glass, nor is a specialization in incantations among people who do not practice them. Not any division of labor will do.

## Burdens

Technological efficiency—getting more output from a given input—might be called getting something for nothing. Beyond such bonus opportunities, the pursuit of aspirations proceeds through allocations in the face of scarcity: not enough to go around. To produce more of one valued performance or object means putting up with less of some others. More medical care, fewer lawyers. If there is more labor in industry, there is less labor in agriculture.

Every allocation of a scarce good or service is burdened—to get something of value, something of value has to be forgone, given up. In all societies, everyone from private citizen to chief executive confronts endless burdened choices. Moonlighting aside, choosing one job precludes the benefits of another. Because our incomes are limited, spending on one assortment of consumer goods precludes enjoying others. For an entrepreneur, choosing one set of inputs precludes choosing others that also would be useful. Collective choice is no less burdened. A central authority's decisions to publish more books or fight a war call on scarce resources that then cannot be employed on other valued programs. It follows that allocative efficiency requires that choices or decisions be made with information on burdens. Without that information, decisions can be wildly inefficient—indeed irrational.

Again, you and I may evaluate the burdens differently. And citizens' evaluations may differ from officials' evaluations. But every judgment about efficiency requires an evaluation of what is received against an evaluation of what is given up.

What has to be given up depends on what options are open. In deciding whether it would be efficient for me to acquire a full-time servant, the answer would depend on how it might be done. If a servant could be assigned to me by an authoritarian state, the cost to me might be near zero. If I have to capture the servant in battle, the burden will be higher. If I can obtain the servant through hiring in the market, the burden will again be different. If officials are engaged in estimating the efficiency of deploying labor to the construction of a dam, the burden—that is, their evaluation of what is to be given up—depends of course on their evaluation of what that labor could produce elsewhere if it were not drawn into dam construction. But that depends on their options. Can they command the unemployed to come to work on the dam? If so, the burden is less than if they have to hire laborers away from other projects where they are already productively employed.

In these words on burden I am referring to cost: about choices that cost, outcomes that cost, costly choice. A burdened choice is one that incurs costs. The burden or cost of controlling inflation is some degree of unwanted unemployment. Highway speed carries a burden or cost of death.

The burden or cost of pots and pans consists of the other valued outputs forgone—outputs that could have been enjoyed if resources were not used to make pots and pans.

Cost is not simply a technical concept of secondary rather than fundamental significance. Nor does the word always refer to money. Some burdens—costs—are expressed in money; but the examples just given show that many are not. Even more important, money costs have no significance except as they represent performances and objects forgone. If you read that in Denmark it costs 200,000 kroner to send a person to college for a year, the significance of the statement is that some persons must carry the burden of giving up the benefits that the 200,000 kroner so spent might have otherwise bought for them.

The key requirement for allocative efficiency is some method of weighing the value of what is to be taken or received against cost, which is the value of what is to be forgone. Obviously a choice is efficient if the value received is worth the value forgone. If that proposition is a commonplace, it is also one of the most useful of all those key and universal propositions through which we cope with the days of our lives. Efficiency requires either the maximum in value to be received from a given cost or the least cost for a given value received—in short, efficiency means least-cost decisions.

If allocations are to be efficient for the whole society, everyone's benefits and burdens have to be weighed. When benefits for some people throw costs not on them but on others, the comparison of benefit with cost is enormously difficult. For example, widespread benefits of automobiles have to be compared with the value of lives lost in accidents. Opinions differ both widely and contentiously on whose benefits warrant whose losses. Still, the requirement for efficiency is inescapable: values or benefits to be received must be compared with burdens, costs, or values forgone.

When costs are unknown, decision making is rendered irrational in the extreme. You do not dare accept an offer of a desired cellular phone if you have no knowledge of what you will be asked to give up if you accept it. As an entrepreneur you cannot decide on the size of your labor force if you have no information on what you must give up in return. Centralists' problems are the same, but magnified. They cannot rationally decide, say, on plans for more rail transport without first knowing the many possible reductions of other kinds of production that would be necessary to make it possible, and knowing as well the value of each.

And, again, what has to be given up—the burden or cost—depends on what options are open for effecting the choice. There is no one correct statement of cost when a person, an official, or a whole society chooses more bread. What the cost will be depends on the means by which more bread can be had. The cost of bread to an official or an entrepreneur will depend on whether bakers have to be paid or can be commanded, their own preferences simply disregarded as irrelevant to an evaluation.

That producing an appropriate combination of products is difficult and requires cost information comes as a surprise to some people. They think it obvious that people need food, shelter, education, medical care, transport, and recreation. No problem, then, for any society: simply produce them. The question facing a society, however, is not whether to produce them—of course they are needed and should be produced. The question is how much of each to produce. Less or more? Should 5 or 20 or 40 percent of the

society's capacity—these are not insignificant differences—
be put into medical care? Whatever figure is contemplated,
it is easy to see that more is needed, just as more is needed
of the things that have to be given up to get more medical
care. Hence, to find and produce an appropriate combination of all is an endlessly complex task.

We almost never compare generally or abstractly the
value of, say, food with that of medical care or of any good or
service. We compare only the value of an increment or a
decrement of a good or service with the value of an increment or a decrement of others that have to be forgone. If I
make a choice between shoes and a jacket, I do not ask myself, as though I had neither, whether on the whole I would
rather wear shoes than a jacket. I ask only whether I would
prefer a new pair of shoes, to be added to those I already
have, or a new jacket, to be added to the clothes I already
have. A planner asks not whether steel or electric power is
more valuable but whether more steel is worth putting up
with less power.

In short, allocative choices are made at the margin.
Choosers compare marginal benefits with marginal costs.
For choice to be efficient, the marginal values to be received
must be worth their marginal costs or burdens.

It would be helpful to individual as well as planners'
choices if human wants and needs were biologically fixed.
Then anyone would know what is worth producing. But
they are not biologically fixed. Biology never specified that I
need television nor, if it had, how many sets of what screen
size. Nor did it specify my choices of food, as evidenced by
how cuisine differs from one society to another. Nor does it
say whether a society should put more of its resources into
education than into health care or vice versa.

## Prices That Measure Cost

Two additional specific requirements for efficiency emerge from the very concepts of allocative efficiency and cost.

First, for comparing benefits with costs, some common-denominator measure of cost is needed, no matter who is doing the evaluations and the choosing. The cost to me of a computer might be stated as "If you take the computer, you will have to go without the value of a new sofa you have been considering." Or, "If you take the computer, you will have to cut back for a year or so on eating out, whatever that is worth to you." But there are dozens or even thousands of other things I might give up rather than the sofa or eating out. I need to compare them all to find the least-cost alternative. Central decision makers face the same difficulties. To plan new resources, say, for air transport, they need a better statement of costs than that they could take the needed resources from the production of motor scooters. They need to know and compare all possible ways to obtain the resources to find the least-cost alternative. Hence market-system participant and central planner alike need a common denominator for the measurement of cost or value forgone and for comparison of it with value received.

Measure every good and service in pounds or tons? As we have already seen, for commodities that is a possibility, but a nonsensical one. That lead is heavier than gold says nothing about its value. And services are weightless. Measure volume? The same objections. For efficient choice, we want a measure not of any physical attribute of goods and services but of value.

Money and prices can offer a common denominator of value. For a consumer or business manager, a price on a cellular phone expresses its cost in a number that can be compared with similar numbers on alternative possible purchases. Looking then at prices on goods and services other than the phone, a buyer can see instantly what can be bought if not the phone—what must be forgone to obtain it. The prices on each alternative permit a least-cost decision. Prices enable a consumer to compare at the margin all alternatives: buying or saving, buying this service rather than that, and buying this brand or design rather than that. Prices enable an enterprise to compare with each other the marginal costs of alternative inputs—shall the product be made with aluminum or plastic?—and compare as well the marginal costs of inputs with the marginal value of outputs.

Because we easily make evaluations every day in the market system, we do not wholly realize what problems we would face without prices. One might think that some choices are easy even without prices—anyone would obviously choose a new car over an old one. The fact is, of course, that all over the world many millions of people make the opposite choice. For the price of a new car says that for them its burden or cost is too great. You might think that any rational person would choose gold over salt. But in the Saharan salt trade, salt and gold were once traded at equal value, ounce for ounce. In the absence of prices, there are no obvious choices, and choices become irrational in their ignorance of costs.

Second, prices must measure cost. It is implicit in what has just been said that prices pulled out of a hat will not do, for prices must in some sense measure value. But since nothing is of value except as someone puts a value on it, we must ask whose values are to be represented in prices.

Imagine that you are a central planner asking yourself

whether a 2 percent expansion of steel production is worth
a 3 percent cut in electric power output that would make
the expanded steel production possible. Worth the cost to
whom? You might reply: worth it to society as I estimate society's needs. Or you might reply: worth it to my governmental superiors, as I understand their values to be. Or:
worth it to millions of citizens as I estimate what *their* values are (quite irrespective of my values, with which they
may or may not agree). The value of steel against electric
power will differ, depending on your reply. The cost of steel
expansion and the efficiency of expanding will also depend
on your reply. There exists no correct value, no correct estimate of cost, no one maximally efficient choice, no correct
price. It all depends on whose values are to count.

I do not know how to establish a set of prices that might
be called efficient rather than arbitrary for a planner willing
to disregard all values except what he or his superiors value.
It has been a curse, one might say, on central planners that
they have no such set of prices. But it is possible to construct
or give rise to a set of prices that responds to the values of
millions of people. To avoid a long disquisition on abstract
points of economic theory, I shall use a shortcut exposition to explain how prices can represent values, though not
equally, for almost everyone in the society.

## Efficiency Prices

Imagine yourself among a thousand or so people gathered
together in a gym for an experiment. With a few exceptions,
each is given one or a few goods that many people want: one
might be given a loaf of bread, another a brick, another an
auto or an insurance policy. Somehow, as though by magic,

most of those gathered are also given abilities and skills as varied as those of lawyer or common laborer. All are then instructed to engage in such trading as they wish. You cannot simply take what you want from others; you can only trade. You have no use for the brick dealt you, so you try to find someone who wants a brick and will give you something for it. It must be something that you value, either because you can use or enjoy it or because you think you can trade it for something you can use or enjoy. Another can offer a contract for legal services in order to obtain an air conditioner. All are to continue trading for as long as they can make favorable trades, stopping only when there are no further possibilities. In this imaginary interchange we assume that people post offers and demands by voice, on bulletin boards, and on computer screens. They move around energetically searching for opportunities, and they have all the time they need.

When all possible favorable trades are completed, observers will see that for each specific exchange, like brick for bread, the final trades are almost all at the same ratio—say one brick exchanges for two loaves of bread. So long as there were exchanges at two different ratios, trading would not stop. For a better offer for bread will, when it is discovered, render all lesser offers futile, thus leave a single ratio prevailing.

At the end of the trading, the prevailing ratio for each traded good or service is of course linked to all other prevailing ratios. A two-for-one ratio of bread to brick together with a one-for-one ratio of brick to package of pencils implies a two-for-one ratio of bread to package of pencils. This set of ratios for all goods and services can be expressed in a set of prices. The price of the brick is the same as the price for the package of pencils. The price of bread is half of that. This is the kind of price that measures marginal values and costs for people who can effect their choices only through the voluntary responses of others.

We can imagine that the managers of the hypothetical game also distribute a kind of money printed for use in the game. All present are then instructed to buy and sell at ratios expressed in money prices, rather than simply engage in barter. Their interchanges will bring them to the same set of ratios that we just saw are implied in their bartering.

Prices of this kind are called efficiency prices because they represent the terms—the prices—on which interchanges from a starting position bring to all participants all the gains to all that are possible other than gains possible by compelling or imposing losses on some participants. They permit an exhaustion of possibilities of advantageous voluntary interactions, given an initial distribution of skills and assets. We can say both that 1) they permit all participants to know the costs of what they might wish to acquire, hence make efficient choices, and 2) they permit everyone in the game to gain from it while imposing losses on no other participant.

Take special note that, with efficiency prices, the cost of anything for a person is what that person must give up to get it, assuming that the only way he can get it is through a voluntary transaction. If he could steal it, his cost might be zero. If he could appeal to an authority to grant it to him, his cost might be zero or perhaps the cost of a bribe or a favor to the authority. Since he can do neither, what any person must give up is indicated by the value of it to other persons from whom it can be obtained only by an exchange. Hence the price each person pays for an object or performance indicates, under the rules of the game, its cost.

The contrast of efficiency price with arbitrary price is fairly clear. Suppose that you and I are on the point of a transaction in which I offer you two loaves of bread for a brick (or an agreed price in the game's money). Such a trade would benefit both of us. But the game managers intervene to set a different ratio or price. You or I do not find it advantageous to trade at that price, and so we both lose the gains that we were on the point of making. The imposed arbitrary price has ruined an efficient transaction. Or suppose that one of the participants in the game somehow intimidates some others so that they do not trade. Or suppose that one participant offering a good somehow silences or excludes from the game some others who offer the same good but on better terms. These are the devices of monopoly, and they too block mutually advantageous transactions.

The prices implied in the prevailing ratios or—if game money is used—actually established through transactions do not, it is clear, correspond to any physical attribute of the traded service or good. They correspond to the frequency and intensity of desires, hence to value. If in the game I must pay forty-five pingos for a shoe shine, forty-five pingos represents the degree to which others value their time and energy.

Efficiency prices will change as people change their minds about what they value. Efficiency prices and costs are also of course greatly influenced by the distribution of income and wealth. As a society grows in wealth one might expect, for example, that the efficiency prices of shore properties in resort areas might rise as wealthy people bid for them.

Capital growth and technological change also greatly alter efficiency prices. Indeed, the pace of change is often breathtaking, running faster than planners can plan but producing, week by week, new efficiency prices to guide the next necessary decisions. Between 1880 and 1890, for example, declining American steel prices signaled new opportunities for steel-using industries, with the result that steel production rose from 1.25 million tons annually to more than 10 million. So fast a pace of change is common, particularly in today's computer and communications industries.

The distinction between arbitrary and efficiency prices is no small distinction. Arbitrary prices often produce shortages and queues, or even gluts, as they conspicuously did in the Soviet Union and China. When governments in developing societies hold down farm prices to favor the urban poor, the effect on farmers is to discourage the very production urgently needed or to induce farmers to hide and hoard rather than sell. When electric power is underpriced, people overload and then have to suffer the inconvenience of blackouts. When irrigation water is wastefully distributed through subsidies, the result is agricultural production not worth its costs, which include taxpayer payments to construct the irrigation facilities. When petroleum, minerals, and other basic resources are arbitrarily priced through subsidies, the whole system's growth may be retarded. When cartels boost the price of milk, the children of the urban poor suffer. When pharmaceutical corporations use patents to achieve monopoly on newly discovered medications, the costs levied on some needy ailing people may be ruinous. Efficiency prices are not simply an economist's toy, nor an incidental adornment of the market system. They are a fundamental requirement for efficiency in the production of services and goods.

Efficiency prices are appropriate for a liberal or democratic society or any society whose authorities want social coordination to proceed as voluntarily as possible. For a corps of rulers who do not care what their subjects wish or value and are willing to compel rather than make use of voluntary interactions, efficiency prices, so called, do not represent the relevant values, and rulers would be efficient to disregard them.

# Market-System Efficiency

In the real world, how are efficiency prices established? Strictly speaking, they are only approximated. How approximated? By interchanges in markets in which, as in the game in the gym, participants can endlessly engage in favorable exchanges. As in the game, it is required that the presence of many buyers and sellers constrains monopoly and that no one has the power to fix prices—that is, government desists on the whole from price fixing. To the degree that these conditions are met, market systems give rise to and make use of efficiency prices.

That is a core claim for market-system efficiency: efficiency requires efficiency prices, and market systems establish them. The brevity with which I have just put it should not detract from its fundamental significance.

This first great and distinctive claim to efficiency is made for all market-system choices where efficiency prices prevail. It is a claim made both for consumer choices and for entrepreneurial choices about what to produce and of what quality and with what inputs. It is also made for entrepreneurial choices on technology and capital investment.

Andrew Carnegie's legendary entrepreneurship is an example of how capital is accumulated and new technologies are introduced in a market system, both hinging on the efficient choices that efficient prices make possible. "One of the chief sources of success in manufacturing," he wrote, "is the introduction and strict maintenance of a perfect system of accounting, so that responsibility for money or materials can be brought home to every man." Between 1875 and 1898 his attention to efficient choice brought the price of steel rails down from $160 a ton to $17, with enormous consequences for growth not only in the steel industry but throughout the economy in the many industries using steel in some form as inputs.

I do not want to overstate or oversell so large a claim as that efficiency prices make market systems efficient. In real-world market systems prices are often distorted by monopoly and government price fixing. And it is a claim only about allocative efficiency in the production of services and goods, leaving questions open about other kinds of efficiency. Still, the claim of efficiency through efficiency prices is a broad and fundamental one. It is a claim that cannot be made for hypothetical physical planning systems without money and prices. It cannot be made for communist systems because, although they use prices for some purposes, their prices are highly arbitrary. Nor are their production decisions governed by prices, as they are in a market system. In short, market systems practice a rough efficiency pricing widely and routinely; other real and hypothetical systems do not.

One might be tempted to believe that efficient choice is less important than that entrepreneurs simply produce more physical capital at technological frontiers. Market efficiency through efficient choice and efficiency prices is too static a picture, one might think; it lacks the color and life of dynamic growth processes.

No question about it, capital creation, technological innovation, and the energetic entrepreneurs who undertake them are a large part of the explanation for market-system accomplishments. Their contribution shows up in growth. But entrepreneurs do not simply introduce new methods in order to pile up outputs and capital without regard to what people want or low-cost ways to create new capital. For example, they do not allow their energies, however creative, to construct a mountainous accumulation of air conditioners or of the machines necessary to make them, to the neglect of all else. Their energies, their capital construction, and their innovations are consequential for growth and efficiency because they are tailored to what people want and to low-cost ways to satisfy them. Without the discriminating choices that efficiency prices make possible for both the enterprise and its customers, a society wastes its resources of electric power, petroleum, or labor, and falters—or turns back—in its growth processes.

But is it not almost certainly true that this year's capital production and technological innovation will contribute more to this year's growth than will improvement in the efficiency of choice? Of course. But that is because they will be guided by relatively efficient choices made possible by efficiency prices. Societies do not choose between entrepreneurship with capital construction and innovation for growth, on one hand, and efficient choices, on the other. The first succeed because they are guided by the second.

Granting the many failures of the market system, understanding that all complex social systems are afflicted with gross inefficiencies, market systems can nevertheless be credited with the great and distinctive merit of efficiency prices that permit a drastically improved degree of efficient choice. They make cost information universally available. And they force cost information on every chooser, for each chooser must pay to effect a choice.

## Motivational Efficiency

If efficiency requires, first, that choosers ascertain costs and compare them with value received, it then requires that choosers are motivated to collect and act on that information. Here then is the second great and distinctive efficiency claim about the market system: its motivations for all market participants. Especially important, however, are its extraordinary motivations for entrepreneurs, who are moved to undertake massive projects, at an extreme the creation of entire new industries, as by the Rothschilds, the Krupps, and Gates.

Informed by efficiency prices, participants are powerfully motivated to act because they gain contingent specific benefits from doing so. A rule of quid pro quo, whatever its inequities and harshness, is a powerful motivator, admittedly not of all kinds of performances, but of market performances. Compare the rule with the usual alternative, motivation by command, the deficiencies of which are often obvious. Commands frequently offend and motivate people to evade. They do not so immediately tap motivations of self-interest as do the motivations of the market system.

Familiar as we are with market motivation, I want to mention several aspects of it. It does what motivation through altruism or good will, even at their strongest, cannot do. To achieve efficiency, it is not enough to motivate people to love their neighbors, do good, or work hard. For social cooperation, incentive systems have to draw people into specific assignments, like welding or managing a janitorial crew. Even under the most favorable circumstances, altruism cannot motivate an allocation of energies to a required variety of different tasks. Market incentives can and do draw people to each of the innumerable tasks to be done in any society.

As for motivating energy in each of the tasks to which people are allocated, the strength of market incentives is noteworthy yet less conclusive. Market interactions hold open a variety of opportunities for movement rather than the few that may be prescribed in the table of organization of a centrally planned system. Millions of people consequently throw their best energies into the roles they play, believing that to be the most effective way to move up to a better role. In simplest logic, if you want a better job, do this one well. I say that this is not conclusive evidence of the efficacy of market incentives because there are also many millions of wage earners whose prospects of better jobs are so slim as to fail to motivate them in their existing jobs.

The authoritative, even authoritarian, management of the workplace is often inimical to employee motivation on the job. I think that we do not know how much inefficiency on the job is implied in employee indifference, frequent hostility to management, fatigue, and despair. Quite possibly the inefficiency is enormous. Yet in the absence of the market system, enterprises would presumably also be authoritatively managed, even more so than in market systems. Authority would be extended to the management of interactions among enterprises and between enterprises and their suppliers and customers, interactions otherwise coordinated through markets. And employees could not simply leave, as they often do in a market system, rather than bear impositions from management. Indeed, one way to reduce managerial authority and its questionable incentives within the enterprise is to introduce internal markets within each enterprise.

Folklore has produced some vulnerable doctrines on incentives. For example, it is an article of faith in some circles that the strict rule of quid pro quo best motivates worker productivity. More than the softened quid pro quo of the welfare state? As noted in Chapter 8, the empirical evidence does not say so. It is closer to denying than affirming the doctrine.

In several familiar distinctive ways, the market system motivates millions of people to become entrepreneurs. It motivates them to accept the challenges, bear the risks, anticipate the gains, suffer the losses—and bring to the society the great benefits of entrepreneurship. For one, the market system multiplies and spreads opportunities for innovation; they are not limited to a few in a hierarchical table of organization, as in a planning system. For each of countless entrepreneurs, there is no restricted list of opportunities, no gatekeeper, no supervising committee that doles out opportunities, as in communist systems. And once embarked on a venture, there is no restricted list of persons or other enterprises whose consent or cooperation is required. An entrepreneur who cannot find a needed supply from an expected source finds alternative sources. While a hierarchical central planning system sets above every enterprise a possible veto at each of every higher level, in a market system almost no such superior authority exists. To accomplish a goal, a manager in a centralist system walks a prescribed path given by the table of organization of a hierarchy. In the market system, an entrepreneur can try dozens or hundreds of paths. And of course the entrepreneur also is motivated by the unhappy contingency that both suppliers and customers can leave if dissatisfied.

Speed and flexibility of action, wide dispersion of opportunities for entrepreneurship, and a multiplicity of paths to explore make for powerful entrepreneurial incentives. These incentives stimulate a proliferation of initiatives—new enterprises, new goods and services, and new technologies, even if, as we shall see, many are of questionable value or are dangerous. At an extreme, it is as though the operating rule for market projects were: "If someone wants it done, do it!" and the rule for government projects: "If someone doesn't want it done, don't do it!" If Fidelity wants to manufacture a new kind of financial service, it does not have to clear its decision with the existing suppliers. But if the navy wants to set new tasks for naval air services, its proposal will often be vetoed by the air force or army.

Market systems produce strong motives for the same reasons that other forms of mutual adjustment do. For one, many problems are solved not head-on but as a by-product of attacks on smaller, easier problems more likely to stir individual persons and collectives to action. In a market system, the distribution of income or the allocation of resources to capital investment is a weighty determination to be made. But it appears on no one's desk for consideration. Instead, it is determined as an unintended by-product of individual decisions to buy and sell. The greatest "decisions" of a market system are not decisions at all but states of affairs reached through millions of individual small decisions. They are not delayed by the size and gravity of these "decisions," as they would be if, in the absence of the market system, they came to someone's desk. Like other forms of mutual adjustment, the market system can move with a speed rare in central coordination, such as the dazzling speed now revolutionizing methods of communication.

These are, as I see it, the keys to such efficiency as market systems achieve: one, efficient choices made possible by efficiency prices, the other, powerful motivations. But there is more to the efficiency story, and what remains to be told will lead to conclusions perhaps not expected.

# 11 Inefficiencies

Some attributes of the market system point to great exceptions or limits to its claims to efficiency in the production of services and goods. I shall not attempt the whole list, for many have already been mentioned and some are too familiar to need discussion. Let us look with a cool mind at the most fundamental—and most illuminating. These are inefficiencies that stir strong emotions and rhetorical excess.

## Spillovers

Perhaps the most telling market inefficiency is that, although efficiency requires that all benefits and costs be weighed regardless of where they fall, market participants weigh only their own. Of course, most individual participants weigh costs and benefits for members of their families. Nonetheless, each market participant, whether an individual or an enterprise, typically weighs benefits and costs narrowly, pursuing what is conventionally called self-interest, or profit. If as a consequence the establishment of an airport goes far to ruin surrounding neighborhoods for whom the noise is intolerable, we can hardly call the decision to establish efficient. Spillovers are so obviously a major inefficiency of market systems that one wonders how it can be that their significance is still widely denied in some quarters.

Think again of the traders in the gym. The exchanges through which A and B each benefit and which we consequently judge to be efficient cannot be efficient if they harm any of the others in the gym. Nor can they be efficient if A and B are indifferent to benefits that their further transactions might bring to others.

The inefficiencies of spillovers are enormous, especially the adverse effects of the great physical energies that enterprises harness with contemporary technologies. Spillovers are of course not all traceable to enterprises. Lake Erie became a dead lake not only because of industrial wastes but because residential lawn fertilizer polluted the water. But given the rise of large enterprises driven by the technological changes of the past two centuries, they typically and generally rather than exceptionally impose large spillover burdens or costs. Every factory must dispose of waste products, and they commonly burden millions of people. Even enterprises that appear to be benign do so. Enterprises now construct, for example, retirement villages and gated towns with far-flung spillovers on the security and freedom of movement on nearby persons not in the community. Air and water pollution, as the most familiar examples of spillover burden, are clearly not exceptional.

Now that spillover effects of fuel consumption and other chemical discharges have reached critical magnitudes, not only writers of science fiction but scientists ponder the possibility that spillovers, if not governmentally curbed, may impoverish or bring an end to human life on Earth. The World Resources Institute joins with the United Nations' development and environmental programs to conclude that the world is headed "toward a variety of potential human and environmental disasters." The United Kingdom Royal Society joins with the U.S. National Academy of Sciences to warn against "irreversible damage to the earth's capacity to sustain life."

Enterprises impose an even wider variety of spillover burdens than those that economic theory identifies as externalities. They impose, for example, burdens of bankruptcy on an enterprise whose customers have abandoned it in favor of a new competitor; burdens are then also visited on employees and suppliers of the bankrupt enterprise.

That everyone weighs benefits and costs almost exclusively for self or family blows an enormous hole in arguments for market-system efficiency. Taking account of the universality of spillover burdens, it does not seem that much can be said for the efficiency of market systems except in comparison with even less efficient systems.

Can we believe the once-dominant opinion—still strongly held in some quarters—that spillovers are unusual, that market transactions typically have little effect on persons not party to the transaction? I do not believe there ever was a market society in which that might have been true. In any case the great energy-using technologies of our era commonly produce widespread spillover effects. Mines blight landscapes, high-rises block sun and view, boom boxes and power lawn mowers destroy tranquility, and autos bring with them congestion, stress, and death.

Of course, people who do not like the fumes from a factory chimney or the racket of a neighbor's lawn mower can move to a new location. They must nevertheless carry the burden or cost of moving, even if it turns out that they like their new locations as well as the old.

Some people deprecate the significance of spillover burdens by claiming that, common as they may be, they represent losses of values of small intangibles, unlike the important solid values for which we are willing to pay pounds or rupees. The values we lose through spillover costs are somehow of a lesser quality, they say, not to be compared with the values of services and goods. A loss of open space because of commercialization of an area or a burden of soot in the air is not important when compared with the values of marketable goods and services. But why do I value and buy, say, a commuter ticket? Because I want to commute from a suburban location where I can enjoy more open space than in the heart of the city. And why do I spend as I do on laundry? Because soot in the air dirties my clothes. What congestion and soot deprive me of, I pay to recover. Spillover burdens are costly and significant in exactly the same way that transport and laundry are costly and significant.

A few economists deny that those spillovers they call externalities constitute an inefficiency of the market system. Instead, they say, they are evidence that the market has not been sufficiently enlarged. If rights to open and clean air, sunlight, and beautiful vistas could be divided up and turned into private property, they would be priced because they would then be scarce and controllable. An enterprise or person would then have to pay me for interfering with my view or polluting my air. If so, every enterprise and person would have to take account of those values now neglected in market decisions.

For many of the values neglected in existing market systems, the "if" is enormous. For property rights cannot generally be established in values like air, sunshine, and security. I agree, however, that they can be established in some important areas in which they are now uncommon. For example, assigning forest property rights to farmers in Thailand has reduced deforestation. Granting property titles to Bandung slum dwellers has greatly improved sanitation—owners can refuse or charge for the use of their domains as a dump. New Zealand has curbed overfishing by assigning transferable fishing rights. Along these lines, there is room for reducing the inefficiencies of spillovers.

Many small enough spillovers, we can also grant, are irrelevant to appraisals of market efficiency. For whatever the social system, all social interdependence generates floods of spillovers. It irks me that you chew gum so visibly, and it may disturb my neighbor that my dog barks. These spillovers are not peculiar to life in a market system. When one wants to compare the market system not with utopia but with other systems, these inevitable spillovers can be ignored. Even utopia would perhaps permit many significant spillovers, for we cannot wish for a society in which people are so isolated that they never inadvertently hurt one another.

Some options to impose significant burdens on others are also highly valued as personal liberties. For my freedom or liberty I am allowed broad rights of free speech, even though I am sometimes greatly hurtful to you. I am also allowed to lock my doors against intruders, even if homeless people sleep on the sidewalks. We do not label the market as inefficient because it permits us zones of liberty that impose spillovers on others.

Governments of course engage in a variety of standing attempts to control spillovers as, for example, through zoning and other land-use restrictions, curbs on waste emissions, programs for employee health and safety on the job, and regulated job termination. The frequency with which the state tries to curb spillovers indicates how common and threatening they have become. It also suggests that hope for an efficient market system, if hope is possible, hinges on state regulation of most transactions of enterprises, abhorrent as the thought is to many people. If, on the other hand, the state is inefficient enough in its regulations—and that is always a possibility to be weighed—then there is no escape from spillovers as a source of gross inefficiency in market system. Under the influence of business, governments often refuse to curb spillovers and often protect the enterprise's prerogatives to create them, as, for example, when they restrict individual suits against corporations as well as, sometimes, public criticism of them.

It is sometimes noted with surprise, as though the opposite were to be expected, that communist systems abused their resources—for example, polluted the air and water—more wastefully than did the market societies. Hypothetically in a system in which production is decided by central authority, that authority looks after such effects as blight and pollution. Entrepreneurs do not. Yet the empirical record shows that the market societies better conserve the environment and the society's amenities than do communist systems. A careless inference is that the market system, for all its inefficient spillovers, is more attentive to spillover problems than is a centralist system. A more careful inference is that the market system, combined with governmental regulation, can deal more effectively with these problems than can central control without the help of market system. That may be true even if that regulation is flawed, as it always is.

The other side of the coin of spillover burdens is spillover benefits. For example, an enterprise trains the employees it hires, and then over the course of months and years some workers are hired away by other enterprises that can then benefit from their training. Or you fashion a beautiful garden, and all passersby benefit. These inadvertent benefits may be no less numerous than inadvertent burdens.

At first glance, spillover benefits seem an obvious bonus, a happy accidental efficiency. But in principle, no less than for spillover burdens, they reveal a shortcoming in market efficiency. They represent gains that could be enlarged if they were taken into account by parties to the transaction, as, by definition, they are not. They consequently represent opportunities wasted. Hence an efficient training program would call for more training than will be provided by the enterprises, each of which understandably does not take spillover benefits into account when deciding on training programs for its own employees. Governmental occupational training programs are a response to such a shortfall.

Spillover benefits and burdens almost certainly do not simply cancel out—plus against minus. If through market neglect of spillover burdens the earth loses its forests or the atmosphere its ozone, or if scientific laboratories unwittingly unleash a deadly pestilence, what spillover benefits can offset these disasters? On this count alone I suspect that the coming decades will see a slow-moving but drastic reconsideration of the market system.

## Transaction Termination

It takes two to tango, and it takes at least two to create a market interaction, each acting voluntarily. But it takes only one party to dissolve a market interaction, and the dissolution imposes or forces a burden or cost on the other party. It is a burden not taken into account by the decision maker, whose decision is consequently inefficient. This is not a spillover to a bystander, to persons not party to a transaction, but a loss imposed by one party to a transaction on the other party.

An obvious example is the sacking of an employee. In market systems many millions of people are never free from fear that this burden will be thrust on them. Nor is discharge necessarily a once-in-a-lifetime burden. They may suffer from discharge again and again throughout their working lives. How severe a cost is this to them? It depends, of course, on what alternative jobs are available. Idealized models of the market system postulate no lack of satisfactory alternative jobs, but just that lack is of course a problem in all real-world market systems, even in what is called full employment. And the weight of the burden depends on whether there are fallback protections, like unemployment compensation.

Other terminations of market relations impose burdens of varying severity: an enterprise leaves a town, a landlord evicts a tenant, or an employer loses a prized employee.

Conventional views of the market system see it as an arena in which people engage in advantageous interchanges. But plainly it is in fact an arena in which people both engage in and are ejected from them. Classical arguments for market efficiency, including mathematical models of idealized markets, show net benefits for all market participants under specific conditions; but they are benefits of transactions when compared to no transactions. Under certain hypothetical conditions, a market system is better than no market system. The arguments do not show that, given a market system, everyone gains from continuing transactions and terminations. Everyone does not.

Terminations are in fact so deeply burdensome that many societies legally restrict rights to terminate transactions. Employers are sometimes prohibited from firing without legally allowed cause. Or they are required to give notice and to pay dismissal wages. Landlords can evict tenants only under limiting rules. In some circumstances, an attorney cannot abandon a client. The telephone, gas, or electric company is restricted in terminating service to customers who do not pay. Clearly market inefficiency on this count is widely recognized.

The burdens of withdrawal or eviction throw light on difficulties in moving into market systems in Russia and Eastern Europe. Millions of people there see the fixed claims they enjoyed under communism being reduced, and they are frightened by employers' new options to terminate their employment.

## Arbitrary Prices

Although the efficiency of market systems depends heavily on efficiency prices, we have already noted that real-world market systems often establish prices that are arbitrary to some significant degree. The practices are frequent enough to reduce significantly the market system's claim to efficiency.

Of the two sources of arbitrary prices—monopoly and governmental controls over prices—monopoly, though perhaps the lesser of the two, is perhaps more frequent. Notwithstanding the complaints, monopoly is a lesser source of inefficiency than commonly thought because, in the extreme form in which it is often imagined, it does not exist. All sellers compete with all other sellers, and each limits the power of the others to manipulate prices. Although in very few markets is there enough competition to make a price an ideal or near-perfect efficiency price, in many markets the approximation is close. In many more it is at least acceptable. Every market is a long way away from single-seller control of price, far from the "mono" in monopoly.

Imagine a society with a single passenger airline. You fly on it or not at all. It can set high fares, as well as lose baggage and generally irritate its customers. Even so, its power to raise prices and its irresponsibility are greatly limited—not satisfactorily curbed but nevertheless limited. Some prices and abuses you will refuse to bear. You will go by train or bus, rent a car or drive your own, in some cases go by boat, or stay home. Such limits on the airline are more effective than might first appear, for it has to worry about the loss of those customers most likely to defect. Though you are compelled by circumstances to travel by air, some other airline customers are not.

The seller's capacity to control prices is constrained by the availability of an alternative or substitute to which the buyer can turn. That is the key idea in understanding monopoly: the availability to customers of alternatives or substitutes. All possible customer expenditures are least distant substitutes for each other. Alternatives to buying a Hyundai include not only a Civic but a remodeling of one's living quarters, an expensive vacation, or dozens of things one could buy with what one saves by not buying a car. Alternatives to an overpriced breakfast cereal include not simply another cereal, but other foods as well. For that matter, they include any other performance or object to which one might turn rather than pay the asked price for the cereal.

Like some other agriculturists, a sheep rancher may be only one of thousands of enterprises offering the same product to buyers. Competition holds the rancher in a vise, with no power over price. In contrast, most enterprises offer—and intend to offer—services and goods somewhat different from those of any other enterprise. Geisha canned pineapple is both slightly different from other pineapple and advertised to be even more different than in fact it is. Consequently, most enterprises hold some power over price, for the customer cannot find exactly the same performance or object from any other source.

Enterprises also create or fall into cartels—explicit or tacit agreements on price and other policies that restrain them from competing with each other to the degree that would push them strongly to efficiency prices. Patents also permit price manipulation, as do many licensing laws and other legally imposed constraints on trade. For all these reasons some degree of arbitrary pricing by sellers runs throughout the market system.

Because it provides the enterprise with some security against competitors and also provides higher returns, monopolistic powers over price sometimes stimulate innovation and therefore should not be simply categorized as inefficient. On the other hand, as enterprises turn increasingly away from providing goods and toward providing services, monopoly may become increasingly exploitative. A consumer is often at the mercy of a television repair service or physician, not knowing just what each will do or how service differs from what other repair services or physicians might offer. Opportunities open to service enterprises to deceive and overcharge are great. This may be a more significant monopoly problem than the overpricing of goods by large corporations.

As an inefficiency of the market system, monopoly hardly compares with inefficiencies from such spillovers as environmental pollution and urban blight. Nor does it appear that the arbitrary prices of monopoly distort prices to the degree that the state does. The two sources of inefficiency are often combined. For example, the state establishes a tariff to wall off foreign competitors, thus granting monopoly powers to the protected enterprises. Or it curbs competition by limiting the number of competing enter-prises licensed to do business. Or it allows the regulation of public utility prices, as for water or electricity, to slide into corruption by industry influence. On the whole, although the state on some points curbs monopoly, it is in many re-spects monopoly's great friend.

Broadly speaking, monopoly includes practices other than selling at a controlled price, practices that may ac-count for more inefficiency than those of conventional mo-nopoly. An enterprise negotiates with a municipality, re-gional authority, or nation-state, offering to establish, say, a factory. In return for tax concessions or other subsidies, it promises to open up new jobs in the area. The corporation can play one municipality or nation against another, induc-ing them to compete in order to attract the enterprise. Euro-Disneyland was the recipient of French subsidies, local and national, estimated to be the equivalent to $1 billion, paid to attract it to Paris. Poor small nations not only offer subsi-dies to attract corporations from overseas but also have to bend or rewrite their laws to win them. In effect, an offering enterprise "sells" job opportunities to a community at a price, in the form of a subsidy. Studies of negotiations of this kind show a general pattern: the community pays a high price for each promised job—in one study of them, $70,000 per job, as it turned out—and often the jobs paid for do not in fact materialize.

Monopoly aside, governments make prices arbitrary in small or large degree through explicit price fixing under-taken for various purposes. As noted, developing countries sometimes force down food prices because they are fearful of urban unrest, which sometimes flares into riots. Or gov-ernments anywhere may impose price ceilings to curb inflation. Such particular objectives may or may not be worth the consequent losses in efficiency.

Governments also create arbitrary prices through subsidies, although not all subsidies have such an effect. Market systems subsidize a variety of industries. The subsidies bring down their expenses with the result that their products are sold at prices that do not cover costs. The political pressure for subsidies is enormous, often for the worst of reasons. Frequently subsidized directly, through tax credits, or through other devices are agriculture, lumber, mining, petroleum, shipping, fish, livestock, and electric power. And many subsidies are large. In Italy, subsidies cover roughly a fifth of the revenues of its electric power companies. Their effects run through the economy, constituting a major failure of market systems to achieve allocative efficiency.

We may as well recognize here that government engagement in price fixing and subsidies often goes so far as to significantly degenerate the market system. In a number of nation-states like Thailand, not an unusual example, enterprises commonly make use of both webs of political influence and bribes to obtain low-cost loans from governmentally controlled banks—or to obtain loans while others are deprived of them.

Subsidies can, of course, be used for excellent purposes: to help distressed low-income farmers, to support an industry that shows promise for the future, to encourage the production of services, like medical care, that many consumers could not otherwise afford. The purposes for which governments announce subsidies are often laudable. But the reason they are often established is, in fact, that they work to the advantage of groups or industries that can exercise the political influence necessary to establish them. Agriculture

subsidies, as a case in point, though often defended as protections for low-income farmers, are paid almost entirely to
high-income farmers or farm corporations.

## Ignorance and Irrationality

Efficiency prices and cost calculation do not make sages of
buyers and sellers. Although we have made much of cost
calculation as necessary to efficiency, market participants
are plagued by the general irrationalities and ignorances
that affect all people in all social systems. That consumers
often do not know just what they are choosing is evidenced
by the complexity of many products. What can a typical
consumer know about the many specific ways in which, behind the covering panels, one washing machine differs from
another, or whether a white-coated physician's diagnosis is
correct?

That consumers often do not even try to find out and instead choose irrationally is indicated by the heavy reliance
of advertising on nonrational and irrational appeals. In this
morning's paper, a phone company offers its services to
"open up the lines of communication with your sweetie,"
as though its rivals cannot. Consumers swim in an ocean of
information and misinformation, often unable to distinguish one from the other. Not simply spillovers but also the
incompetence of all market participants—the two joining
together—promise occasional disasters like thalidomide
and the constant risk of others.

One might put these considerations aside, simply holding that efficiency is to be judged by what consumers think
they want, irrespective of their incompetence in knowing
what they want or need. An incompetent consumer, one
might say, is a better chooser than even an ostensibly com-

petent government official. But consumers themselves believe that they are often incompetent. Hence in market systems people turn to the state to impose constraints on their
own purchases. They compel family breadwinners to spend
in such a way as to feed and clothe their children or, say, to
hire someone to haul away their garbage. Almost no one
seems to believe that the consumer always knows best.

Of course every social system is inefficient because people—as family members, consumers, entrepreneurs, or cabinet members—often make bad decisions even when they
have cost information. Even our small private decisions do
not come out as intended: we kill a houseplant by overwa-
tering or inadvertently teach a child to lie to escape parental
punishment. Both governmental and corporate decisions
typically bring societies to unwanted consequences and in
that sense are always to a degree inefficient. By almost
everyone's values, building Chernobyl was a mistake. Given
the values that many people hold, the euro may turn out to
be a mistake.

Poor market choices do not just constitute simple errors, such as producing big cars when customers want
smaller ones. Greater wastes arise through distant choices. A
wave of caution in decisions to buy or not buy can inaugurate
depression, throwing millions out of work and reducing output. Global financial decisions that seemed sound in New
York or Hong Kong have caused massive capital with-
drawals from Indonesia, again with great losses in employment and output. Farmers' calculated decisions to irrigate
their lands have often over the years salinized their soil and
destroyed its productivity. There seems to be no end to what
can go wrong with choices made in the market system.

Consequently, the market system is grossly inefficient.
Critics who say so are right. To cope with the enormous

complexity of the social world, participants in any social system, including rulers, bring only fallible capacity, even when that capacity is extended through devices ranging from pencils to computers. Infinite problems, but only finite brains. Again, we can only point to the market system's attributes, like efficiency prices, that give it an advantage over alternative systems.

## Inequality

A topic that refuses to go away is inequality in distribution—of income and wealth, as well as of position and opportunity. With their quid pro quo rule, market systems produce great inequalities A United Nations estimate is that one-fifth of the world's people consume 86 percent of the world's services and goods, the bottom fifth less than 3 percent. The World Health Organization estimates that the world spends $56 billion annually on health research. Less than 10 percent of the money goes to research on the diseases of the poor 90 percent of world population, a population with distinctive diseases—tropical, for example. Within industrial nations, inequalities in wealth are reduced (within socioeconomic classes but not much between classes) but of course not eliminated by the redistributions of the welfare state. Taking those redistributions into account, the richest 1 percent in Britain in 1989 held 13 percent of British wealth; the richest 1 percent in the United States, 22 percent of American wealth.

But inequality characterizes all large-scale social systems other than those imaginary ones in which equality is written into the blueprint. Past and present market systems do not remove and sometimes exacerbate the inequality characteristic of large-scale social systems. Yet through taxes, transfer payments, and other methods, any existing market society can significantly reduce or restructure inequality if its people or rulers wish to do so. For these reasons, the inequalities of existing market systems do not constitute a reason for abandoning it.

Is inequality inefficient? Or does it pose, as many economists propose, only a problem of equity or justice, not one of efficiency? Efficiency, it will be remembered, turns on the relation of valued output to valued inputs. If the valued result of social organization is taken to be a collective value, such as "the good society," then inequality is an efficiency problem. Or, looking at the market system as a method of allocating Earth's and society's resources for the benefit of humankind, one can indeed question whether a high degree of inequality is an efficient allocation. Considering the poverty of much of the world and the affluence of parts of it, one may reasonably ask whether the market system is efficient to leave so many in squalor.

Either way, though, whether inequality is viewed as an equity problem or an efficiency problem, some people are not disturbed by it. Others are frightened by the slow historical movements of societies away from it—they like inequality and would prefer to hang on to it. Others regret inequality but believe it necessary for incentives and at least on that score efficient. On the other side, many people—according to survey research, great majorities in many societies—want to go on reducing inequalities. Of these, many do not think abstractly about patterns of distribution but want to reduce specific ills of inequality, such as obstructions to education, inadequate medical care, or the income insecurity of the aged.

Considering inequality either abstractly or with reference to specific social ills, no one can persuasively declare market systems to be acceptably efficient without facing it. In its distribution of cooperatively produced services and goods, the market system serves the needs or wants of some people far more than others, at an extreme leaving many millions without such elementary requirements of the good life as hygienic sewage disposal. One has to cope with—accept, qualify, or reject—the simple allegation that on this score market systems allocate resources in a pattern inefficient for the good of society, no matter how good is defined.

## Entrepreneurial Motivations

Finally, those very strengths of motivation that contribute greatly to the efficiencies of the market system often plunge it into inefficiencies—and they are not typically small. I see no reason to believe that the excesses of the American tobacco industry or of Swiss banking derive from unusual moral failures of their executives. Assuming these entrepreneurs to be neither less nor more moral than most of us, their behavior is a consequence of the power of market incentives. Entrepreneurs will bring the same determination and inventiveness to product misrepresentation as to introducing a new product. Similarly, if their governments will not approve their food or pharmaceutical products for domestic customers, they will ship them abroad and there advertise their claimed virtues. And, of course, not all the losses of spillovers are attributable to the ignorance of entrepreneurs, say, regarding what industrial wastes are doing to the environment. Their market incentives tell them to go ahead anyway.

The power of their market motivations energizes entrepreneurs to struggle inventively and endlessly to avoid regulation. It also often drives them into a "sordid story of greed and manipulation." In Japan in 1991, for example, the president and chairman of Nomura, the chairman of the Sumimoto Bank, and the president of Nikko Securities were all removed in various scandals. At the same time, the Guinness Affair had just wound up in Britain, France had to cope with illegal insider trading, and criminal proceedings against entrepreneurs in Germany were on a sharp rise.

In short, entrepreneurial motivations, powerful as they are, create not only marketable products but also such "products" as blighted communities and theft. They also produce, through sales promotion, some of the irrationality and ignorance that makes the market system inefficient. Because the strength of these motivations brings to a society both benefit and damage, it is not clear what level of strength is desirable. I know of no evidence that any existing market society has chosen an efficient level. That being so, any judgment that, generally speaking, the level of strength of entrepreneurial motivations in market society is efficient would be premature, not obviously true, and not even probably true.

# 12

## Too Little, Too Late

Suppose there were no spillovers, no compulsory terminations, no monopoly, no price fixing, no ignorance and irrationality in choice, and no motivational failures. Could the market system then achieve a high degree of allocative efficiency? One might think so, but the answer is no—unless, of course, efficiency is simply redefined to make the answer come out yes. There remains a barrier to efficiency, for the market system can operate only within a limited domain. Many efficient allocations consequently lie beyond its capacity.

The principal limitation on its domain, we already know, is that it can coordinate only those allocations that are voluntary. Market participants can obtain objects and performances only through offers of benefits, with both buyer and seller acting voluntarily. The market system can coordinate the construction of a skyscraper or the coordination of 10,000 workers to provide financial services to investors. But it cannot coordinate—purchases cannot achieve—the acquisition of land for a highway. At least some owners must be compelled to surrender. Nor can it accomplish a planned transfer of money income or wealth from one group to another. Nor the education of children whose parents cannot afford to pay for it. It cannot do these and many other things efficiently because it cannot do them at all.

To get them done, the market system often requires help from the state—for example, taxation in order to redistribute income so as to allocate more production to the poor. For some tasks the market system is almost wholly out of the picture. It cannot, for example, assemble a team of representatives to write a constitution, nor can the market system thereafter enact it.

One might say, however, that this is not an efficiency issue. We do not say that a hammer is inefficient because it will not bathe a baby or carry telephonic messages. Nor, then, is a market system inefficient because some tasks of coordination lie outside its scope. The inability, however, of the market system to coordinate through compulsion is turned back into an efficiency issue when broad claims of market-system efficiency are made. For example, it is a common broad claim that the market system achieves an efficient allocation of resources. Investigating or weighing that claim—which is, to repeat, a claim about efficiency— one discovers that it is false. For the very best that can be said is that the market system is efficient only in such allocations or resources as can be achieved through voluntary transactions. In other words, the limited domain of the market becomes relevant to judgments about its efficiency because claims about its efficiency make it relevant.

Another overstated efficiency claim for the market system is that it generally permits people to pursue their aspirations, whatever they may be, through voluntarism rather than through compulsion (as though all aspirations can be pursued in that way, if people so choose). The correct statement is quite different. It is that the market system is constrained to the voluntary track; and when, for the pursuit of aspiration, voluntarism is not enough—and it is often not enough—the market system will not do. The incapacity of the market system again is made into an efficiency issue because of an overbroad claim to efficiency.

Another common overstated claim is that the market
system is efficient because it responds to popular preferences regarding allocations. The fact is that at best it responds only to such preferences as can be expressed by voluntary offers of skills and assets. Change the allocation of
skills and assets, and the preferences to which the market
responds will change correspondingly. A new and higher
evaluation of, say, educational services in a market system
does not necessarily mean that participants have reconsid-
ered the value of education; it may mean only that assets
have been compulsorily redistributed. Again, the limited
capacity of the market system disproves the broad efficiency claim.

There has grown up around market systems an ideology
that declares compulsory allocations undesirable in any
case, hence the market system is deemed actually efficient
because of its incapacity to compel. But as became apparent
in Chapter 6, societies cannot survive and prosper without
a broad range of compulsions. They need taxation, of course.
They also need such compulsions as are implicit in procedures like elections, which compel outvoted minorities to
accept the decisions of the winners.

Market systems not only fail to achieve compulsory allocations necessary to efficiency, but their existence obstructs the efficient use of such other mechanisms as the
state. The taxes necessary for an efficient allocation of resources—to education or public health, say—will often act
as a disincentive to tax-paying entrepreneurs. Entrepreneurs hotly declare that environmental legislation will discourage new investment, or even drive some enterprises
into bankruptcy. Historically they have brought the same
objection to government regulation of child labor, work
hours, occupational safety, and against every other exten-

sion of the hand of the state. Sometimes the complaint is valid, sometimes not. Either way, to maintain a high rate of activity in the market sector, societies often will move only timidly in the nonmarket areas, such as education and health, where at least the compulsion of taxes is required. The result is market efficiency within market-system domain that comes at the expense of inefficiency in other domains.

We may note in passing that the frequent objection to state "interventions"—that they obstruct market efficiency—is invalid because incomplete. Suppose an income tax induces a singer to curtail performances, thus depriving audiences of what they highly value (as indicated by their willingness to pay). Whether the tax is on balance an inefficiency depends on its effect on both the singer's choice and on whether the tax funds are used to reduce an inefficiency in resource allocation, such as inadequate medical care for some segment of the population.

## Prior Determinations

To achieve efficiency, the necessary compulsions are not simply those of taxation and the welfare state. They include a more important category of compulsions that I shall call prior determinations. These are beyond the capacity of the market system, and they greatly alter—and reduce—claims of market efficiency.

Market systems require two sets of decisions or determinations. One set consists of market transactions. The other consists of those "prior" determinations of the distribution among people of assets and skills that are then offered in market transactions. These prior determinations come from custom, law, and historical accident; and they are largely compulsory. Both sets of decisions are current—the contrast between them is not one between present and past. To be sure, personal liberties and property rights in a society may have first been well established two or three hundred years ago, but it is the current or present custom or law on them that matters for the market system. Some of these determinations are being revised today, and they will continue to be so day by day indefinitely into the future.

Market transactions cannot be undertaken until these prior determinations have been made. Market transactions do not start from scratch. Until it has been somehow decided, by custom and law on property, that certain assets are yours, you cannot offer them in the market. Nor can you offer your labor until it is somehow decided, by custom and law on liberties, what options you are to enjoy to do so.

Although custom and law withhold some things as assets for the state, in market systems most assets are of course assigned to persons. The assignment may be no more than some clothing or, at the other extreme, it may be land, buildings, securities and collectible loans. Custom and law on liberties in our era usually forbid offering anyone's labor other than one's own—slavery is thus prohibited, although many market societies permit parents to put their children's labor on the market. Custom and law also try to forbid some occupations: hired killers and drug dealers, for example. More than law, custom closes off some occupations to members of a racial or ethnic group; and both custom and law on, say, admission to universities, open for some young people but close for others opportunities for social mobility.

The pattern of the assignments of assets and skills through the path of history and inheritance varies from society to society, with one society favoring some groups, another society others. The pattern is never wholly fixed, but in important respects, all market societies are similar. They all assign individual rights to land rather than hold it all collectively. The same goes for rights to shares of assets of corporations. And all societies assign assets unequally.

A first conclusion, then, is that *one cannot explain the pattern of output or results in any market system by pointing exclusively to market transactions, for the pattern is always a result of both the transactions and the prior determinations taken together*. Whether, for example, market transactions result in large expenditures on luxuries or large expenditures on necessities is in large part decided by the pattern of prior determinations.

Every current generation sits on an accumulation of assets produced by a sequence of earlier generations. In industrialized and postindustrialized societies, the accumulation is mountainous. The assets are distributed largely through custom and law governing inheritance. The distribution on the whole is not thoughtful, nor has it been calculated to achieve such an objective as the public interest or common good. What each of us inherits, aside from genetic factors, is in large part shaped by a long, long history of war, conquest, looting, deceit, and intimidation, and law on property and inheritance. I am the great-great-grandson of Swedish peasants. The small stock of assets they possessed was in large part decided by historically distant pillage and conquest that shunted their ancestors and them down the path of peasantry. What they left to their son, my great-grandfather, was accordingly limited, sufficient only to permit his migration to America. The law eventually handed his limited assets on to my grandparents and subsequently their assets to their son, my father, whose small total of assets vanished in the Great Depression.

A second conclusion then, is that *the prior determinations operating at any time are not efficient.* They are what they are largely by historical accident and by laws governing inheritance, themselves not subjected to a weighing of benefits against cost.

From the two conclusions we can draw a major inference about market efficiency. Given an existing set of prior determinations, market interactions at most give participants opportunities to make efficient decisions on how to use whatever skills and assets have already been allocated them. They do not permit people to erase or escape from the inefficiencies of prior determinations. In that sense, market efficiency is too little and too late. It kicks in when earlier decisions not made with an eye to efficiency have already largely determined the results. In its dependence on prior determinations, the market system is like a car with an efficient engine that can operate only with a fuel that must be towed behind in quantities that degrade the performance of the engine.

Think again of the traders in the gym to whom a donor allocates objects and skills that the beneficiary can either use or try to trade for something better. The donor makes no attempt to suit the gift to the recipient; there is no attempt at efficient choice. When the participants have finished their trading, each will be better off as a result of it, or at least not worse off; and we may be tempted to call the outcome consequently efficient. Nevertheless, the result or outcome may be wholly unsuited to the wants or needs of participants because of the pattern of the original gifts. The original allocation by the donor was arbitrary, not efficient, and trading can improve it only to a degree.

One may be tempted to allege a critical difference between the hypothetical game and the real world of markets.

In the game, one might say, the original allocation is arbitrary and makes no particular sense other than to start the game. In the market system, the original allocation to each person is given. It is what one "owns" together with certain liberties and prohibitions with respect to what one can do with one's own labor. It is a mistaken distinction. What each person "owns" is a result of allocative processes—that is, historical and current social processes. They have created and from time to time reshaped the right called ownership or property. That allocation is not, like the Himalayas, just "there;" it is a product of human activity, and no less so than the allocations achieved by market transactions. The same is true for those rights that bear the name of liberty or freedom. That people enjoy returns from their own labor is possible only because people make prior determinations that allocate liberties to them.

Let me make the point in another way. Imagine two methods of achieving efficient choices on allocations of assets and skills, as well as on products and services to be produced with them. In one the state does not allocate productive assets like land and capital to individual persons or private organizations. Intending to achieve efficiency in the use of assets to satisfy its citizens, state officials allocate them to various lines of production they plan. The officials may achieve an allocation and production plan widely regarded as efficient; or, given the magnitude of their task, they may fail. In either case they have approached efficient choice on the allocation and use of the society's resources as an integrated problem.

In the other, officials do not want to try to achieve an efficient allocation or production plan, perhaps believing that the task lies beyond their competence. So they simply assign productive assets to members of the society and leave it to the recipients to make the most of their shares. How do they decide on sizes of share to each citizen? They look at historical precedent, patterns in other societies, politically feasible patterns, and the like; they shrink from asking questions about efficiency. Watching what ensues, they see that recipients create a market system through which, by trading, as in the game in the gym, each efficiently improves his or her position.

Of the first case we can say that, since all choices are approached as problems in efficiency, the level of efficiency achieved will depend on the competence of the officials. Allocations may reach a high degree of efficiency, although they probably will not, given limits on the human brain and the complexity of the task. Of the second case, we can say that there is no hope for efficiency. All that can be hoped for is that the society achieves those limited improvements in the original distribution that can be achieved by voluntary exchanges. That is a small claim when put in perspective.

Our third and final conclusion is, in short, this: *Market systems, wisely or foolishly, largely in effect give up the possibility of an efficient resource allocation and pattern of production. They settle instead on inefficient allocations improved to the limited degree that voluntary transactions make improvement possible.* That they make such a choice is ordinarily hidden from the eye. But the choice process has recently been conspicuous and flagrant in Russia. There the move toward the market system has set in motion an extraordinary and harsh struggle over the "prior" determination of who is to have the assets once owned by the state. Power, greed, and corruption are creating a highly inegalitarian allocation of assets that will shape market-system outputs indefinitely.

Am I saying more than that the market system is rooted

in its own past? Yes, I have added the simple point that its limited domain is a limit on its capacity to achieve efficient allocations.

I have also added that the market system requires a set of conditions, like property law, without which it cannot exist and yet which drastically limit the efficiencies that it can then achieve. Its distinctive efficiency is efficient voluntary choice, yet such choices require a prior set of largely compulsory "choices." To achieve the efficiencies of the market system requires that a society bear the inefficiencies of prior determinations.

I can add too that through redistributive taxation and transfer payments, as through unemployment compensation, market societies can, if they wish, greatly improve the efficiency of prior determinations. That would make the market system, in its tandem relation with prior determinations, a far more effective instrument of efficiency than it has ever been. Here again we find a reason for believing that market systems can be better than any are.

Yet I have added too that the market system itself obstructs some improvements in prior determinations that would otherwise make market-system results or outcomes more efficient. The market is in that sense a peculiar institution. Confined by its foundations in custom and law, it inhibits many of the changes in them that could make outcomes more efficient.

## Persistence of Prior Determinations

Might the prior allocations themselves be outcomes of earlier market transactions rather than allocations by law and custom? Might I hold, for example, assets not because custom or law allocated them to me but because I bought them in the market with my earnings? Yes, I may have bought them. But if so, my earnings were shaped by earlier prior determinations. Custom and law prohibited some kinds of earlier transactions while permitting others. They also decided, through taxation, how much of my earnings I could keep; more important, they decided whether I entered into market life with my parents' assets. Law and custom on inheritance represent a mammoth prior determination of market outcomes. There is no escape from death or from the effects on each participant of custom and law on inheritance. Every generation begins its market life with a set of assets, tiny or massive, specified by custom and law on inheritance.

What one can produce in or take from the market system is always a consequence of a network of prior determinations even wider than we have discussed. Henry Ford was able to provide millions of people with low-cost cars only because the state undertook massive road building, without which the market demand for autos would not have grown as it did. Bill Gates could not provide the objects and services of Microsoft nor become a billionaire by doing so if his society were illiterate. That a society is not illiterate is in some large part the consequence of nonmarket decisions through custom and law, among them those on education. The results of market performance, even of an industrial genius, depends in part on prior determinations that are never overridden or washed over—they never expire.

In the theater of efficient social coordination, Act I belongs to the state, in which, half blindly and not efficiently, it makes the prior determinations that set the course for the next act. Act II belongs to the transactions of the market system. A long act with much audience participation, it moves not to but in the direction of an efficient ending. It cannot achieve that ending because it is limited to playing out the consequences of the first act. Act III again belongs to the state, which tries in its often blundering way to bring everyone the rest of the way to an efficient ending, largely through the redistributions of the welfare state. The state is only half aware that the obstacles are not only the failures of Act II but its own performance in Act I. It is a long-running play in which Act III always becomes Act I of the next performance, for which a new Act III is then written.

# 13   Freedom?

As I read and listen to what people say about the merits of the market system, whether in scholarly publication or the heat of argument, a key claim is that it gives a society not only efficiency but freedom.

To determine the attributes of the market system that bear on freedom or liberty, we had first better say something about what these great words mean. Even in the most tyrannical of societies, life showers everyone with more freedoms or liberties than can be counted. We are all free to do countless things of little or no impact on others: to sing to ourselves or do push-ups. But mere numbers of liberties are not enough to qualify a person as free. Some important freedoms, such as free speech or choice of occupation, are required. On the other hand, some severe impositions on our choices are not counted by most people as deprivations of freedom. Most people believe that a person is free even if he is legally compelled to pay taxes, free even if conscripted for the military. Aware that we are all controlled by family, market, state, and other interactions, we draw distinctions. Some controls are judged to be consistent with freedom, others not.

Clearly, then, to say that a person is free is not just to state a simple fact, such as height or hair color. It is to say that, controlled as we are in many ways, choices judged to be important or valuable are not closed off. Which choices, then, are valuable or important? Opinions differ. And those differences send the analysis of freedom or liberty into a cloudland of abstraction and argument that, no matter how tightly reasoned and illuminating, remains inconclusive.

In this one chapter we cannot join the great debate on the what and how of freedom. We can, however, nail down a few points critical to understanding the connections and disconnections between market system and freedom. I want here to look only into market liberties, setting aside for now discussion of political liberties, specifically, the possibility that the market system facilitates political democracy and that democracy in turn protects freedom. Regardless of the presence or absence of political democracy, what attributes of market exchange either enlarge or curb valuable options of market participants?

The standard answer to that question is pretty well given by definition of the market system. The market system is a method of coordination by voluntary interchanges. Contrast the market system with a hypothetical physical planning system bereft of money and prices. In such a system it is not free choice but command that determines which goods and services are to be produced, to whom and in what shares they are to be distributed, and to what jobs people are to be assigned. In such a hypothetical planning system, whether a book would be published and whether you could have a copy would depend not on whether there were freely choosing buyers but on an administrative decision. Whether you could, say, take a bus from Bangkok to your apartment in the suburbs or pick up a few groceries on your way would not depend on your spending but on permissions granted or denied.

No matter how one might torture such terms as "free" and "command" to show that they mean somewhat different things to different people, the distinction just drawn between command, on one hand, and choosing in markets, on the other, is a solid one. The distinction can also be put as one between command and inducement. Market relations, chiefly of inducements, are, by almost anyone's concept of freedom, more free than are command relations.

Yet the proposition needs to be put in its place and whittled down.


## Market Liberties Without Market System

A first qualification is no small one. For many market liberties—if we could count them, we would probably say most—the market system is not necessary. The liberties can be had without it. While moneyless physical planning does not permit free choices, we can easily imagine hypothetical money-using nonmarket systems that do.

The two kinds of market liberties that most people practice are occupational free choice and consumer free choice. Absent a market system, central planning not only can allow both but will find good reasons to do so—narrowly or broadly.

*Occupational free choice in a nonmarket system.* Having scheduled various lines of production, planners have to draw workers into the scheduled lines of production. They might draft labor to each planned occupation, industry, firm, and location. But hiring willing and qualified workers is easier than asking a labor authority to find and assign an appropriate person to each job. It is difficult enough to draft an army; drafting an entire workforce can hardly be imagined. Instead, wage offers will ordinarily attract the necessary employees without the compulsions and resistances of conscription. Wage premiums can be offered to recruit for positions otherwise hard to fill. Responding to offers, workers are free to choose among jobs, just as in a market system.

The several advantages of occupational free choice in central planning are not simply hypothetical. Authoritarian as they were, Soviet and Chinese planners made heavy use of conscription and other methods of formal and informal compulsion. That included forced movement of workers from urban to rural areas, massively in Mao's Great Cultural Revolution. But they also made selective wide use of occupational free choice. Their methods of job assignment were mixed, as, for that matter, they are mixed in market societies though in entirely different proportions. Market societies limit occupational free choice, for example, when they conscript an army or assign young physicians, whose training has been paid for by the state, to rural areas.

*Consumer free choice in a nonmarket system.* Having planned and produced an output, central planners must devise a method of distributing the planned output. Giving everyone equal shares of each commodity and service would be grossly wasteful. Some persons need clothes and toys suitable to their infancy, others need the services of schoolteachers, and others need geriatric physicians. Rationing through distributed coupons is clumsy, wasteful, and annoying—and gives rise to black markets. In a central planning system, the simplest and easiest method of distribution of output is to distribute money incomes to all in whatever pattern of inequality or equality the people or their rulers wish, and then sell the produced outputs at whatever prices will clear the market for each kind of output. That grants to consumers the same kind of free choice they practice in market systems.

Again, this is not merely hypothetical, for communist systems in fact practiced consumer free choice, but they did not do so broadly, as in the market societies. They often assigned housing, for example, and many other goods and services were so arbitrarily underpriced as to give rise to shortages. The result was that consumers had to engage not in simple market purchases but in special legal and illegal relations with suppliers. Yet people obtained a great range of goods and services through market choice. Not for lack of consumer free choice but because of political tyranny were the subjects of communist regimes unfree.

If authoritarian communist systems practice a range of consumer and occupational free choice, democratic planning systems, hypothetical as they seem to be, presumably can do so, and much more broadly. I make the point not to advocate such systems but to make clear that these market liberties, although they require markets, do not require the market system. Democratic central planning is, of course, not wholly hypothetical. Today's market societies are marked by "central" planning of production to the degree that subsidies, regulations, and prohibitions—from shopping malls to medical care—give the state a strong central hand in resource allocation and output determination yet leave the consumer with free choice.

We can conclude that these freedoms do not belong to market systems alone but are found in both authoritarian and democratic forms of central planning.

A frequent confusion is to be avoided. When planners offer consumers free choice among those goods and services that central decisions have chosen to produce, they do not offer what economists call consumer sovereignty. By definition, central planning denies consumer sovereignty. The distinction is between a system in which consumers choose (consumer free choice) among those objects that planners have chosen to produce and a system in which consumer purchases themselves determine what is to be produced (consumer sovereignty). Although both systems practice consumer free choice and both make use of markets for consumer goods, only the market system practices consumer sovereignty.

One might believe that, if our choices as consumers do not control production, we are not really free, no matter how free we are to choose among the many services and products the centralists have planned. I think that position almost impossible to maintain, given any ordinary concept of freedom. In a market society you do not through your purchases or in any other *proximate* way control your town's production of trash-removal service or your nation's investment in space exploration or road construction. But that does not make you unfree, although you would claim political unfreedom if you had no control of any kind over the government officials making the decisions. I suspect that most French and British consumers do not even know whether outputs of milk and certain other farm products in their countries are controlled by the volume of consumer purchases or by the size of governmental subsidies for these products. Nor do they regard their liberties as threatened, because either way, they are free to choose from what is offered. Indeed, the citizens of the democracies have often asked their governments to decide outputs and inputs. They have done so, for example, by taxes and expenditures through which the state rather than consumers determines the production of irrigation water or air transport or some other product. Given democratic governments, the possibility that officials might or do plan some outputs does not warrant a charge of unfreedom, as the terms are usually used. We can even imagine a highly democratic society that chooses to leave the determination of outputs and inputs entirely in the hands of the state, yet broadly practices consumer free choice.

## The Authoritarian Enterprise

A second qualification on the alleged tie between market system and liberty is that many employees see themselves as free only when they are not at work. Any claim that markets support freedom has to take account of the unfreedom of the workplace, itself a command system, as we have seen—an island of authority in a market sea.

The conventional defense against the charge that workplace authority curbs the employee's freedom is that the employee freely agrees to accept that authority in return for a wage. And the conventional response to that defense is that the market system requires that people thus agree to surrender some of their liberties each workday. Even if the transaction is freely entered into, it is a transaction to sell some of one's freedom. With some qualifications that do not challenge their basic rough truth, both positions are correct.

Of course, workplaces in nonmarket societies are also command systems. Workplace authority is after all not distinctive to market systems. If hierarchical organizations are necessary for at least some lines of production, then there is no escape from authority-obedience relations in them, market system or not. Some observers dismiss this prospect as an unhappy fact of life that says nothing about freedom. Others see hierarchy, authority, and obedience, however necessary, as profoundly limiting freedom—and tragic in that they cannot be escaped even in the market system. The two positions do not necessarily disagree on the facts. But one proposes not to use the concept of freedom to analyze the situation; the other chooses to use it.

Either way, the enterprise is not an unrestrained tyranny, for management typically wants to limit its commands to those necessary during working hours to organize production. Management cannot ordinarily give orders to employees—nor does it usually wish to—on their off hours. Yet evidence of invasions of freedom outside the workplace in industrialized societies ranges from managerial attempts to compel employees to vote as management wishes, to corporate controls, often subtle, over how their executives dress, where they live, with whom they associate, and their politics. In many parts of the world, managerial authoritarianism is still much like that in isolated mining towns, with their company stores and company housing.

The main curb, of course, on managerial authority is that employees, while agreeing to practice obedience to management in return for a wage, can quit. How well that constrains management depends on what alternative jobs employees can find. Governmental regulation of the workplace arises because that constraint is not sufficiently effective. In all market systems a weak but persistent demand for worker participation in management attests to continued discontent with workplace authority. Sometimes it is a strong demand for "industrial democracy," as, in one of its forms, in German employee membership on supervisory boards of enterprises.

If competition for workers is vigorous enough, an employer who commonly makes coercive demands will fail to hold employees. But it does not deny the coercion latent and often practiced in employer-employee interactions because employers can selectively coerce—that is, can do to a few of their employees what they cannot do as a general policy. They can fire, for example, "agitators" or union organizers.

## Compulsion in Transactions

A third qualification on the tie between market system and freedom: Quite aside from workplace authority, many kinds of market interchanges impose burdens not freely chosen, burdens that would be rejected if choice were free. Most are by now familiar.

*Spillovers.* Just as a spillover represents an inefficiency, it is also a compulsion. A morning paper reports the distress of Manhattan apartment dwellers whose view of the Hudson River and access to sunlight is being curtailed by a wall of new apartment houses they obviously did not choose. The market system is not entirely composed of free choosers; it is populated by people compelled to accept the consequences of injurious choices made by others.

*Terminations.* Similarly, market freedom fails because of the compulsions of unilateral terminations of market interchanges. The bankruptcy of an enterprise when its customers abandon it is hardly an example of free choice for the entrepreneur. A fired employee is not practicing free choice; the employer made the choice. Can we brush this compulsion aside by holding that the employer is under no obligation to continue the job? No, the employer is not. Nevertheless, to be discharged is to be compelled. What is worse, the threat of discharge has often been made an instrument of other compulsions: for example, obstructing employee freedoms to organize a union.

*Compelled to work?* Markets also compel or coerce people to work. No, not compelled! some will retort. Work is simply a fact of life, and most people must work to survive. The issue is an example of inescapable difficulties with concepts like freedom and coercion. The quid pro quo rule tells us that to survive in a market system one must make a particular kind of contribution—a marketable one. No other alternative is open; no choice. Most adults in a market system, then, work or perish. If it is a fact of life that in any system, market or not, most people must be compelled to work, then the market system is one way to accomplish the required compulsion. In that respect the market system succeeds not because it leaves people free but because it does not. The classical economists applauded the market system because it coerced the masses to work, doing so by the "silent, unremitted pressure" of hunger, as one of them, William Townsend, put it.

*Inequalities of income and wealth.* As everyone knows, inequalities permit some market participants to compel or coerce others. For lack of income, people have felt compelled to sell themselves or their children into prostitution or slavery. When inequality is extreme—in poverty, for example—and I cannot obtain what I need, cannot afford to move about to find employment, or cannot provide for my dependents, many people will judge that I am not free. For lesser inequalities not everyone will infer that freedom suffers. Low incomes render no one unfree, they will say, only less privileged than others. Yet many others hold that, even if one is not poor, for lack of more income one may not be free to go to college, not free to choose one's neighborhood, not even free to take a desirable job that requires one to bear immediate expenses of relocation.

*Inequalities in market position.* Somewhat separate from inequality of income and wealth are compelling or coercive inequalities in the influence or power that each par-

ticipant brings to a market interaction. The most frequent
great inequality of this kind is in the employer-employee
interaction; but it goes beyond the unfreedoms of authority
over those in the workplace. Employers who hire hundreds
or thousands of employees can easily refuse employment to
any one applicant and can often compel an applicant to accept the employer's conditions. An applicant has no reciprocal power over a prospective employer except in those
cases in which one offers the employer a unique talent or
service for which the employer cannot find a substitute.
Hence employer powers overwhelm the market powers of a
factory worker even if not the market powers of a Michael
Jordan. All over the world, job applicants have often been
compelled to accept conditions of work that they regard as
coercive, including high exposure to risks to health and
safety.

Claims that markets facilitate freedom rest on the assumption that every buyer and every seller can turn to alternatives. Buyers will be free from compulsions by sellers
only if they, the buyers, can get what they want from many
sellers and are not dependent on one. Similarly, sellers will
be free only if they enjoy a multiplicity of customers or employers and are not dependent on just one. But of course alternatives are often limited. Monopoly is a form of compulsion. Intimidation, compulsion, and coercion in market
relations because of inequality of position are consequently
commonplace. Many of us have experienced at least touches
of it in dealing, say, with a corporation indifferent to a complaint brought by us as a customer. If an enterprise wishes to
ignore us, its assets and income permit it to do so without
compunction, and we are often compelled to accept defeat.

*Ignorance and manipulation.*   Is a choice merely inefficient or is it in addition not free when choosers misperceive

their alternatives and do not get what they thought they were choosing—new shoes losing their soles in the first week of wear? Or if in ignorance they overlook what otherwise they would have chosen? A borderline unfreedom, some would say. They would be more willing to acknowledge compulsion when market participants deliberately deny information, misinform, or confuse in order to control the behavior of others, as is common in sales promotion. Even there, however, they will more probably claim only that choice is not genuinely free; it is choice without the values that we usually associate with freedom—a degenerate kind of free choice. Perhaps most people would not go so far as to call it compulsion or coercion, although many critics do. Again, we cannot call up a single definition of freedom.

If we say that manipulative sales promotion obstructs a more genuine free choice, perspective requires us to acknowledge that political choices—referenda and elections—are also degenerate. Parties and candidates want not to enlighten but to control the electorate. In what they communicate, they intend to induce people to vote as they, the communicators, wish. In that respect they are not at all different from sellers who want to control people—to induce people to buy what the sellers propose to sell. Both deal heavily in myths, misrepresentations, and lies. They practice diversion and obfuscation to obstruct what could be a more informed and thoughtful free choice. Increasingly, political manipulation has taken up the same techniques as sales promotion. The similarities do not at all reduce the charge that in the market system manipulation undercuts free choice. Instead, they suggest that elite manipulation of mass is at war with free choice wherever it is found—in market, politics, education, religion, even science.

Do all these many considerations understate the freedoms allowed or encouraged in market systems? Freedom,
you will correctly say, has not in fact been as greatly curtailed in the market systems of Western Europe and North
America as I seem to indicate. No, it has not, because the
state has in many ways stepped in to protect the liberties
that the market itself fails to protect. States—that is, most
states—do not permit people to sell themselves into servi-
tude, and they impose limits on discharge of employees,
such as advance notification and dismissal wages. Unions
and other private groups also often intervene. That they and
the state intervene so frequently traces back to the frequency of market offenses against freedom.

## Two Remaining Cautions

Clearing a slum or providing homes for impoverished elders
requires that some people be compelled, at least to pay the
necessary taxes. A free people, one might suppose, need to
be able to pursue such collective ventures. If they cannot,
they are not free. Take note of what might look like sleight
of hand. In three sentences I have shifted from liberty of individual choice to liberty of collective choice, suggesting
that people are not free if important collective choices they
wish to make are not open to them. They are free as a people
only if under appropriate circumstances they can compel:
for example, a majority compelling a minority to acquiesce.

Market systems, we have seen, do not make a place for
collectively imposed compulsions. Claims about market
freedom tie individual choices to the market system but fall
silent on collective free choices. They simply fail to confront the difference between a society of free people and a
free collectivity, both thought desirable. Although you and

I individually may be free to choose in market systems, it does not follow that "we the people" are free to choose. The market system gives us no freedom, for example, to take a family's land for a highway or to impose an elementary education on every child. Only the democratic state, if democratic enough, gives a people freedom of that kind of collective choice.

Having suggested that most of us are interested not simply in a high count of miscellaneous freedoms but in important kinds and patterns of freedom, I now add a final suggestion that we not confuse the freedoms of individual persons, which are generally to be prized, with freedoms of institutions, which are not. Societies would make a disastrous mistake in granting general or broad freedom to such an institution as a police force or parliament. The vision of their running free is a nightmare, no less so than a vision of the tax office or the air force running free. Institutions or organizations, both governmental and private, have to be put under such controls as are necessary to hold them to their responsibilities, to limit powers that could otherwise be irresponsibly and dangerously exercised. That holds for all kinds of organizations—government agencies, unions, and philanthropic institutions.

It holds too for business organizations: They need supervisory controls and are entitled to no general freedom. No one who is not hopelessly confused in thinking wants businesses and business executives to be free from controls over them. Market systems work only because enterprises are controlled by their customers, employees, and suppliers through the interactions of the market system, as well as through government controls. Free enterprises—that is, businesses not under market controls and free to produce without regard to what people want—that is a prospect we can hardly imagine and that makes no sense. Societies need enterprises that are not free but are compelled, at the risk of extinction, to respond to people's wishes.

The propositions in this chapter do not provide a complete analysis of market-system impact on market freedoms. Given the various meanings attached to "freedom," and for other reasons as well, the end of the road cannot be reached. We may, however, have captured fundamental connects and disconnects between market system and freedom— gone some miles down the road.

# 14

## Personality and Culture

I do not hear of anxieties about the effects of the market system on personality and culture from as many voices as declare that it makes us prosperous and free. Yet for some observers of the market system, concerns about personality and culture are intense.

At his touted best, market man is blessed with a multiplicity of choices of career and life style. He is informed on the burdens of each of the choices he might make, and he is free to choose. Admirable! But is he ever at his best? For 150 years many critics have said no. Not only Marx said no, but so also did art critics like John Ruskin, psychotherapists like Erich Fromm, and social scientists–philosophers like Herbert Marcuse, among many others. Adam Smith himself joined the lament. Not often challenging market-system efficiency in output, they deplore the effects of its daily processes. To listen to their critiques or to go back to Aristotle's warnings against excesses of greed is to find a deeply disturbing picture of market man. If historically, at least in some societies, the female personality seems less corrupted, it may be only because males engaged in the market system while females long pursued their tasks within the household.

How do critics paint the portrait of market man? They allege that he excessively pursues the lower rather than the higher values of life. They accept his pursuit of food and shelter but find him excessive in pursuit of ever more goods and services, as well as money for its own sake, to the near

exclusion of things of mind and spirit. To the classical
Greek values—the true, the good, and the beautiful—he
gives hardly a thought, so fully engaging are his lesser and
corrupt materialistic values.

He is small-minded, petty in calculation of advantage.
He is more cunning than thoughtful or wise. He thinks in-
vidiously. His moral code, insofar as he follows one, consists less of the rules of good conduct derived from the
Greek-Judeo-Christian or Eastern traditions than of the
self-serving rules of an aggressive game.

He is an egoist, yet not skillfully so. His narrow pursuit
of market advantage makes him crass and shallow. He is in-
sensitive to the costs to himself and his family of the pattern of living he has chosen or drifted into. He does not recognize his loneliness, nor how difficult he finds it to think
"we" instead of "I." Of all participants in the market system, entrepreneurs most fully engage in it and hence most
fully take on these attributes of character. Who admires not
their achievements but their character?

I recognize the portrait. But granted that it is a face often
encountered, is it typical? And if typical, typical of what?
Not necessarily of the market system; perhaps typical of
the urban man in industrialized societies, market system or
not. The portrait expresses the painters' disdain for some
ugly aspects of modern life that they may not have carefully
traced to their sources.

What the critics, for all their insights, do not know—and
nobody yet knows—about the connection between their
portrait and the market system reduces my ambitions in
this chapter. We do not know enough to conclude that the
market system does or does not degrade personality or culture. But with a sample of allegations we can begin to show
that the critics have brewed an inconclusive mix of percep-

tion and misperception. At the end of the chapter we will still not know as much as we would like about the effects of market system on personality and culture. But we may have made gains in coming to appreciate how serious the charges are, in appraising how much we do not know, in finding that much of what some people claim to know is either unfounded or false, and in deciding which hypotheses are most worth further thought.

At least since Plato, a procession of philosophers and theorists, including Marx, Maine, Spencer, and Durkheim, draw some such distinction as Ferdinand Tönnies' contrast between *Gemeinschaft* and *Gesellschaft*. Roughly, they distinguish two forms of peaceful and cooperative human association. One is through the multilateral relations of kinship, shared values, and affection. The other is through heavily unilateral relations and formal organizations that make deliberate efforts toward coordination. The first takes the form of a community in which community life itself is an end. The second takes the shape of formal organizations like state, bureaucracy, and corporation, all of which pursue purposes other than the life of the community or of the organization itself. In the last three hundred years in Western Europe and North America—fewer years in some other parts of the world—they believe they have seen societies move away from the first and toward the second of these two forms of human association.

Although the transformation coincides with the rise of the market system and almost certainly alters personality and culture, it does not permit inference about the responsibility of the market system. For the transformation also coincides with industrialization and technological innovation. Also with urbanization and bureaucratization. It also coincided, although usually after a time lag, with the rise of political democracy. If it is agreed that these movements fed on each other, just how does one sort out cause and effect? Clearly industrialization, urbanization, technological innovation, and bureaucratic organizations took off on a track largely independent of the market system in the Soviet Union. Hence the market system cannot be credited or debited. That begins to undermine confidence in any hypothesis that ties contemporary aspects of personality and culture to a source in the market system. We are left not with a connection but with a headache.

Thus, if many people come to spend their workdays under a supervising authority rather than under the control of community and custom, perhaps one has to attribute that specific change not to the rise of the market system but to the rise of large commercial and industrial organizations. Nonmarket systems organize big enterprises no less than market systems do. The bureaucratization of production is worldwide, in communist as well as in market systems. The boss is not an animal peculiar to the market system.

One can even question the three-hundred-year transformation as it is described. In the transformation from a world of community toward a world of purposive organizations, the market system is usually seen as belonging to the later world but not the earlier. Something is wrong. Market relations take the form of multilateral, widely diffused interchanges among most adults. They are not at all limited to the relations, heavily unilateral, among participants in a formal organization. They are not, to be sure, quite the relations that characterize tradition-bound communities. Like them, however, they take the form of webs of multilateral control tying people together in innumerable connections.

The contrast between the two forms of society—community or purposive organization—would be more demonstrably valid if three hundred years had brought us all the way. We would then see an unmistakable contrast between traditional community and the tragic terminal of a homogeneous society coordinated largely by the purposive authority of the state. But except for the fascist and communist world, the change did not go anywhere near that far. It turned out that there was a third alternative: the market system. It provides large-scale social coordination beyond the possibilities of community yet does not require the subordination of humankind to purposive organizations. It is that third alternative—the market system—that makes it possible to escape the purposive authoritative state as the way to coordinate on a large scale. As a societywide coordinator of persons and organizations in the contemporary world, the market system preserves some important features of earlier societies. It preserves especially the multilateral character of social interchange, thus the minimization of unilateral authority characteristic of purposive organizations.

## Hypotheses

In light of these cautions, we can examine a few hypotheses about market-system effects on culture and personality. They will show how careful one must be in laying responsibility on the market system yet not denying a responsibility.

### MATERIALISM AND COMMERCIALISM

The first common thesis—that market systems push participants into the pursuit of material ends—is absurd if taken literally. As noted in Chapter 6, ends are not material—that is, not physical objects. They are sought states of mind, like feelings of security and satisfaction, including such pleasures as friendship and adventure. Food—is it not material? Yes, but its material qualities, weight, volume, or solidity, are not what we want. We want such nonmaterial intangibles as satiation, taste, and novelty. Clothing? We dress to conform and to display. But do not the states of mind we pursue require physical objects? Yes, as does all of life. But they also require services more than they require material objects. An avaricious market participant will pursue physical objects less avidly than medical, legal, and financial services, bank accounts, and rights to income and wealth in the form of stocks and bonds. In the pursuit of our objectives we make use of things, services, ideas, and decisions; material objects are only one category.

That the market system pushes participants toward materialism is usually a clumsy way to say either that it pushes them toward the pursuit of money or toward acquiring those performances and things that money can buy. That is an allegation that cannot be dismissed. It suggests an excessively commercial and therefore corrupt culture.

The great instrument for interaction in market society is money. Who can deny that in market systems people revolve around it? The question is what to make of our central pursuit of money income. Money is on some counts a great liberator, opening up vast choices; spending is the route to any among an extraordinarily wide array of ends. Money is of course limited in its capacity to allow people to win friends, find inner peace, or achieve immortality. Yet people spend money even for these purposes. They make a contribution to their college in exchange for a name on a building; and some people have even tried to arrange to be frozen and then awakened in a thousand years. In market systems, so many aspirations can be approached with money that people prudently pursue it in advance of plans for using it, saving it in order to hold possibilities open. So far, however, this is a picture of wide-ranging choice and rationality rather than of corruption of personality and culture.

But it is perhaps only a short step to postponing forever a consideration of many alternative ways to live one's life, letting the pursuit of money displace all the other alternatives. It becomes possible to go through life as though through a tunnel. The pitfall in such a hypothesis is that life in a tunnel may be in actual fact infrequent rather than common. Good survey research seems to indicate that for most people in market societies aspirations for a challenging job, friendships, and the pleasures of children and family life rank higher than do aspirations for more money or more market products. The research is a major challenge to the common view that the market system corrupts our aspirations.

Perhaps people commit as much time as they do to the pursuit of money and purchasables not because their aspirations have been narrowed but because it is easier to pursue aspirations through the market system than through the state or civil society. If one wants one's municipality to convert some vacant land to a public park, one faces a formidable and, even in the best circumstances, time-consuming task. One must enlist allies, will almost surely make enemies, and will often fail. If one wants a closer set of family ties or a broader congeniality among acquaintances, one may not know how to go about achieving it. In contrast, in the market system one simply buys what one wants, or, lacking the money, puts the aspiration aside. One may behave this way because one is thoughtful and clear-headed, not because one's aspirations have been distorted by market life.

These alternative interpretations illustrate the difficulty of appraising market-system impact. Perhaps the very ease with which people turn to market transactions to pursue their aspirations is seductive and puts a stamp on the society. It becomes a society of people alive to what they can obtain effortlessly from the market and dead to what collective choice will yield only uncertainly. Participation in community or collectivity declines and people become, as Aristotle would say, less human. Do we know that much? We know that rates and kinds of participation in community differ from society to society and that they change over time. But we do not know that the differences are attributable to the market system or that they make us less human.

## INSTRUMENTALISM

We often give no more personal attention or affection to a person who sells us a railroad ticket than to the ticket-vending machine that often replaces the human being. Nor, while we treat the plumber with civility, do we usually make the plumber our friend. In market interactions, it is often said, participants regard each other only or largely as instruments. In a market transaction, you are simply a means to my ends: I am interested in you only if you can offer me something I want. In contrast, nonmarket relations are said to be warmer and less instrumental. The interacting parties find each other on some points interesting in themselves; they each accept certain obligations of respect; and they are often joined in friendship.

In this contrast we see what appears to be the obverse of

the rule of quid pro quo. If the rule says "you take out only according to what you put in," it also seems to say "you put in only in order to take out." I do nothing for you except obtain things from you. My interest in you is no different from or greater than my interest in a vending machine. Both you and the machine are instruments of my purposes.

Plausible as it sounds, the instrumental thesis is full of pitfalls.

Nothing in the market system or in the rule of quid pro quo prohibits voluntary interactions other than or beyond transactions. Nothing prohibits sociability, friendship, or love. Are market participants too busy buying and selling to have time for other interrelations? Research suggests that participants in the market system interact with and enjoy a wider circle of interactions than did their ancestors in pre-market societies. Although family ties decline in modern society, that is not true of interactions in general.

In comparing market with premarket societies, it is easy to contrast the coordinating interactions—buying and selling—of contemporary market systems with the pleasurable leisure-time interactions—drinking and dancing, among others—of the earlier societies. But compare the coordinating interactions of market systems with the coordinating interactions in earlier societies. In the absence of a market system, coordination, say, of agricultural production required authority and command. Lord and clergy provided it and of course exercised it to their own advantage. It would be difficult to establish that they treated their subjects less instrumentally and more warmly than people treat each other in contemporary market interactions.

The instrumentalist thesis is also questionable because it is too broad. Market interrelationships are of many kinds. Mindful of the legendary used-car salesman or the undertaker, one is tempted to generalize that market relations are not only instrumental but predatory. Often they are. But the market relations between one dairy farmer and another and their relations with the cheese producer to whom they sell their milk are of a different kind. The relations are distant, so distant that the farmer may not see himself as having any relation at all to other farmers. He may not know them or have reason to think about them. He does not see them as instruments, nor can he exploit them. And, then again, some market relations are very warm. Friendships sometimes grow out of repeated interactions. Shoppers sometimes count among the pleasures of shopping their conversational interchanges, enjoyed for their own sake, with sellers. In the variety of interrelations it offers, the market system is a good deal more complex than the now weary elephant to whom the three blind men seem destined forever to be attentive.

If, however, many market relations are distant and impersonal, then at least those relations are not warm, as many nonmarket relations of sociability and friendship are. And Internet shopping may further lower the temperature. But again, these cool or cold interchanges leave room for warm nonmarket relationships that flourish, as survey research tells us, in market societies. And again, not all nonmarket interactions are warm: compare a sales brochure with a summons from a draft board.

Given urbanization and industrialization, are interactions warmer in nonmarket societies than in market societies? Were they warmer in the Soviet Union and communist China than in Western Europe market societies? Not likely: witness the legendary indifference or rudeness of retail clerks and waiters in the USSR or the cold maneuvering of Soviet consumers to get their hands on scarce commodities. A big difference in structure of interchange should not be missed. In recent and contemporary nonmarket societies, a relatively small elite or cadre of rulers and managers treats the whole adult population as instruments for the achievement of elite ends. Market system or not, then, we are all instruments of others. But who the others are differs from system to system. Who plays the instruments? In market systems, almost everybody. In other systems, a very few.

In market systems, however, one pervasive cold instrumentalism is prominent: sales promotion. It is matched in communist societies by the instrumentalism of rulers intent on subduing a population by pageantry and propaganda. But sales promotion probably pushes cold instrumentalism further than it is carried by ruling officials in democratic systems. For although democratic rulers devote much of their effort coldly and instrumentally to persuading the electorate to allow them to remain in office, they do not persist so relentlessly and with so great an avalanche of persuasive messages as does the sales-promotion industry. If communications from political elites try every week or day to manipulate me, communications from sellers try several to many times each day.

DEGRADATION OF WORK

Work in the market system is degraded, some critics hold, because its ennobling purposes are either lost or subordinated to gaining income. More immediately, they are subordinated to the purposes of the employer. If you are a wage earner you cannot indulge a passion for excellence except to the extent that it serves an employer's purpose. You cannot take satisfaction from having produced a product, because your efforts are anonymously mixed with those of thousands of others to produce, for example, a refrigerator that you may never see, let alone admire. Although your supervisor may repeatedly remind you to speed output and keep costs down, you will not be invited to reflect on the joys and dignity of work.

Points well taken. But they need to be laundered and shrunk. They derive from memories of a society of self-subsisting families, their implements designed and fabricated by members of the family. The complaints point to consequences of large-scale social cooperation, not consequences of a market system. Compare again communist systems. Supervisors and managers? Of course. Setting standards of quality and cost, whether low or high, to which workers must accede? Of course. Not seeing and claiming the finished product? The same as in a market system. Opportunity for and encouragement of reflection on the meaning of work and life? Perhaps in utopia, but not in any recent or contemporary nonmarket system that we know.

The most conclusive refutation of the degradation-of-work thesis puts all these considerations aside and simply points to attitudes toward work in premarket societies. To Aristotle, labor was degrading, a judgment dominant into the nineteenth century, as illustrated in English upper-class contempt for both work and trade. It is only with the rise of the market system that the contempt begins to die away.

## Market Ethics

As they move toward market systems, China and Russia are laying down a record of corruption, elite greed, and business practices not easily distinguished from gangsterism. Since the abuses seem to exceed those of established market systems, one may consider dismissing them as transitory. And one may find some of their sources in the inadequacy of law rather than the inadequacy of market system. One might also believe that we are seeing in these countries nothing more than the displacement of elites, who practiced these abuses quietly, by new elites, who are noisy in seizing places for themselves. Notwithstanding these and other reassuring interpretations of the sorry spectacle, we may indeed now be seeing a sample of the worst consequences of market life for personality and culture. In the established market systems, similar consequences may be obscured yet no less damaging. We do not know, but the possibility is too dismaying to be ignored.

Less flamboyant corruption in established market systems, some critics say, has come to be protected by an ethical code, a set of moral rules that tries to justify it. Market systems, they say, are governed by a code of conduct that represents a constant attack on and erosion of those beliefs and attitudes necessary to humane civilized society. From ancient Greece through the Judeo-Christian tradition, as well as through other cultural traditions, the best minds have taught the virtues of compassion, charity, conscientiousness, love, and social responsibility. Market ethics instead applauds gain, looking after only one's self and family, competing and winning, with social responsibility and charity only at one's convenience. In the great tradition, good society is a community. In the ethics of competition, it is a contest. In the former, one is asked to "love thy neighbor." In the latter, one has no neighbors, not even the family in the adjacent apartment on the same floor.

The market ethic, so the argument goes, does not simply justify an indifference to the welfare of others. At least some of its adherents go further, as in the novels of Ayn Rand, to celebrate the positive virtues of greed. It does not simply justify an executive in firing employees in a down-

sizing or in driving another enterprise out of business. It
calls on him to do so both for market virtue and for the efficiency of society. Market ethics turns the inhumane quid
pro quo into a moral virtue.

For entrepreneurs the market ethic permits—or encour-
ages—a disregard for the welfare of executives in other enterprises, of employees (except for benefits necessary to recruit them and obtain output), and of customers (except for
benefits necessary to recruit and hold them). It is prudent
and not unethical for the executive to misrepresent what
the enterprise offers, to play cynically on customers' emotions, to disparage what other enterprises offer, or to rattle
customers' minds with irrelevancies that will attract them.
Within some broad limits the market ethic permits or en-
courages enterprises to undermine broad social interests
by dodging taxes and evading legal regulations. To anyone
other than fellow entrepreneurs in the enterprise, market
ethics puts the executive under no obligation of candor, reasoned discussion or communication, compassion, sympathy, or responsibility except in those circumstances when,
and to the degree that, it pays. To take a simple clear case, it
puts no burden on a corporation to carry a surplus workforce because dismissal would cause the workers great
hardship. And that example excellently displays the force
behind the ethic. In its foundations it is a persuasive ethic of
survival for the enterprise—fire the surplus workers or go
under—that conveniently also sanctions a never-ending,
never-satisfied drive for more wealth.

Ugly as all this sounds, there is another side to the story.
Market ethics is one of a number of necessary role ethics,
sets of ethical rules suitable for the guidance of people who
play specialized roles in society. A role ethic contrasts with
the great ethical tradition, which is a universal code seek-

ing the same conduct from everyone, irrespective of role. A role ethic draws necessary distinctions. The role ethic of a judge requires that he be impartial and unemotional. Perhaps allowing a dilution of the harshness of a decision with the milk of human kindness, we nevertheless do not want the judge on the bench to be moved by appeals of kinship or friendship or of love and forgiveness. On the bench, many of the universal rules of ethics are forbidden. Similarly, role ethics permits an attorney to defend a guilty client. It may be that a common difficulty in maintaining popular control over government officials is that they lack a well-defined role ethic sufficient to make their behavior predictable, hence controllable.

That the market system gives rise to a special market ethic is not sufficient reason for it to be deplored. The great ethical tradition is as inappropriate a guide to entrepreneurial decisions as the universal rule "see no evil, hear no evil" is for a judge. To enjoy the benefits of social cooperation societies have a stake in cost control, innovation, and winnowing out of technologies or enterprises that have lost their usefulness. In many appropriate circumstances a dismissal of workers no longer needed deserves approval. A society should not shrink from the market role ethic simply because it endorses efforts to maintain an enterprise or make it grow. The financier George Soros has explicitly recognized the distinction between the two ethics, arguing for a moral obligation to keep them separate and to be guided by each in its place.

Having said a good word for a market role ethic in its appropriate place, I want to add that, necessary as a market ethic is, the existing market code of ethics will to many observers look as grossly defective as it does to me. It gives credence to those who claim that market life corrupts a so-

ciety's ethics. The objection at this point is not that the
market ethic justifies the quid pro quo rule. For I see no
great social ill in a combination of a market ethic that calls
on entrepreneurs to follow that rule with a universal ethic
that induces us to make state provisions to protect those
who are injured by it. No, my objection is that the market
ethic—not the kind of ethic that I have been describing but
a defective edition of it that actually exists—becomes in
large part a rationalization of questionable practices. In
their role ethic, physicians, for example, put themselves
under ethical obligation not to expose the incompetence of
a colleague. Similarly, entrepreneurs put themselves under
obligation not to undersell each other and in other ways try
to make monopoly ethically acceptable. For more than two
hundred years Adam Smith has warned us of these practices. One might also consider the possibility that, so central is the entrepreneurial role in market societies that their
market ethic overweighs the universal ethic—the domain
of the market ethic expands as the universal ethic contracts. Or continuing conflict between the market ethic and
the universal ethic reduces the efficacy of ethical rules of
any kind.

We are thus brought not to an easy formulation of the effect of the market system on a society's ethics but to great
questions beyond our present competence.

## Common Defenses

A few claims to benign effects on personality and culture
find voice from time to time. Some ride piggyback on the efficiency claim. They allege that, because the market is efficient, it creates wealth as no other method of coordination
has been able to do; and wealth in turn brings positive ben-

efits for development of personality and character. Wealth—
here compare Western Europe with much of Latin America—
raises the level of education, widens the range of experiences that people enjoy, acquaints them with various life
styles from which they can choose, and possibly turns them
away from invidiousness.

Some stereotypes of the wealthy are insulting, yet they
may represent some truths about the personalities of people
whose wealth is much greater than that of those around
them. But research suggests that when whole societies become relatively wealthy, as in Western Europe and North
America, they tend to develop in their members the kinds
of personality traits that Western thought has long prized:
higher levels of moral reasoning, self-reliance, sense of responsibility, and capacity to handle cognitive complexity.

Some research makes an even stronger claim: that not
only wealth but market participation itself tends to produce
these and other qualities of character. Market participants,
engaged as they are in never-ending choices, see themselves
as in control of themselves and their lives. They see their
own decisions as making a difference to both the near future and to life aspirations. In a market system they attribute to themselves—even if with some touch of self-deceit—power, autonomy, or independence, all together with
responsibility. And these attributes of personality, noteworthy in themselves, then support self-esteem, often considered the fundamental human aspiration. In the absence
of money and markets, the situation on these several scores
would be transformed. Centralist coordinating decisions
would displace many of their own individual decisions.

How much of a burden of choice and self-reliance can
market participants carry? Sixty years ago the psychoana-
lyst Erich Fromm argued that Germans fled into fascism

partly to escape the impossible burdens of decision making and consequent anxiety that the market system imposed on them. And in the conversions in recent years of communist systems to market systems, many Russians and Eastern Europeans fear not only the insecurities of the market system—the quid pro quo requirement—but their new burdens of decision making. They must take up new responsibilities for finding jobs, housing, and medical care. In those systems, obtaining these necessities always required initiatives of decision and action, but the retreat of the state from as full a responsibility as it once carried has stepped up the need for individual self-reliance.

To these observations research has added the probability that stimuli up to a point raise the mind's competence to cope with complexity but overload decreases it and may cause cognitive regression. Market systems do indeed stimulate, as do the pace and breadth of change. So also does job seeking or making the many provisions necessary for the family's future. But the research does not yet go far enough to tell us whether on balance these stimuli do or do not overload.

One last positive claim for the market is often confidently put—and we have encountered it before: the market system gives people what they want. A more correct proposition is that it gives people what they want to the degree to which they have money to spend. And, of course, it gives them only the kinds of benefits that markets can provide, for some benefits cannot be bought. Waiving these qualifications, which we have already looked into, is it true that the market system gives people what they want?

That it does is a preposterous claim, for people do not know what they want. What human beings want has been a source of speculation for at least 2,500 years. Although we still do not know what they or we want, observers do know that they practice self-deceit, contradict their own words with their actions, struggle with conflicting desires, create myths, long for insights denied them, and often claim more laudable motives than actually move them. That is enough to demonstrate that they do not very well know what they want, or whether, given the various meanings of the word, they would want what they want if they could have it.

We cannot even say that the market system gives them what they think they want, for what people think and what they do often diverge. No more can be claimed for the market system than that it gives people a distant approximation to what they choose in their market choices—only a distant one because of the defects in market choice canvassed in preceding chapters. It saddles them with burdens not chosen, as in spillovers. Or it compels them to accept rather than choose, as when workers can find no jobs to choose among.

All of this bears on a larger question that I have chosen not to tackle: Does the market system make people happy? That is a question for someone else's book, or perhaps it is too great a question for any book. Worth mentioning, however, is a striking fact. All over the world—and it is a world increasingly marketized—in response to inquiry from researchers, people are reporting declining happiness; and many countries report rising rates of clinical depression. Something is amiss, and the market's responsibility has to be pondered.

# Persuading the Masses

There develops in market systems a distinctive or pivotal form of interaction to which we have given only passing attention. It bears on efficiency, freedom, and personality and culture. Entrepreneurs—think of them again as market elites—greatly engage in unilateral communication to influence mass. It is a pattern of interaction far removed from the celebrated "competition of ideas" of democratic theory, for mass cannot reply. The pattern represents not an attempt to enlighten the masses but to induce them to buy what market elites are in a position to sell.

Now if it were consequently true that consumers buy not what they really need but what sellers persuade them to buy, then the market system would be circular and could hardly be called efficient. And one might not feel confident in calling participants wholly free if they can be so successfully manipulated. One might also then regard the great mass of people as duped, their personalities reshaped in a culture of constant elite manipulation.

"If it were true." Is it? That is what we now look into.

Let us walk through some elementary facts about market-elite communication with mass. To begin, although families and friends engage in multilateral communication, the dominant form of communication engaging masses of people in market systems is indeed highly unilateral. Small numbers of entrepreneurs and their agents send messages to vast numbers of people. It is a pattern that came with literacy. Until people could read, no one voice could reach millions. With broadcasting, the size and frequency of audience for a unilateral message took another jump. It was a new world of torrential unilateral communication. Mass is drenched in product ads and other sales promotions, institutional advertising that praises or defends the enterprise, and political messages.

Although you and I as ordinary citizens can hypothetically reach vast audiences through press and broadcasting, doing so is too expensive. Speech is costly rather than free. Newspapers and broadcasting stations are owned and operated by market elites. For the most part, only other elites can afford to buy print space and broadcast time. You and I do not often talk back to the entrepreneurs who every day address us. We do not much discuss their products with them. But morning, noon, and night we read and hear what they choose to say about them.

The intention of the market elites is to control. The intention is to induce people to buy or to induce them to think well of the enterprise and ill of its enemies, who are often identified as politicians. Or it is to persuade people to throw whatever weight they may have in politics—at least their votes—into support of policies favorable to enterprises. We have all been taught that communications are a method of conveying information, that communications edify. In fact, communication often intends no more than entertainment—we laugh at a comedian rather than take notes. But whether information is entertaining or informative, both purposes are subordinated to achieving control.

Even in multilateral communication the control motive may be dominant. "Eat your spinach!" does not edify; it tries to control. Clearly a politician intends not edification but control when declaring unilaterally "We all have to join together to get the job done." So also an advertiser, who pretends to edify customers by repeating that the product is "six ways better" but never tells them even one of the ways. A candidate's "I will not raise your taxes" is intended to capture your vote. "New and improved!" only pretends to be informational.

As a method of control, persuasive communication is powerful, although like other exercises of power it does not always succeed. One indicator of its power is that entrepreneurs spend staggering amounts of money to sell their services and commodities. The United States, at an extreme, spends more on sales promotion than on higher education. Another indicator of the power of persuasion is the use of propaganda by ambitious politicians—Hitler, Lenin, Stalin, and Mao—to win control over entire societies. They showed their appreciation of its power also by prohibiting communications that challenged them. With the rise of political democracy and democratic aspirations in the early twentieth century, dictators found outright command harder to enforce and have turned more heavily to inducing political obedience through propaganda and other forms of persuasive control over the citizen's mind. Unlike command, persuasion is almost universally accepted as a legitimate form of power. It consequently reaches everywhere. Multitudes of people submit to it because they do not even recognize that it is a form of power.

## Market Circularity

With this elementary preface in mind we now ask: Is it possible that market elite control of the mass mind goes so far as to create, as is sometimes alleged, a high degree of circularity in the market system? By not responding to customers, do entrepreneurs induce them to buy what they, the entrepreneurs, wish them to buy? Such a circularity thesis has been voiced off and on for at least a hundred years.

At best, it is an extreme exaggeration. Despite the great promotional influence of sellers and their advertisers, it seems clear that consumers continue to eat, dress, and sleep in beds at night for reasons other than that advertisers have persuaded them to do so. Nor have unadvertised products dropped out of shopping lists. Nor is the world's desire for medical care or electronic equipment exclusively an accomplishment of advertising. Advertisers do not even wholly control consumers' choices of brands, for on that point consumers receive conflicting messages that compel them to exercise choice. Panasonic sends a persuasive message to me, but so does Sony. Confused or ignorant as I may be, I make the choice. Consumers obviously have not wholly or largely lost control.

A sensible statement—not indisputable but plausible— is that consumer control is not destroyed by but shaped and weakened by the appeals of sales promotion. That is worth looking into.

People in the sales-promotion industry often claim credit for keeping the market system in good health. Advertising, they say, induces people to buy more and—although they often do not say so, it is logically implied—save less. Big spending means more jobs and prosperity. The argument is simple-minded, for many societies need not more spending but more savings to stimulate growth. That aside, stimulated spending and reduced savings probably do follow from sales promotion, but the evidence is not all in. If they do follow, it is only a weak circularity, however, for how much one saves is more governed by one's culture and circumstances. The Japanese are savers and Americans are spenders. The rich save, the very poor do not.

Sales promotion presumably sometimes shifts purchases toward luxury services and goods: haute couture for the wealthy, and designer underpants for everybody. But a shift is only a shift, not an abandonment of underwear in favor of tailored shirts. And shifts toward luxuries and the pursuit of fads and fashions have multiple causes, such as competitive spending, "luxury fever," and trend setting by wealthy or conspicuous consumers. There is not much evidence of a binding circularity, even when wealthy and conspicuous consumers are enlisted in advertising campaigns.

As noted in Chapter 5, the sales campaigns of market elites are not driven by desires to block or reshape mass demands. In pushing sales these elites are unlike political elites intent on protecting their advantages of wealth, power, and status. Market elites want profitable sales; they care very little what they sell so long as consumers will buy it. To respond to consumers, however, usually requires capital investment, hence lead times to gear up for production. Having committed capital to the production of whatever consumers want, corporations, we saw, do not want potential customers then to change their minds. And, of course, they want the maximum returns that they can obtain from the capital commitments. Hence entrepreneurs will often spend heavily to achieve the sales they have planned. Although this is a kind of circularity, it is not very threatening to consumer control over market elites. At its best, it is a circularity that makes it possible for market elites to put great commitments of capital where consumers want them.

## Assault on the Mind

Some sales promotion is informational—it tells a consumer what is for sale, where, and at what price—but the problem is that much of it is noninformational or misinformational. As is evident to all of us who are appealed to by sales promotion, much of it is designed to move the consumer by emotional appeal, to thwart rational deliberation, and to obfuscate. Pepsi is an "up thing" according to an ad, something to be identified with good spirits or perhaps the phallus. The message is in any case not informative on what the drink contains or in what respects Coca-Cola is the same or different. It is mind-rattling rather than helpful to thoughtful choice. The problem posed by the steady flow of seductive communications from market elites, then, is not that they decide for consumers what they are to buy. It is that they degrade the mind or, more precisely, degrade the human capacity to use the mind.

Can that be proved? No, I think not. But it is a conclusion also hard to deny. A reasonable suspicion—to understate it—is that the messages of market elites constitute a twofold assault on the mind, the effects of which are all the more grave because government elites join in the assault. The first assault might be called distraction. Market elites in particular cry constantly for the attention of customers and drench them in torrents of persuasion. Sales promotion and public relations, both commercial and political, are industries in themselves. Their communications everywhere catch our eyes and ears. Market elite persuasion of mass is so persistent and relentless, so widespread, and so inventive in its appeals that one must ask how much room it leaves in the mind for thinking about other things—or thinking at all rather than simply reacting. What room for conversation, introspection, speculation, creativity? How much room for thinking about anything other than possible purchases?

The second assault is obfuscation. As we see it about us, sales promotion and political persuasion deal heavily in im-

ages and slogans. They often intend to confuse rather than
clarify, giving not a reason to choose but a reason-overriding
impulse. They throw an array of influences at our minds
that one might think to be a checklist of tactics for render-
ing a mind incompetent. Yes, they are often entertaining.
But perhaps, as in a recent book title, we are "amusing ourselves to death."

You can judge the strength of these two assaults by
counting and reflecting critically on the messages that will
reach you, say, in the next twenty-four hours. For sales messages, you know that usually you are asked to buy not for a
reason given but in response to visual and aural patterns.
And you know that you will often be lied to: "Only Bayer
can . . . " is not true.

Much of the time, recipients or targets do not realize
that they are receiving a message. Teaching materials provided by corporations for the classroom often leave children
and teachers unaware of their ideological content. The children do not distinguish ideology from other content, and
teachers often do not pause to reflect. In the "oil shocks" of
the 1970s, when oil shortage in the United States stimulated new proposals for government regulation of the petroleum industry, few television viewers noted that petroleum
commercials played up with new emphasis the capacity of
the industry to find all the oil needed—pictures, for example, of heroic workers on storm-ridden offshore oil rigs. The
commercials made no explicit reference to government or
any political issues, but the message to consumers was one
of confidence in the industry. Nor do Americans realize
that frequent recent editorial opinion on the excesses of lit-
igation—depicting America as becoming a nation of quar-
relers—derives from public relations efforts of business
groups hoping to weaken government regulation.

As early as 1950 in the United States, nearly half the contents of the best newspapers and nearly all the contents of the lesser papers were estimated to come from public relations releases. That is in addition to paid advertising space. Is this assault on the mind becoming intensified? World over, advertising has grown three times faster than the global population. And many observers call attention to what they consider a continuing degradation of discourse. Public issues are increasingly aired not through the exchange of sustained coherent argument but by fragmentary question-and-answer or by soundbite sloganeering. The average interval of uninterrupted speech on television by U.S. presidential candidates dropped from an already deplorable 42.3 seconds in 1968 to an abysmal 9.8 seconds by 1988.

All over the world, the days when a candidate or official could educate constituents, thus playing the classic leadership role, seem to be receding. Politics, it is now often said, is huckstering. As for communication from the market elite on products, its mixture of emptiness, confusion, and deceit may have descended to a level below which there is not much room to drop further. The indisputable benefits of literacy and the mass media have come at a heavy cost.

Some of these trends in relations between the market elite and customers may be slowed or stopped by a new growth of multilateral communication through the Internet. A consulting firm, addressing prospective business clients, reminds them: "In the new electronic economy, potential buyers can print out a dozen independent reviews of your product in minutes with a few clicks of a mouse." To which it adds: "Knowledge is power, and suddenly your customers are awash in it."

In some quarters, feelings run high and biases deep on the effects of the sales-promotion and public-relations industries on the minds on which they so steadily seek to bring their distracting and confusing efforts. Some people cannot bear to acknowledge that these industries, especially sales promotion, are rivals to public education. Nor will they reflect that this industry is at war with the education "industry": the one assaulting the mind, the other often seeking, among its other functions, to inform and exercise it. The sales-promotion industry's disposition toward truth is roughly the same as its disposition toward misrepresentation, falsehood, and obfuscation: within some legal limits, use it if it works. The education industry tries to give to the pursuit of truth a standing denied to misrepresentation, falsehood, and obfuscation.

If we simply look about us at both sales promotion and the political appeals of market elite to mass, especially those now in the hands of specialists in public relations, we cannot escape some fears that they are systematically undermining that respect for truth or honesty long argued to be a requirement of civilized society. Perhaps the traditional endorsement of honesty is no more than a pablum that we intend only for the very young. In any case, veneration for truth is always shaky and highly qualified. Still, there appears to be a worrisome problem here of market impact on culture even though it receives far less attention than the other impacts just discussed.

In the United States, the judiciary long ago accepted as legal some degree of product misrepresentation. "Puffing," the court said, is to be expected in commercial transactions, hence hardly to be outlawed. The court was insightful: misrepresentation is to be expected as a widespread practice. The decision was a telling commentary on market society.

Just as societies now usually forbid a market in children, prohibit slavery, and begin to curb industrial pollution, so also might they curb the sales-promotion and public-relations industries. Many nations now control sales promotion for some products: for example, drugs or stocks and bonds. I make this point not to advocate such a policy here but simply to point out that the two industries are not in their present form an inherent requirement of a market system. In principle, a market system can operate across a vast array of social interactions without either a market, say, in children or without a market like the present market in persuasive messages from elites. Market systems need a wide distribution of information, and that in turn imposes some limits on state supervision of that distribution. But that is not to say that the present form of the industry is essential to the market system. Assuming no nibbling at free speech, the key to curbs, if desirable, on sales promotion and public relations is a distinction between the rights of individual persons and the prerogatives of organizations, a distinction drawn in Chapter 13.

## Political Circularity

Finding an assault on the mind but not circularity in the market system, we may have been looking in the wrong place for circularity. Perhaps it is to be looked for less in the market system, where market elites contest with one another, than in democratic politics on issues on which market and political elites join in trying to control their ostensible controllers. A visible and audible feature of elite communication to mass is agreement between market and political elites on some of their messages. They do not join in promoting sales of kitchen appliances, but they do join in defense of the established social order. And where the assault through sales promotion often leaves the consumer more confused than persuaded, the assault through political messages, though it too is both distracting and obfuscating, is also persuasive. Perhaps consequentially it creates a political circularity in which, even in the democracies, masses are persuaded to ask from elites only what elites wish to give them.

This is hardly a novel thesis. Down through history, many of the great minds have been troubled by distortions in thought that bear on social organization and elite manipulation of mass. Plato spoke of shadows in caves rather than reality, Francis Bacon of "idols," Kant of "tutelage," Locke of "insinuations," Rousseau of "capturing volitions," and Marx of "false consciousness." In our time Schumpeter speaks of "manufactured will," Habermas of "distorted communication," and Schattschneider of the "heavenly chorus" that sings "with a strong upperclass accent."

Elites defend their political communications as a contribution to a competition of ideas such as has been prized in liberal and democratic thought. But the competition of ideas works, if at all, only when several conditions are met. First, the messages must challenge each other. And, in the contestation, loud voices must not silence others. Third, each of the contesting messages must contain some empirical content. Finally, the contestants must not depart too far from a respect for truth. All of these conditions are in varying degrees violated in elite political messages.

Between and within each of the two elites, mutual challenge is frequent, but not on the fundamentals of the social order. The two elites speak almost unanimously, though of course not explicitly in every message sent, on the "obvious" virtues of hierarchy and inequality, the competence of elites, the necessity of social solidarity, and the dangers of political agitation. Nor on the functions, privileges, and offenses of elites—clearly questions about fundamentals—do they challenge each other. The failure of a competition of ideas on fundamental institutions is a particularly American problem. Ideological homogeneity puts a touch of impropriety on questions about the "American Way," the Constitution, the private enterprise system, the corporation, and equality.

Compared to those of the elites, the voices, say, of consumer and environmental groups are infrequent and weak. The voice of labor unions, though strong in some nations, rarely speaks so frequently and loudly as the voices of entrepreneurial and governmental elites. The two elites overwhelm all other contributors to what consequently fails to become an illuminating competition of ideas.

If elite assaults on the mind go so far as to make ostensible political democracy actually circular, their success may owe a great deal to a long history of elite manipulation of mass. Elite attempts to control mass of course antedate the rise of the market system and the rise of democracy. In fact, much of earliest recorded history is a story of tyrannical exploitation of mass—Plato's *Republic* is a blueprint for ostensibly benevolent elite control of mass. Medieval Europe is a picture of collaboration between the secular and the religious for control of mass, always seen as threatening to elites. A historian writes of the Renaissance: "Fear of insurrection was a steadily nagging irritant within the lives of those with power or property to lose." And on state-church cooperation to control mass, "from the mid-sixteenth century this co-operation became closer than ever." Even the founders of the American democracy—that elite, too—struggled with fears of mass and found ways to curb the influence of masses in the new constitutional order.

The larger picture of elite control becomes a picture of

class conflict in which the advantaged members of society
and their elite leaders struggle for the minds of the less advantaged in order to protect their own advantages from in-
cessant mass demands for a larger share in all the benefits of
society, including goods and services but no less so status,
influence, and power. In James Madison's eyes, governments have to be constructed to curb the demand of the
"majority faction" for an equal division of property. The
struggle continues in our time, conspicuously in recent
class-motivated attempts to cut back the welfare state. Tac-
tical moves aside, it is to the advantage of the advantaged to
persuade the disadvantaged to be satisfied with the many
benefits that market society has already bestowed on them.

Elite efforts endlessly teach—once through shamans,
then chiefs, then nomadic raiders, then through lord and
bishop, and now through contemporary elites—the virtues
of inequality, hierarchy, authority, loyalty, obedience, docil-
ity, trust, and faith. If each of these in its modest place is in
fact a virtue, an indiscriminate endorsement of them is a
formula for mass deference to elites. The steady and indiscriminate overendorsement of these virtues is supplemented
in every period by additional messages relevant to the culture of the time. At one time they taught the divine right of
kings; in our time they teach the doctrinal correctness of
capitalism. Elites of course end up persuading both themselves and their own children. Hence all over the world the
elite message, in a largely unilateral flow of communication, displays a high degree of continuity.

Some radical critics of the market system see elite communication as successfully "selling" the market system to
the masses. Elites, they would say, succeed even though the
market system is in fact an exploitative social process for
locking mass into such limited shares of society's benefits

as are permitted by the rule of quid pro quo and the rights of property. That is a kind of circularity. And they would look cynically at the claim in Chapter 3 that the market system is a peacekeeper. In highly inegalitarian societies, they might say, its peacekeeping, though undeniable, intimidates and oppresses the disadvantaged. Elites have persuaded the disadvantaged to accept from the market system the small shares so peaceably allocated them rather than risk a struggle and defeat if they were to challenge them. That again is an allegation of strong circularity.

# Necessary to Democracy?

Like political democracy, the market system establishes mass control over elites. They constitute the twin alternative methods by which millions of people can exercise popular controls over those relatively few people—entrepreneurs and government officials—who actively make the proximate decisions.

The two are of course intertwined. And it is widely believed that a democratic nation-state is impossible if not linked with a market system. If there is no market system, then there is no democracy. In this chapter we shall try to find out whether that is true.

So far in history, no democratic nation-states have existed except those tied to market systems. The world has never seen a democratic centrally planned system. Market system without democracy is common—Indonesia and Saudi Arabia, for example—but no democracy without market system. So firm is the historical connection that some observers predict that Russia cannot achieve democracy because it put democratic reform ahead of market reform and still lacks a market system that can support democracy. China, they say, is on the right track: market first. Before long it will have a suitable market-system base for democracy, if its rulers then permit democracy.

At one time the world had never seen a democratic nation-state of any kind. In time, such a state proved to be possible. That as of today the world has never seen a democratic central-planning state does not at all deny that it too may be possible. Perhaps the tie between democracy and market system is merely a historical accident and will in time disappear. What do we know about the historical connection?

A frequent answer is that, if a state through central planning puts an end to the market system, the state then becomes so powerful as to destroy democracy. The postulated sequence is democracy, then removal of the market system, consequently the end of democracy. Since never in history has there been a democratic central planning state, no such sequence is to be found in history. It cannot explain the historical tie.

What *might* happen *if* a democratic state abolished the market system is an interesting question even if it cannot explain why in history the two are tied together. The common hypothesis is that a state powerful enough to engage in central planning in the absence of a market system would, because of its powers, destroy democratic controls over it. It is an appealing argument but embarrassingly simpleminded. It says that more power in one location—the government—implies less power elsewhere—among citizens. But the proposition that more power at one location means less at another is not generally correct, even though it holds in some circumstances. If citizens are to exercise power over the Internet, for example, that will require new powers, not fewer, in the hands of regulatory agencies, national and international.

Historians have often noted that the power of citizens to compel their governments to undertake programs desired by citizens requires not weak governments but authority strong enough to tax and administer. The citizens of India, for example, and of other developing nations are often frustrated by the weaknesses of their governments. Citizen power requires strong governmental powers.

Moreover, whether governments abuse their authority depends on the rules, rooted in custom or law, that in each nation govern the political behavior of elites. In well-established democracies, chief executives do not call out the army to maintain their power after losing an election. And they know that if they were to call the army, it would not answer. In less well established democracies, the effectively operating political rules are different; coups are possible. How the civil service or the judiciary behaves similarly depends on the rules they follow. Nor does a large, hence "powerful," army threaten democracy more than a small one. The size of the threat depends on the customary and legal rules that officers and those under their command follow.

Democratic governments today exercise much greater powers than in early to mid eighteenth century: powers to tax, to manage money and credit, to regulate enterprises, to transfer income through social welfare payments, and the like. Democracy has not suffered from these powers—the democracies have not been on Hayek's "road to serfdom." Many observers would argue that these very powers are evidence of growing democratic control over the state. Nor has the repeated vast exercise of wartime powers, including military conscription, undermined democracy.

## What Needs Explaining

It is a second remarkable fact—perhaps we should say astonishing—that no democratic nation-state has ever attempted to eliminate its market system. That is the hard fact that needs explaining: not why democracy requires the market system—perhaps it does not—but why no society has tried democracy while dispensing with the market system. The wave of socialization of key industries in Western Europe immediately after World War II was not an abandonment of market system but a move from private to public enterprise, the enterprises remaining firmly fixed in market-system buying and selling. Governments have of course altered the domain of the market in tax policy, social insurance, and regulation of business, for example. French "indicative planning" of a few decades ago and the detail of Italian government regulation of business today represent some movement away from the market system. So also did India's succession of five-year plans, though the plans were largely targets for government investment only. No democracy has ventured into any displacement of the market system greater than its occasional partial displacement by wartime economic mobilization.

How is it possible that no democratic state has tried—or even tried and failed—to dispense with the market system? One would expect two hundred years of history to reveal at least one wise or foolish democratic attempt, even if aborted, to end the market system. Market critics offered powerful arguments for doing so—not only Marxists but democratic socialists like the English Fabians. Repeated depressions stimulated debate on alternatives. The catastrophic severity of the Great Depression of the 1930s might have been expected somewhere in the world to stimulate a democratic government to try central planning in that period of anguish.

Even if we believe that it would have been an excessive risk or a mistake for any nation to have abandoned it, we must wonder why no democratic nation ever took such a risk or made such a mistake. For nations—even democratic ones—often run great risks and make grave mistakes. Democratic states let Nazi Germany rearm without themselves rearming, and almost lost Europe as a consequence. It was a democratic state that risked exploding the first nuclear bomb, a venture that carried some probability, even if small, that it would end life on earth. A democratic state ran a risk of nuclear war by demanding the Soviet withdrawal of missiles from Cuba.

Why do democratic political systems never, either wisely or foolishly, go so far as to test the possibilities of abandoning the market system? They do not do so for a simple reason: a remarkably high degree of conformity in thought endorsing or accepting the market system—by no means unanimity but so great an agreement that antimarket citizens and their leaders never win, not once anywhere in two hundred years.

That without exception citizens and their leaders always chose to hold to the market system is a fact about their state of mind, not about how the market system works. *The historical connection rests on a state of mind, not on the mechanics of market system and democracy.*

## How To Explain Uniformity of Opinion

One can accept opinion uniformity as a sufficient explanation of the historical connection between democracy and market system. Or one can let curiosity persist in trying to explain the uniformity. It cannot be explained by evidence that the dominant opinion was right and the dissidents wrong. For throughout the two centuries both advocates and dissenters have mounted highly informed arguments in a continuing debate in which neither side can demonstrate its correctness. And even if the market advocates were

right, that does not explain their two-hundred-year dominance—many dominant opinions are false, and many
truths never become dominant opinion.

In recent years, it is now sometimes said, communist
failures have finally persuaded citizens and elites in all
countries of the necessity of a market system. But communist failures in the late twentieth century cannot explain
why in earlier democratic societies, to whom those failures
had not yet been revealed, opinion in favor of the market
system was already dominant. In any case, the failure of authoritarianism in communist nations has little to say about
what democracies can and cannot do. It does not explain the
uniformity of opinion.

One can understand that the many millions of people
who live well in market systems and observe that market
systems are wealthier than nonmarket systems would not
wish to displace the market system. But millions of market
participants do not live well, are not obviously better off
than they might be in a nonmarket system. Yet even they
do not join in turning against it. Even in the misery of the
Great Depression of the 1930s, in some countries only a
minority of the unemployed called for ending the market
system.

Nor is the dominance of pro-market opinion to be explained by the absence of an existing alternative system the
defects and merits of which could be compared with those
of the market system. Without a successfully operating alternative system to turn to, no doubt some people and their
governments would not want to make a leap into the unknown. But such caution hardly explains why no people or
their government at any time chose the nonmarket unknown. The establishment of the United States, the French
Revolution, the Russian and the Chinese revolutions all

demonstrate that at least now and then masses or elites look for new forms of social organization.

Another proffered explanation is that a people who enjoy the democratic political liberties of free speech, thought, and movement will also want to enjoy the market liberties of consumer free choice and occupational free choice. This explanation is tempting but mistaken. Central planning, we know, can allow both consumer free choice and occupational free choice, as to a limited degree did the Soviets and Mao's China. To give these market freedoms to everyone does not require a market system.

In my search for an explanation of this steady uniformity of opinion, I find only one possibility. It goes beyond the domain of this book, but it at least suggests where an explanation may be found. The explanation is the assault on the mind of the preceding chapter, assault not only by market elites but also by their allies among governmental elites. They urge the market system on society because any alternative to it would bring an end to their powers and advantages. The market system operates by a set of rules and customs that limit the power of the state. Such rules and customs block, for example, great transfers of wealth. They also require a diffusion of power to entrepreneurs rather than their displacement by central planners. Any society not governed by either a landed aristocracy, where a market system has not yet been established, or by a revolutionary elite, where a market system has been abolished, will be governed by a diffuse elite whose privileges and power depend on the rules and customs of the market system. This elite may not support democracy at all but instead directly govern. But if it does take the democratic route it will defend itself, through an assault on the mass mind, by teaching mass allegiance to the market system.

I can suggest some supporting detail. Royal authority, custom, and legislation long stood in the way of market transactions, not wholly blocking them but greatly constraining them. In the seventeenth and eighteenth centuries an English merchant class intent on enrichment from such transactions as were permitted clamored for more market opportunities, such as those consequently granted by royal authority to the Dutch East India Company and the British East India Company. The merchant class was not without power to win them. For royal authority needed funds for waging war and for ordinary administration—greater funds than a weak tax system supplied—and turned to merchants both for helpful loans and new tax revenues. Merchants responded, but only conditionally, making funds available only in return for new freedoms to exploit market opportunities. Entrepreneurs thus eventually accomplished, in a mixture of inadvertence and deliberation, new constraints over king and over established landed elites. Power over government became diffused, and merchants enjoyed and profited from their range of liberties. The emerging market system operated to their enormous advantage.

Not surprisingly, the new order had the effect of stimulating other groups in society to demand some of the self-governing freedoms and rights won by merchants. The merchants then faced a choice: suppress the epidemic of demands, as in nineteenth-century Germany, or coopt and make allies of those who made the new demands, as in Britain. The latter choice put the English merchants on the path to political democracy.

Having allowed or encouraged minimal democracy to

develop, merchants—now called entrepreneurs—had every reason to fear that those who had been empowered would use their votes to take from entrepreneurs their wealth and powers. Commenting on franchising the masses through the Second Reform Bill of 1867, a member of Parliament expressed the fear that the working classes "now have in their hands, if they know how to use it, the power of becoming masters of the situation." Market elites consequently began and still persist in a deliberate "education" of the masses on the virtues of private property, private enterprise, elite stewardship of society, hierarchy, inequality, or, in short, the supporting beliefs of a market system. They undertake in public discourse, in the schools and churches and in the mass media an assault on the mind designed to create a conformity of thought endorsing the market system. In short, challenging to elite power as it is, democracy is curbed by an assault on the minds of the masses that persuades them to live within the rules of the market system rather than become "masters of the situation."

The full story, of course, needs qualification. Democracy has in more recent times been imposed on nations defeated in war: Japan and Germany, for example, at the end of World War II. And some developing nations—India, among others—have opted for democracy without going through an earlier stage in which merchants challenged central authority. In these cases too, however, the demands of the market elite for market opportunities have put its educational or propaganda resources in support of the market system rather than in support of central authority. And when the Russian Revolution appeared to make communist authoritarianism the only likely alternative to the market system, elite efforts to convince the masses of the merits of the market system were intensified.

The market system is, then, by this hypothesis, historically tied to democracy by elite assault on the mass mind.

Given the assault and its consequent uniformities of thought, the democracy to which it is tied is a minimal or low-grade democracy rather than a highly developed one, blighted as it is by the incapacity of its citizens to think. That this minimal democracy exists at all seems to owe a great deal to merchant and entrepreneurial political energies that curbed the powers of the authoritarian state before then undertaking an assault on the mind that obstructs a fuller democracy. In all this we find no convincing evidence or argument that, except in the mind, the market system is necessary to democracy. Not having found it, we acknowledge that nevertheless it may exist. There may be connections that we have missed.

# Enterprise Obstructions to Democracy

Whether market elites did or did not historically make a contribution to minimal democracy and do or do not continue to do so, they blight a fuller democracy through their assault on the mind. The market system holds democracy down to a low level in other ways too, obstructing a more genuine yet feasible democracy.

If genuine democracy requires, by definition, at least a rough equality of political influence or power among citizens in their attempts to control elites, then any significant economic inequality among citizens is an obstruction to democracy. Inequalities in income and wealth create inequalities in opportunity to run for office, in launching candidates, in capacities to use the mass media to influence voters, in lobbying, and in social interchange with party and government officials. Because market systems produce inequality of income and wealth, they obstruct democracy. Q.E.D. That communist or other nonmarket systems also produce inequalities of income and wealth does not refute this conclusion.

Beyond that fundamental market-system obstruction to democracy are several others that hinge on the position of the enterprise, especially the corporation, in the political system. They provide the agenda for this chapter.

## Oversized Citizens

Set aside the mom-and-pop grocery and other small enterprises whose prerogatives in a democratic political system are hardly distinguishable from those of individual persons. It is the large enterprises that pose obstructions to political democracy. Through their spending and their relations with government officials they exercise much more power than do citizens. Their power swamps the power of all but a few enormously wealthy citizens.

If an enterprise incorporates, it then enjoys certain additional rights. Limited liability, for example, limits losses to stockholders if the enterprise fails. Investors thus protected, corporate executives can acquire from them—and then spend—funds far larger than possible for wealthy individual persons, even larger than possible for some nation-states. The corporation plays the role of an oversized, greatly empowered citizen. The role does not threaten a conspicuous breakdown—certainly no paralysis—of democratic regimes but a mammoth violation of the political equality ordinarily deemed necessary for genuine rather than spurious democracy.

A striking example: In response to citizen action on environmental issues, enterprises in Canada, Australia, Britain, and the United States in about 1970 began to sue individual persons for circulating petitions, attending meetings, writing to public officials, and engaging in other citizen activities adverse to the enterprise. The suing enterprises know that they will win very few of these suits, because citizen activities are protected by law, especially laws on free speech, in democracies. But they also know that a suit can be effective simply because of the threat of legal costs that will fall on the defendant, who of course does not have enterprise funds to draw on, as does the plaintiff. These suits often constitute frightening intimidations that obstruct free speech and participation in public affairs. More familiar examples of corporate activity inconsistent with political equality are corporate spending on election campaigns or to cultivate close relations with government officials.

Enterprises enjoy advantages beyond size itself. They can draw on "public" funds while members of other groups must spend out of their own incomes. These public funds they throw into political activity are public in the sense that they are drawn from the receipts of the enterprise, thus from customers and stockholders rather than from the personal income of enterprise executives. The individual citizen is on his own. Laws sometimes limit executive use of "public" funds, but it takes little ingenuity to escape them.

Enterprises, corporate and other, enjoy the additional advantage that they are already organized, ready and able to move, while ordinary persons are still struggling to raise funds and organize. In a moment, a corporation can assign executives to political tasks, while citizen groups must search for qualified staff. And corporations persist, for they are not mortal. They may persist in their political activities for one generation after another, while their mortal adversaries lose their energies or die off.

Although the law varies from one country to another, it generally grants corporations as legally fictitious persons many of the rights, including rights of political participation, that one might think appropriate in a democracy only for living, breathing persons. Corporations are legally entitled to engage heavily in political activity, even if they cannot vote or run for office. Theirs, too, are legal rights of free speech and of communication with political elites.

Corporation as person is a fundamental fact about

democracy or, more precisely, about undemocracy, even though its implications are often more timidly than bravely studied. The transformation of corporation into citizen can hardly be dismissed as insignificant on the ground that enterprises are, after all, composed of individual persons. The effect of granting the enterprise a citizen's rights in addition to the rights already enjoyed by participants in the enterprise is to confer great special powers on groups of enterprise executives, who can make use of corporate assets and personnel in addition to exercising the rights and powers they enjoy as individual citizens.

Other than by redefining democracy, I do not see how it is possible to reconcile democracy with the practice of conferring on institutions the rights and powers of real persons. The rationale for democracy is rights and powers for living, hurting, and aspiring persons whose assigned rights and powers give them protection as well as opportunities to pursue their aspirations. It would make no sense, on democratic grounds, to assign such rights and powers to fire hydrants or computers—they neither suffer nor aspire. Neither does a corporation suffer or aspire. Only the people in it do. To them alone would a democratic state assign the rights and powers of persons.

For the performance of the functions that societies assign to corporations—to organize air transport, for example, or extract ore—corporations need certain rights and powers such as to buy and sell and to manage a workforce. I see no necessary obstacle to democracy when corporations hold those rights and powers. The obstruction of democracy arises only when the additional rights and powers of free persons are granted to corporations. Every society minimally recognizes such a principle—I do not know of any society that permits, say, a corporation to run for and hold po-

litical office. But democracy requires other restrictions of
corporate political participation—that is, other applica-
tions of the same principle. The designation of corporations
as legally fictitious persons stands in the way.

Societies do not permit their taxing authorities or their
military forces or their ministries of agriculture to claim
the civil rights of individual citizens. They are instead constrained to pursue their assigned purpose and no others. By
any usual definition, democracy similarly requires similar
constraint on corporations and other kinds of organizations. Unlike individual persons, organizations are presumably servants, neither fellow citizens nor masters. Contrast
that democratic requirement with the position of an organization like Unilever, which like all large corporations, in
some respects acts more like a state than like a person or
servant. Only with a legal status and a set of rules appropriate to its functions will it and other corporations meet the
requirements of political democracy. In a democracy, a corporation would not go into court as an injured person but in
its role as a social institution.

## Corporations in the International Order

In the emerging international order, the corporation has become increasingly visible as a challenge to democracy. A
significant change in its political role may be riding the
back of new structures of international trade and finance,
the spread of multinational corporations over the world,
and the energies of governments engaged in protecting and
promoting them.

Among the corporations, we have already noted, are
many whose resources and volume of production are

greater than those of many nation-states and who, consequently, can bring more power to bear on those states than the states can bring to bear on them. Beyond that, market elites from corporations and banks have joined with state elites to establish institutions that are assigned certain powers of central direction of the international economy: the International Monetary Fund and the European Central Bank, among others. This poses at least three problems for democratic government.

First, to some extent these institutions become the domain of technically proficient elites—bankers, financiers, and economists—over whom often less technically qualified officials in the member governments cannot exercise sufficient control. The policies of the International Monetary Fund in forcing fiscal orthodoxy on developing nations is a case in point. Not many nation-states possess either the competence or the power to share effectively in control over it.

Second, even when member nation-states do achieve effective control, the control is then in the hands of political elites in those nation-states. These international institutions remain far removed from the voters in the member nation-states, who on many issues are close to powerless. The new European Central Bank is deliberately designed to be insulated from politics in part, it appears, so that it can pursue not high levels of employment, as masses of people might wish, but the price-level stability favored by market elites.

Third, these bodies, although far removed from voters, are easily accessible to corporations. When the European Commission, for example, permits enterprises to dispose of toxic and radioactive wastes by diluting them for recycling into consumer products or by using them as fertilizers, it will have heard from interested corporations, whether or not ordinary citizens mobilize to be heard.

In large nations, democracy at the national level is difficult enough and only partially achieved. Whether and how democratic control over international institutions can be achieved for an "electorate" of several billion people of diverse aspirations and understandings is an almost frightening question. Perhaps it cannot be established. How these market-regulating institutions will shape international trade and finance in the twenty-first century remains to be seen. In the meantime, corporations, banks, and international political elites make momentous decisions under little democratic control.

## Authority Within the Enterprise

Corporations, we know, operate through an autocratic rather than democratic internal structure. The structure has been sustained by corporate rights to private property in productive assets. At the edges, the law has whittled away at those rights. It has permitted unions to bring some small measure of democracy into industrial relations, and some nations have established employee councils, though of highly limited authority.

The idea that in a democratic society every large corporation should internally be organized as a democracy, its employees playing the role of citizens, thus choosing, removing and in other ways controlling the active managers, continues to attract a steady following. An appeal to consistency is a formidable argument for it: if democracy is a good idea for the state, it is also a good idea for corporations that are in many respects like states. But only a few nations have ventured into formal employee control, as in Germany's legal provision for employee membership on corporate supervisory boards even though not on the more active managerial boards.

I would proceed cautiously in appraising the authoritarian workplace as an obstacle to democracy. Workplace democracy is on some points at odds with democracy for the whole society. It is not at all clear what range and degree of "industrial democracy" is necessary to the larger democracy.

Would one on democratic grounds advocate turning the army over to the control not of legislature or cabinet but of the soldiers in it? Would one turn tax policy over to the employees of the tax-collecting authority? Would one turn decisions on where to construct new highways over to the workers who construct them?

The appropriate constituency for military, tax, or highway decisions is, roughly speaking, "all of us," not just those who do the work, even though those who do the work have intense interests in how it is organized and done. How many television sets of what kinds ought to be produced is a decision that impinges on all persons who want a set or something else instead, not just on those who make them. Decisions on rates of pay in a factory affect all claimants to shares of the society's production, not only on the employees in that one factory.

If employees were to replace stockholders as proximate controllers of corporations, their new managers, whom they would presumably elect, would need to continue to practice a responsiveness to market controls as well as a responsiveness to new employee controls. The two controls would conflict, as when employees might want to drain the firm of its liquid capital by taking wage increases while market controls call for investing the capital for growth.

Even if the road to more democracy in the corporation is not well mapped, some nations find it worth exploring. Many of the autocratic practices of the workplace are unnecessary, as well as obstructive to feasible popular control over executives. Examples are racial or ethnic discrimination in hiring, discharge without sufficient cause, arbitrary wage differentials, excessive executive compensation, and secrecy about workplace threats to employee health and safety, among many others. Although some nations have curbed some of the excesses of internal autocracy in the corporation, people at the end of the twenty-first century may look back with astonishment on our era's discrepancy between democratic principle and autocratic practice in the corporation.

## The Soulful Corporation

Democratic criteria call corporate philanthropy into question: contributions to education, research, environmental protection, the arts, and aid to the poor. Superficially, there is no problem. One might believe that neither on democratic grounds or for any other reason need the generosity of the corporation be regarded with anything but gratitude. Although consumers and stockholders in fact pay for what the corporation spends on philanthropy, they are not taxed to do so, nor need they be aware that they are footing the bill and are not the recipients of corporate generosity. Confused or inattentive, they welcome corporate largess in the belief that they are getting something for nothing.

These areas of corporate activity raise the issue once discussed as the "soulful" corporation. Societies have a choice. They can hold corporations closely to the production of what they sell and to the expenditure only of those funds necessary to the production of it. Or they can permit them to spend "public" funds without restriction, presumably for good purposes that need the help of philanthropy. Societies have tended toward the latter.

Although corporations operate under market control with respect to what they produce for sale, they are little controlled with respect to what they give to various causes and institutions. In the market system, a consumer can vote for or against the production of tomatoes or vacation cruises but neither for nor against a corporate contribution to the city's orchestra, a corporate refusal to support research on soil contamination, or a corporate program of private-enterprise propaganda in the schools. In the absence of control over them, corporate executives are not democratically positioned to channel "public" funds and instead simply channel the funds into their own personal choices. What is more, like all groups, they are influenced by characteristic biases, such as are displayed in their disinclination to finance research critical of the business community. Philanthropy raises great issues on the competence and propriety of corporate choice in democracy, similar to issues on corporate political expenditure.

Might, by definition, a more genuine democracy require that corporations be curbed not only in overt political and philanthropic activity but also in institutional advertising— that is, messages that tout the corporation as an institution? Might it even forbid any massive advertising other than informative messages about products? To some observers, steps like these look like a democratic way for a society to cope with a torrent of corporate communications that obstructs the genuine competition of ideas long thought necessary for democracy. To others, they go down a slippery slope to the extinction of free speech. Democratic theory has not been developed to the point at which it provides criteria for judgment.

## The Privileged Political Position of Market Elites

Beyond these familiar market obstructions to democracy is another: a privileged position of market elites in the political system. Special privilege is always suspect in a democracy, but here we go beyond mere suspicion in a line of analysis that is consequential even if disputed.

Among the things the state does to make a market system work is to stimulate entrepreneurial energies through a great variety of aids to enterprises. Although enterprises can be ordered to "cease and desist," commanded not to produce, they cannot, some special circumstances aside, be commanded to produce. They must be induced. Governments offer diverse inducements: among many others, tariff protection, loans, outright cash grants, government purchases, patents, tax concessions, information and research services, subsidized advertising, governmental negotiation with or military intervention in other nations to open up markets. Governments also adapt the school system to the needs of enterprises. The state is strongly motivated to provide whatever enterprises need as a condition of doing their work. A contemporary popular derogatory term for much of it is corporate welfare.

Governmental benefits or inducements to business run larger than most people imagine. To encourage transcontinental railroad construction in the United States in the late nineteenth century, the federal government gave as gifts to the railroads one fourth of the land of Minnesota and Washington; one-fifth of Wisconsin, Iowa, Kansas, North Dakota, and Montana. The total of land gifts was an area larger than either France or Germany. Contemporary estimates of the value of inducements run into many billions of dollars but vary wildly depending on what is included in the total—on such questions as how much of governmental expenditure on public education should be counted as a benefit or inducement to business.

If enterprises falter for lack of inducement to invest, hire, and produce, members of the political elite are more likely than those of the entrepreneurial elite to lose their positions. The consequence is constant attention by the political elite to the needs of the market elite, as evidenced by the practice of presidents-elect in the United States to convene a meeting of major corporate heads even before they take office to provide assurances that the new president will be sensitive to their needs. It is an assurance not offered to farmers, labor unions, municipalities, the military, or any other like group. On many issues and many circumstances, the needs of the market elite take priority over democratic demands on the state. The electorate is often slow to respond to disappointment and often forgets a disappointment by the time of the next election. Disappointed members of the market elite may almost immediately reduce production, cut the workforce, or shut down and move abroad.

Here and there other groups can influence government by withdrawing or threatening to withdraw their services if their needs are not met. Subway workers and garbage removal workers can extract concessions from a city's government by the threat of strike. Governments have been persuaded by threatened discontent among physicians to yield to them on health policy. But governments do not so broadly, deeply, and constantly depend on the performance of such groups as they do on the performance of market elites to make the wheels of industry turn fast enough to keep the population employed and political incumbents in office.

All this gives to the market elite a special voice, a special privilege not granted to others in the political system. It appears in several arenas. In the national arena, it shows up not only in specific benefits to market elites—tax concessions, for example—but also in the general reluctance of the state to override market elite objections to broad issues of policy on which entrepreneurs agree. In municipal government, it confers tax relief and other benefits on enterprises that otherwise will locate elsewhere or threaten to do so to extract these benefits from the municipal government. Over the globe, the size of some corporations and the consequent job opportunities and other benefits they offer to small nations permit them sometimes to overwhelm their governments by threatening to withdraw or indicating reluctance to invest. Confronted with a threat by Philips Electronics to move one of its many factories to Poland, the Dutch minister of economic affairs explained: "I think this behavior of Philips is common for corporations that operate in international markets. . . . The only thing a government can do . . . is provide for a maximally attractive place of business." One can almost see the minister impotently wringing his hands.

The privileged political position of market elites constitutes a flaw in democracy, a grant of power or influence that violates political equality. It also helps to explain why political elites tend to join with economic elites in a homogeneous defense of existing political and market institutions. And that throws more light on why neither political nor market elites in any market society have ever chosen, or even blundered into an attempt, to abolish the market system.

The privileged political position of the market elites is strengthened, I suggest, by popular perception that public policy must accommodate their elite needs. Masses of people who might otherwise support, for example, a higher legally required minimum wage do not do so for fear, not necessarily irrational, that its effects might be to induce employers to reduce their hiring. Or however unjust they may think tax reductions for the wealthy may be, they may still support them for fear of weakened incentives to investment. They know—but they are also taught—that "business confidence" is a plant that can either wither or flower. One sees their acknowledgment of the need to give business elites a privileged position in their frequent acceptance, however reluctant, of what is called the trickle-down theory. It promises that gains will trickle down from elites to mass if elites are well enough treated. If that is how gains are to be had—and often that is in fact how they are to be had—the immediate requirement then, is that elites first enjoy some gains. Hence a popular perception develops that market elites need a special position in politics in order to protect their gains.

The privileged position of business can on one great count be strongly defended: it is necessary to make the market system work. The defense grants that the market system does indeed obstruct democracy. It then goes on to say that this downgrading of democracy is a price worth paying for making the market work.

Up to some point, it makes sense to dull democracy in order to stimulate the market system, all the more so because they are both systems of popular control. Whether market societies in practice accept greater limits on democracy than are necessary to stimulate the market system is a question that these societies have rarely asked. Granting that some trade-off between the systems is required, the defects of democracy accepted in the trade-off are, however, more than skin deep. They imply a substantial wrenching of the political process to meet the needs of market elites, either by overriding or manipulating popular political demands. An example of both appears to be the many new advisory councils that the British Labour Party has installed in British government since 1998. They bring corporate executives into closer relations with the ministries, with some loss of power, it seems probable, by the established appointed officials. A society has to pay heavily for its market system in some loss of democracy.

For all the obstructions to democracy attributable to enterprises, especially corporations, few people propose to dispense with them. Most of us can hardly imagine a world without something very much like a corporation. Despite its obstructions to democracy, the corporation has been and continues to be a productive institution; and each society will perhaps shape an appropriate future with some form of it. Frankenstein created a crazy monster, but it was an insignificant accomplishment, even as allegory, when compared to mankind's collective creation of the corporation. For the corporation is sane enough to survive and flourish, as the monster was not. It is also immortal, as the monster was not. And it is capable of bestowing benefits or wreaking havoc the world over, as the monster was not. One can imagine a better democratic harness for the corporation. But how well it can be harnessed depends heavily on the corporation itself, for to escape the democratic harness it will run on its strong legs as freely as it dares.

# Thinking About Choices

# 18

## Alternative Market Systems

In France, market and government elites cooperate more intimately than in the United States, where they more often look on each other as adversaries. Or contrast Japan's long inattention to environmental pollution—it was once the "most polluted nation in the world"—with Britain's government-business cooperation to curb it. From multiple causes, new forms of market system emerge, sometimes hardly winning the attention of policy makers, sometimes their deliberate creation.

In the twentieth century, while policy makers were concerned with other choices on their agendas, the place of the market system in our lives was changed in deeply consequential ways by a massive movement of women into the workforce. Their tasks would now in large part be set by market demands rather than by the authority of husband or family tradition. With their new money income, women now buy in the market many of the services—and some goods—earlier produced in the home. Equally weighty unplanned changes may in the twenty-first century emerge from the Internet and new technologies of multilateral communication. Internet auctions, for just one example, greatly widen the range of choice open to market participants and probably increase the volume of market activity.

In this chapter I look at some of the choices open within a market system. What I shall say will sometimes make a persuasive case for certain alternatives over others, but that is not my purpose. I discuss alternatives because they illu-

minate the market system on some attributes so far ignored
or passed over too lightly.

Drawing on earlier chapters, we can deal with a number
of specific alternatives quickly. Hypothetically, at least,
every market society can choose a market system with very
little, more, or a great deal more state control of

- spillovers
- monopoly in its many forms
- corporate powers other than monopoly, including political powers
- managerial authority within the enterprise
- entrepreneurial motivation
- investment
- distribution of income and wealth

The alternatives are not limited to small differences.
They range from the intimacy between state and corporation in Japan in the 1960s to the continuing turbulent state-
corporate relations of the United States. And within any
one national system, on each of these variables wide choice
is open and consequential. How large nations like China,
India, Russia, and the United States choose to deal with
spillovers may be pivotal for the whole world.

Hypothetically, I said, a society can choose. Whether in
actual fact it can depends on how well the state, which is
the main lever for working on the market system, can be
harnessed either by a ruling elite or, in a democracy, by citizens. The odds are not encouraging, for the state itself is
deeply flawed. Among other obstructions stands the corporation. In its role in government it is itself a major barrier to
a better market system.

Among the aspects of the market system that have given
rise to choices on degree and character of state control, to-

day's most intense debates are on redistributions of income and wealth that depart from the rule of quid pro quo. The redistributions range from free public education through those of the welfare state, such as unemployment compensation and family allowances.

A colleague flatly declares to me that "the welfare state has proved it doesn't work." Clearly, the programs of the welfare state are often in trouble. Medical care is an especially telling example. Unwilling to consign lowest-income citizens to inadequate medical care, many market societies offer them subsidized or free care. But then how are demands for care to be held down to a feasible level, the price of care to the consumer no longer high enough to impose the necessary constraint? The welfare state is also plagued by government disposition to spend more than planned or anticipated. Welfare expenditures add to historically frequent excesses of spending, for example, on celebratory public works, on the military, on luxury for rulers, or on corporate welfare. But even taken by themselves welfare programs are the subject of increasingly severe questions when, with the aging of the population in many societies, the number of earners available to support beneficiaries continues to decline.

Nonetheless, these distributions appear to be here to stay. Market societies can choose among various designs of the welfare state, from stingy redistributions to careless excesses. A United Nations estimate rates the United States as the world's richest nation (per capita income), yet its welfare programs leave poverty at its highest level among industrialized nations. But abandoning the welfare state is not a choice. That welfare is judged necessary is a product of something called "civilization." It is also a strategy through which elites placate a potentially radical mass.

The welfare state has not yet had to cope with the prospect of permanent exile from the market system of able-bodied workers neither aged nor injured nor temporarily displaced but insufficiently productive. It is a frightening possibility: the rise of a new underclass consisting of millions of people with insufficient skill or capital to offer the required quid to win the necessary quo. If it forms, it needs not only income but jobs, together with the status that goes with jobs. Those not in the underclass are not likely to tolerate and support it in its idleness. Those in it are not likely to accept their idle exile quietly. Difficult choices may have to be made. Two legal scholars have recently presented a proposal to provide to every young adult American a once-in-a-lifetime $80,000 share in the capital wealth of that society, thus creating a society of stakeholders. One would expect significant national differences to emerge if the industrialized nations have to face a future of able-bodied market exiles.

## Two Visions

Your choices—mine too, or a society's—on each of the listed and other aspects of the market system are probably guided by a theory or model—not precise but roughly sketched in the mind—of a preferred relation between state and market system.

A common model or vision places the market system front and center, leaving the state with two subsidiary roles. The first role is to establish the legal foundations without which the market system cannot operate. In this model, that first state role raises few questions and is for the most part dismissed. The second role is captured in such words as "interference" and "intervention," or words less critical yet still negative in coloration, like "regulation." The model conceives of the state as a discordant element, at best a partly successful tinkerer, at worst a disrupter. Market participants consist of individual persons. The state is not a participant but a regulator, thus an influence from "outside" the market system and on that account to be regarded with suspicion. Insofar as the state tries to satisfy collective needs neglected by market purchases, it is inefficient. For it pursues such purposes as social amenities and environmental protection, which are of less value than marketed goods and services. It also often compels citizens who, the model postulates, should be free.

Among models alternative to this one, I choose a particular one not to advocate it—though its superiority to the first model will strike most readers as obvious—but to illuminate by contrast. In this second model, the state, a deeply imperfect institution, establishes, as in the first model, the legal foundations of the market system. But its support of the market system goes much further. That support—not interference or regulation but support—is constant and wide ranging. It includes the management of money and credit, subsidies and tax concessions, research and development, and opening up and protecting overseas markets, among many other aids. The state also plays a regulatory role, as in the first model; but that role is no more frequent or strong than the supportive role. The state is also a redistributor of income and wealth.

On top of these state roles in the second model are two other roles overlooked in the first model. The state is a market participant as buyer and seller. What is more, it is the largest buyer and seller in the system, buying the services of teachers, researchers, and highway contractors, as well as farm products, computers, and trucks. The state is also a

price setter for many goods and services. It sets minimum
prices on some farm products in order to bolster farm income. It sets maximum prices on electric power in order to
curb monopoly. It uses tariffs to set high enough prices on
an import to protect domestic producers of it. Price setting
is sometimes part of the state's regulatory role, sometimes
part of its supportive role, and sometimes a part of its redistributive role. As a multipurpose price setter, the state becomes a constant participant in markets, just as it does in
its role as buyer and seller. Both roles make the state an insider rather than a force from outside the market system.

In this second model, the collective purposes pursued by
the state are no less valuable than those pursued by individual participants in the market system. In fact, they are usually the same purposes. One of the reasons people who can
afford to do so buy houses in the suburbs is that they want
some of the amenities that more congested urban life does
not give them. Or they want an immediate environment of
green rather than of buildings and paved surfaces. Or they
want quiet rather than noise. These purposes are also the
purposes of collective choice in the hands of the state:
amenities and environment, among others. Because in some
circumstances they can be pursued effectively only through
compulsion—public education requiring, for example, the
compulsion of taxes—state compulsion is an accepted element in the model.

I prefer the second model and also find it more realistic.
Whether you do or do not, there is an implication in it that
greatly helps clarify our choices.

## Market System as State Administrative Instrument

By implication in the second model—and in reality too—
the market system is the major administrative instrument

of the state. It is by no means its only instrument, for often the state proceeds through outright commands and prohibitions. But it is the nearest thing to an all-purpose instrument. The state's use of it is routine and commonplace. Does the state intend to increase the provision of medical care? Then lower its price. Stimulate research? Then provide funds for it. Clean the air? Then put a charge on industrial-waste emissions. Reduce ethnic conflict? Then curb ethnic discrimination in hiring. In short, the common rule for state administration is: use the market system.

Many of us have been on the wrong track in identifying the market system with individualism, as though it could not serve collective purposes or could do so only exceptionally and badly. Clearly the state pursues a great variety of collective purposes. It does so—usually, typically—with controls made possible by the existence of a market system. The future of the market system is not bound up exclusively with individualism but with collective ventures as well. Understanding that is a prerequisite to making a clearheaded choice.

I think it worth while to walk through an explanation of exactly why and how the market system becomes the major administrative instrument of the state because, although everyone knows, most of us do not know that we know.

How might a government induce its citizens to do as they or their rulers believe is necessary? One answer is that it prohibits by command, forbidding undesired behavior, like excessive highway speed or arson. But how does it obtain positive performances from its citizens—how, for example, to get laborers to build highways? For positive performance, command is used only in limited circumstances, as in military conscription. Even authoritarian governments cannot effectively command more than a few of the positive performances they want from millions of citizens. There are better alternatives.

In one, the state buys the performances it wants just as you and I do when we pay a hairdresser to cut our hair. Directly or through contracting enterprises, it buys the varied performances necessary for new highways, medical care and production of food for the poor. And it buys or hires the tools and equipment people need in order to do what they are paid to do.

Thus the *purchase*, simple as it is, is a powerfully and precisely effective governmental administrative tool. As an administrative device, it is in most cases superior to command—more precise, more widely usable, less frequently escaped, and far simpler in use.

Two other common methods by which governments induce positive performances operate through altering the prices that shape the behavior of citizens. One way to do so is subsidize: subsidies to apartment construction, health care, shipping, farming, or any other industry producing services or goods for which markets and prices are already established. The subsidy supplements the purchase as a fundamental administrative instrument.

If subsidies can induce desired performances, an easy inference is that specific or targeted taxes can discourage performances not desired. Taxes on goods and services can, for example, curb polluting industrial emissions or specific kinds of international financial transactions. The tax then supplements the purchase and the subsidy as administrative instrument.

For whatever collective purposes the government might intend, ranging from national defense to beautifying the landscape, the administrative trio—purchase, subsidy, and tax—is at hand. Thus state purchases of recreational areas or physicians' services, common in market societies. Or Holland's remarkable subsidies to artists, Italy's subsidies to heavy industry, and Norway's regional subsidies to keep northern Norway economically alive. And in many societies, taxes to protect consumers from their own incompetence. Although that requires some outright prohibitions as well, as in food and drug regulation, it might call for a tobacco tax or, as has been proposed, even a heavy tax on aggregate family spending in order to curb the excesses of keeping up with the Joneses. Taxes and subsidies are sometimes disguised. Subsidies to middle-class housing, for example, are obscured in tax deductions for home-ownership expenses or for interest on mortgages, although in magnitude they may dwarf conspicuous outright subsidies to low-cost housing.

To supplement the trio, governments also use other devices that make use of prices rather than administrative commands. For example, by issuing to enterprises tradable or marketable limited permissions to pollute, government can raise the income and outputs of nonpolluting enterprises (they can sell their permits) and lower the incomes and outputs of polluting enterprises (they must buy additional permits). Or through a treaty, a group of nations can assign marketable pollution permits to each nation, thus encouraging each nation to curb emissions in order to be able to sell its permits and escape the necessity of buying any.

Purchase, subsidy, tax, and related devices can be used wherever citizens or their rulers want the state to intervene. And they can be used to make precise choices, as in subsidizing the production of a specific pharmaceutical product; or broader choices, as in subsidizing child care; or still broader ones, as in subsidizing savings rather than consumer spending. They can be used to transfer responsibility for choice from person to state, as when a tax is imposed to reduce tobacco consumption, or to transfer it from state to person, as through the use of vouchers that permit parents to choose a school for their child.

They can be brought to bear anywhere in the chain of production, as in subsidies to or taxes on a specific input— say, subsidized employment of partially disabled workers— rather than on an end-of-the-line consumer service or good. The state may choose, say, to reduce auto production by taxing each auto, or reduce production of large autos by taxing according to their weight or length, or reduce the steel used by the auto industry by taxing the metal rather than the car. Or it can use subsidies to schools or students to raise the level of education generally, or to increase the numbers of students in mathematics and science, or to open up opportunities for disadvantaged students.

In the world's market systems, taxes to raise or lower the production of a good or service are not so common as subsidies yet nevertheless frequent: for example, in the form of tariffs or other import charges to curb imports as part of an economic development strategy. Subsidies are more widespread less for good reasons than for lamentable. They are distributed largely at the initiative of recipients, usually enterprises, who mobilize political influence and then join to it an at least superficially plausible reason for a grant.

No line separates a defensible subsidy from a political handout. Using tariffs and other import restrictions, Japan subsidized a number of industries as part of what might be called planning for a new role in world markets. But it then went on in the 1970s to subsidize industries largely irrelevant to such an aspiration: cement, glass, steel, and petroleum refining. Subsidies to the logging industry have the unfortunate effect of speeding deforestation, but they are supported both by political influence and some genuine concerns for the welfare of communities that would transitionally suffer if logging declined. Indefensible or hard to defend subsidies are tucked away here or there in more industries than not, gifts to influential industries and enterprises, occupational groups, and communities.

State purchases, taxes, subsidies, and other devices for dealing with spillovers increasingly present societies with major choices. A society troubled with urban congestion and blight, at least occasional threat of epidemics, falling soil fertility, declining forests, exhaustion of mineral resources, and uneasy about global warming might be expected to step up its efforts to control spillovers. That describes almost every contemporary society. The growing magnitude and threat of spillovers has already stimulated a round of environmental legislation from North to South America through Europe and Africa to Asia. The market systems of the world are heavy users of taxes and subsidies, as well as outright prohibitions, to cope with them. The Dutch government, for example, now subsidizes antipollution devices in enterprises in Poland and the Czech Republic in order to reduce the air pollution that reaches Holland from them.

I do not intend here to enter into the contemporary debate on when to use market controls and when to use outright commands and prohibitions to cope, say, with environmental problems. My point is simply that all governments in fact use the described market controls broadly for collective purposes and that every society has choices to make on how to use them. Obviously nonmarket mandatory controls have their place.

If we contemplate not only the use of state purchases, subsidies, and taxes to cope with spillover and other problems but also for programs for reducing poverty, dampening the greatest inequalities in wealth and income, and softening the hardships of the quid pro quo, the market system alone is in some respects like an unfinished apartment building in which people can live if they must, but not well. It is not habitable until internal partitions, heat, light, and other amenities are installed. Without them, most people find it too dark, cold, and insecure.

With purchases, taxes, and subsidies, societies make the market system livable. But just as the apartment's heating system may turn out to be a contractor's rip-off or the internal partitions too flimsy, what the state attaches to the market system may range from inconvenience to disaster. If the market system is a structure to which the state can attach many improvements, nations differ greatly in what they attach and with what success. In this respect, every market society has always had and continues to have great choices.

It is no small point, however, that such improvements (the governmental programs) need the structure (the market system) to which they are attached.

# An Alternative to the Market System?

Within a market system, we can see—and I have noted—some alternative forms of it. These will continue to develop as each nation copes in its own way, with such problems as spillovers, corporate power, and inequality. But is there in our time an alternative to the market system as a whole? A choice between market system and . . . ? Well, that is our question. What is the present alternative, if any? Do societies face such grand choices as the old ones between capitalism and socialism or between market system and command system?

As an overarching method of social coordination, the clumsy mechanism I called physical planning—no money, no prices—is out. Nowhere in the world does there appear to be an interest in a moneyless system of central determination of production together with a governmental allocation of goods and services in which individual persons and families have no immediate choice. Or, to say it another way, everywhere in the world the advantage of consumer market choice, for both consumer and harried government official, is acknowledged. However production is controlled or planned, there seems to be no general method of distributing the output than by permitting each person or family to buy what is wanted by drawing on a sum of money that represents the person's or family's share in the total cooperatively produced output. It spares both administrator and consumers the irritations, arbitrariness, and inefficiency of ration coupons. Of course, some goods and services require special arrangements—some kinds of medical care to be distributed free, for example. But the superiority of consumer market choice as a general rule is now recognized. We noted that even authoritarian communist systems found it advantageous to make use of consumer choice. We can also imagine a system of central planning that makes near universal use—far beyond communist practice—of consumer choice.

Similarly, almost nowhere in the world is the case being made for recruiting a labor force by command, other than in special circumstances like military conscription. Again, both administrators and citizens find occupational choice far superior to conscription. Again, even authoritarian communist systems found it advantageous to make use of it. And we can imagine a central planning system making near universal use of it.

We can hardly doubt that, in addition, all societies will make use of purchases, subsidies, and taxes as administrative instruments of the state. Again, communist systems selectively did so. And we can imagine a hypothetical centrally planned nonmarket system making very wide use of them.

For societywide coordination, *the only alternative to a market system is, then, a system that in many respects looks like a market system. It too uses money, prices, consumer choice, occupational choice, and various market operations.* What difference then between the two look-alike systems?

The most common statement of the difference is that, despite these similarities, market systems use money, prices, and market operations to put the control of production in the hands of masses of market participants while the alternative system uses them in order to put the control of production in the hands of governmental authorities or planners. The market system does not centrally plan production; the alternative system does. In the market system, production responds not to central decisions but to consumer purchases made at efficiency prices—or at approximations to them.

The distinction is valid as far as it goes. The trouble with it is that, models of pure market system aside, all real-world market-system societies practice a great deal of central planning of production, whether it is called that or not. Despite the ascendance of the market system as the twenty-first century opens, national planning of production is not dead either as idea or practice, anathema as the word is in some circles. I mean by national planning those procedures through which a society or its rulers make efforts toward informed and thoughtful governmental choices about both the near and distant future. Whether or not one likes it, all societies make such efforts. Planning, so defined, has never been absent. The tyrants of antiquity sometimes practiced it; so did the Mercantilists, against whom Adam Smith made his case for the market system. So did the allied democracies to mobilize for the First and Second World Wars. Indeed, it is so commonplace that it might be said to need no label. We might just as well get over our nervousness about the word. It is within human cognitive capacity to make planning thus defined a tolerable success—but also of course within other human capacities, like avarice, to make it a failure.

Not fully realizing what they are doing, contemporary governments in market societies find themselves practicing planning as just defined—in industrial policy, for example. They also make some deliberate choices—sometimes wise, sometimes not—to engage in it, as in environmental policy. And we have just seen that governments in market systems often plan through purchases, taxes and subsidies.

So we had better say that a difference between any real-world market society and the alternative is that the market society engages less in central planning than does the alternative.

Although this reformulation diminishes the difference between market and nonmarket systems, it retains a mammoth distinction. For it tells us that central planning is suited to the pursuit by government of governmentally decided or collective goals while the market system is suited to the pursuit, sometimes by government but more often by millions of market participants, of a mix of collective and individualistic goals. Since human beings everywhere want to pursue both collective goals like the construction of roads and individualistic goals like food and entertainment, the advantage of the market system on this point seems obvious.

This is a fundamental—and on the whole highly useful—distinction between central planning and market societies if it is understood to be only roughly true. It is not wholly true, because government officials or planners, although acting for the collectivity, often set out to achieve the same individualistic goals, like better nutrition, that people seek through market purchases. And participants in market systems often organize collective organizations like gated communities.

Widely accepted as roughly valid, this distinction too does not go far enough. We need to add a further contrast—between planning method when the market system is used for planning, and planning method in the look-alike system. The contrast is not obvious and is less familiar than the first distinction just drawn.

Absent a market system, central planners either make decisions without regard to prices or guide their decisions by arbitrary prices that do not represent costs. In the market-system society, central planners, like individual consumers, face a set of efficiency prices (again, more precisely, approximations to efficiency prices), hence make their decisions in response to the cost information that the prices provide. *In short, efficiency prices guide market-system central planning but not the alternative form of planning.*

A third difference separates the two systems. Central planning without efficiency prices requires an enormous hierarchical structure of decision-making to coordinate the many lines of production decided on by the planners. Having determined what to produce, the centralists have to carry out its production and make an allocation of inputs to each line of production by issuing commands that reach down to all levels of an administrative hierarchy. Not so in planning through the market system. In the market system planning decisions are limited to raising or lowering prices to call for more or less of a product. Hence market planning leaves in place a multitude of entrepreneurs who produce in response to the planned prices just as they do to the unplanned prices of a market system without planning. *At the center of market planning is the price-watching entrepreneur, not a production planner, not a government official.*

## Market System as Planning Instrument

The market, of course, is not primarily a governmental planning system, and many people applaud it for just that reason. Yet when we say, as in the preceding chapter, that it is the major administrative instrument of the state, we are acknowledging that it is a major instrument of governmental central planning; and we can greatly advance our understanding of the market system if we see in a little more detail how market-system planning contrasts with older or more conventional concepts of planning.

For production destined not for sale or other distribution to millions of individuals or families but for collective purposes—research, recruiting a military force, building highways, and the like—decision makers or planners in a market system enter into markets to buy what they have decided needs to be produced. Unlike planners in a nonmarket system, they do not command, do not set production targets, do not assign inputs. They buy rather than command the goods and services they want. Efficiency prices tell them the cost of every choice they contemplate. And buying rather than commanding permits them to implement their decisions not through the coercion of commands but through the inducements of purchase.

For production destined, on the other hand, to be distributed to millions of consumers—food, housing, entertainment, and the like—market-system planning takes a different turn. We could imagine decision makers again simply buying production in the amount they think needed (and then selling it off to consumers, who for each product can in total have only what the planners have decided on). But we have seen that a much simpler method—and the one actually practiced in all market systems—is that decision makers raise the price paid to suppliers of a service or good for which they wish to increase production, and lower the price paid when they wish to decrease production. The former they do with a subsidy; the latter with a tax. Thus with a subsidy they increase the availability of housing or with a tax decrease the production of automobiles.

In both these methods of planning, market-system planning differs from the look-alike.

*Within the market system.* Market-system planning differs, first, in that it is, as is plain, embedded in an operating market system. It is not a rival to the market system. Nor are money, prices, and markets mere adjuncts to planning, as in the hypothetical alternative or as they were in the USSR and Maoist China. In mere numbers of decisions, most by far continue to be made in markets by consumers, workers, and entrepreneurs rather than by planners outside the market system.

*Efficiency prices.* It consequently differs, as we have already said, because those who make central decisions on production, whether cabinet members, legislators, or civil servants, possess cost information in the form of efficiency prices. In the look-alike, prices are arbitrary.

When officials tax and subsidize to modify or override the market choices of market-system participants, they are of course bringing collective values to bear—that is why they act. That means that, for any good or service in question, they regard market evaluations and efficiency prices as inadequate measures of cost. But efficiency prices nevertheless tell them what masses of participants value and the costs attached to every individual market choice. That is precious information. It permits them to compare existing market evaluations with their own. It also enables them to plan not by ignoring market evaluations but by amending them—by adding or subtracting rather than displacing. In the absence of a market system, they would have no such information, no such guidelines, and no such possibility of amending rather than displacing individual evaluations. They would have no efficiency prices to inform them about individual or popular evaluations.

*Sequential decisions.* Market-system planning differs in that it proceeds without a comprehensive plan for production—no five-year plan, not even a one-year plan. Instead it proceeds, as observation of it in any contemporary nation shows, with a sequence of decisions or plans for one or a few segments of the market system at a time, each segmental decision made in the light of earlier segmental decisions and in anticipation of those to come.

Some will deny that sequential decision making without a comprehensive plan deserves to be dignified with the word planning. Theirs is the old—and I think now antiquated—theory of planning. To see why nonsequential planning with five- or one-year plans is antiquated, you can usefully pause to compare national production planning with decisions on your own household expenditures.

If you were asked to write a family one-year plan—specifying what quantities you want of each service and good—you would find it hard to do. If you did manage to specify each, you could not be confident that you had anticipated changing desires, unanticipated circumstances, changes in costs, or availability of new services and goods. You do not know your family's medical needs in advance, or that the roof will begin to leak this year, or that you will want some new computer software that will appear on the market in July.

Happily, you never need to practice such all-at-once planning. Instead, the market system offers you a sequence of choices, each choice to be made whenever it suits you to decide. You weigh each choice in the light of choices already made—avoiding lamb chops two days in a row—and in the light of options in the near and distant future—if you buy a car, you will need insurance. Your choices are manageable, and you can reach a much higher level of competence on them than in the pursuit of a one-year plan. Very likely you have in mind elements of an overarching rough set of constraints for the year's spending, one that specifies, say, a limit on your year's spending on entertainment. But your planning is almost entirely specific to choices at hand and is sequential.

Although you can be as careless as you wish—and suffer the consequences—you can on the other hand study each possible decision with extended careful attention to past and future decisions relevant to it. Interdependence among decisions need not be slighted but can be examined free of the need to make simultaneous decisions. One decision at a time is all that is required, each decision as broadly and deeply studied or planned as you wish.

In older ideas of planning, national planners or decision makers are thrown into making all decisions simultaneously in a five-year or one-year plan. In that assignment, we have seen, they flounder. A more manageable and rational form of national planning permits decision makers or planners to confront in turn each of a sequence of decisions one at a time. That raises their competence, just as your opportunities to make endless sequential market choices raise yours. Their attempts to consider the interrelations of segments is eased by their release from the obligation of simultaneous decisions in all segments. Like you with your choices, they can study, do research on, and debate the desirable interrelations on each occasion on which they confront a single segmental decision.

Commenting on this distinction between the two forms of planning, a colleague declared to me that, given perfect information and unlimited human capacity for calculation and analysis, the two forms of planning would work equally well—would both work ideally. He misses the point. Human beings do not possess perfect information and unlimited analytical capacity. It is because they do not that the second form can accomplish—not ideally, but comparatively—what the first cannot.

*Discriminating scope.* A final distinction between the two methods of planning is in scope. Market-system planners are not God-like in the scope of their controls over society, and they routinely count on the market system to carry most of the burden of social organization. Despite their frequent pride in their plans, their efforts are those that are typically only marginal amendments to—marginal reshapings of—the results of the market-system coordination. Society loads on conventional central planners all the major allocative decisions on what is to be produced and, for each line of production, with which resources. In contrast, market-system planning limits central decisions on production to those lines of production for which a central decision is, in the eyes of citizens or their rulers, superior to decision by consumers in the market. On this point alone, the latter kind of production planning is simpler and more manageable—and less intrusive—than the alternative form. Not spread so thin, planners or decision makers can better and with less bruising do whatever they do.

Note, too, that in any line of production in which the market planners see no reason to plan, their choice to remain inactive does not leave a void or disorder, as would a failure to act in the alternative look-alike system. It leaves an existing market system operating. If they choose to subsidize mass transit, it is not because without their decision transit will come to a stop but because they believe they can improve an ongoing transport system. The transit system can operate without their decisions; the trains do not wait for them.

## A Reckoning

Contemplating, then, the difference between market system and its alternative—the latter a look-alike yet without efficiency prices and without an entrepreneurial core, is there a case for the market system? I do not doubt it. There is of course a case for the market system as an alternative to central planning, yet also, as we have just seen, as an instrument of central planning when that is desired. I have not, however, claimed that the market system with its prior determinations is generally efficient, even if efficiency prices give it at least one distinctive efficiency. Or that it is necessary for those freedoms of consumption and occupation that seem most often prized. And I have feared its offenses against democracy. And at least expressed concerns about its impact on personality and culture.

Our interest in recent chapters in attributes of the market system like its efficiencies and inefficiencies or its consequences for freedom should not obscure its most fundamental attributes discussed in the earlier chapters. Nor should the role of market system in planning do so. To recall those attributes, let us suppose that we agree—as most of us in fact do—in desiring to make some large room in our lives for cooperation, whether to arrange a car pool or day care for our children, build a house, or bring coffee from Colombia. Even if some of the desired cooperation requires the organizing hand of a central authority, we know that much of it can be left to individual efforts coordinated by mutual adjustment. We know that people will find many opportunities for cooperation that would never come to the attention of an authority, as well as many other opportunities that they can efficiently and happily seize without engaging and empowering a governmental authority. The

bedrock case for the market system rests on the merits of
mutual adjustment as a fundamental social coordinating
process.

Sometimes in mutual adjustment we will enter into cooperation—join a neighbor in repairing a fence—because a
project is pleasurable in itself. Sometimes we can arrange
mutually adjusting cooperation by no greater effort than
persuasion: "Can you give me a hand with this—I can't
quite manage it by myself." But usually more is required.
We need some stronger method of influencing others, especially in lasting mutual adjustment, in order to obtain their
cooperation, whether it is a performance or an object we
want. Most of us agree that threats of violence, physical
force, and other compulsions have to be forbidden as a general rule. What then is left? Only one rule or procedure:
each person can induce desired assistance from others by
making contingent offers of benefits to them. A simple,
great, and fundamental rule of social coordination.

I cannot imagine any reason for generally forbidding voluntary mutual adjustments of this kind nor any reason not
to expect great gains to follow from them. The benefits are,
as we have seen, enormously enlarged when money and
credit appear, together with entrepreneurs. Thus the most
basic argument for the market system is established. If individuals, families, and other groups are to enjoy a great array
of noncoerced opportunities for taking initiatives to arrange
cooperation, they need a market system.

The categorical case against the market system, then, is
dead. A society without any market system at all is not
worth considering for our futures. Lying beyond this general
claim for the market are the many particular claims we
have surveyed, some powerful, all to be matched against defects we have surveyed. The particular claims and alleged

defects are, perhaps, more disputable than the one general and underlying claim.

The general claim does not say that the market system is enough—far from it. Nor is it an endorsement of any existing market system, grossly deficient as they all are. It is only a claim that, among other institutions and social processes, some form of market system for some sphere of human interaction is of great value. It of course has to be supplemented by other forms of social coordination such as state, family, corporation, and the interactions of civil society, to which it must often give way.

The market system is consequential for all dimensions of our lives. It accomplishes what our forefathers would have considered to be an astonishing cooperation engaging the whole society, national and global. It helps keep peace in society. On the other hand, its rule of quid pro quo challenges the very notion of society. No, I am not smuggling into this paragraph a summary of the book, I am only sounding an earlier note. Think society, not economy. The market system can be understood only as a great and all-pervasive part of the structure and life of society.

What kind of society do you want?

# Notes

## Chapter 1. Market System Ascendant

The one great book on the market system, many would say, is Adam Smith's *An Inquiry into the Nature and Causes of the Wealth of Nations*, published in 1776. Others claim that ranking instead for Karl Marx, *Capital*, volume 1 of which was published in 1867, volume 2 in 1885, and volume 3 in 1894, the second and third after Marx's death through the collaboration of Friedrich Engels. Both books are available in many editions in many languages.

On the historical rise of the market system and differences among historians on its story, see Winifred Barr Rothenberg, *From Market-Places to a Market Economy: The Transformation of Rural Massachusetts, 1750–1850* (Chicago: University of Chicago Press, 1992).

On privatization, see John Vickers and Vincent Wright, editors, *The Politics of Privatisation in Western Europe* (London: Frank Cass, 1989).

In applying my definition of physical planning as planning without money, prices, or markets, use caution. The same term is elsewhere sometimes used to denote all planning, both with and without money, prices, or markets—that is to say, all alternatives to the market system.

For recent appraisals of the state of the market system: Robert Kuttner, *Everything for Sale: The Virtues and Limits of Markets* (New York: Knopf, 1997); and Robert Gilpin, *The Challenge of Global Capitalism: The World Economy in the Twenty-First Century* (Princeton, N.J.: Princeton University Press, 2000).

On the European common market, see Peter B. Kenen, *Economic and Monetary Union in Europe: Moving Beyond Maas-*

*tricht* (Cambridge: Cambridge University Press, 1995). See also Robert L. Heilbroner, *The Nature and Logic of Capitalism* (New York: W. W. Norton, 1985).

## Chapter 2. Society's Coordination

On how social order is achieved, Percy S. Cohen, *Modern Social Theory* (New York: Basic Books, 1968), is illuminating, especially chapter 2.

On mutual adjustment generally but especially in the biological world, Richard Dawkins, *The Blind Watchmaker* (New York: W. W. Norton, 1986) is extraordinary. On mutual adjustment in politics, see Charles E. Lindblom, *The Intelligence of Democracy: Decision Making Through Mutual Adjustment* (New York: Free Press, 1965).

The Polybius reference is to his *Histories* 6.10, trans. W. R. Paton (Cambridge: Harvard University Press, 1923).

## Chapter 3. Market-System Coordination

On market-system coordination as it actually develops in history, you might want to sample the descriptive and analytical riches of Fernand Braudel's *Civilisation Matérielle, Economie et Capitalisme: 15e–18e Siècle* (Paris: A. Colin, 1967); English ed. trans. Sian Reynolds, *Civilization and Capitalism: 15th–18th Centuries* (New York: Harper & Row, 1981).

## Chapter 4. Bones Beneath Flesh

Writers on the market system are largely in agreement on just what the subject is—just what a market system is. Yet readers will find the various accounts strikingly different from one another. Contrast my chapter, say, with the overall view of the market system that introduces many textbooks in economics. Or contrast my exposition with that in John O'Neill's *The Market: Ethics, Knowledge, and Politics* (London: Routledge, 1998) and both with John Kenneth Galbraith's earlier *The New Industrial State* (Boston: Houghton Mifflin, 1967). Different as these accounts are, if you allow for the inescapable (at least so far) imprecision of language in social discourse and even in social science that exaggerates disagreement, you will find a solid core of agreement. O' Neill's *The Market* includes an excellent bibliography on the market system in its relation to "ethics, knowledge, and politics."

If almost everyone seems to know that legal freedoms to make choices are necessary for a market system, a long history of controversy over property rights, in which property rights are attacked as a pernicious feature of an exploitive capitalism, leaves a legacy of confusion. To make market choices, consumers have to have property rights in money, as well as in the things they buy. The attack on property distinguishes property rights in productive assets, in the "means of production," from these personal property rights. The means of production, the argument goes on to say, ought not be in private hands.

Whether the means of production are in public or private hands, to organize production through a market system requires that some persons or authorities, whether government officials, corporations, or individual entrepreneurs, have legal rights to make use of, sell, buy, or rent productive assets. These legal rights will necessarily be very much like present rights to private property.

Some objections to property rights are of a different color: the objection is not to the rights but to the grossly unequal distribution of them in all existing market systems, an inequality that might be greatly diminished in future forms of the market system.

On property, see Tom Bethell, *The Noblest Triumph: Property and Prosperity Through the Ages* (New York: St. Martin's, 1998); and Gregory S. Alexander, *Commodity and Propriety: Competing Visions of Property in American Legal Thought, 1776–1970* (Chicago: University of Chicago Press, 1997).

## Chapter 5. Enterprise and Corporation

On corporate size and structure, see Bennett Harrison, *Lean and Mean: The Changing Landscape of Corporate Power in the Age of Flexibility* (New York: Basic Books, 1994); and Scott R. Bowman, *The Modern Corporation and American Political Thought: Law, Power, and Ideology* (University Park: Pennsylvania State University Press, 1996).

The remarkable story of the savings-and-loan debacle is in William Greider, *Who Will Tell the People: The Betrayal of American Democracy* (New York: Simon & Schuster, 1992), chapter 2.

Schumpeter's analysis of popular control of market elites and political elites is in his *Capitalism, Socialism, and Democracy* (New York: Harper & Brothers, 1942), chapter 21. An interesting short study is Richard Rose, *Accountability to Electorates and to the Market: The Alternatives for Public Organizations* (Glasgow: University of Strathclyde Center for the Study of Public Policy; Studies in Public Policy 144, 1985).

On the variety and extent of state regulation of enterprises the world over, John Francis, *The Politics of Regulation: A Comparative Perspective* (Oxford: Blackwell, 1993), is a good introduction.

On the move to teamwork and other horizontal rather than vertical methods of internal control, see Thomas Petzinger, Jr., *The New Pioneers: The Men and Women Who Are Transforming the Workplace and Marketplace* (New York: Simon and Schuster, 1999).

Do corporations grow because they are efficient or because of advantages of monopoly and governmental favor? Alfred D. Chandler, Jr., takes, with qualifications, the efficiency explanation in his *The Visible Hand: The Managerial Revolution in America* (Cambridge: Harvard University Press, 1977). William G. Roy takes, with qualifications, the alternative explanation in his *Socializing Capital: The Rise of the Large Industrial Corporation in America* (Princeton, N.J.: Princeton University Press, 1997).

On the frequency of various forms of enterprise ownership, see Henry Hansmann, *The Ownership of Enterprise* (Cambridge: Harvard University Press, 1996).

On privatization, see John Vickers and Vincent Wright, editors, *The Politics of Privatisation in Western Europe* (London: Frank Cass, 1989).

On troubling questions about the corporation, see David C. Korten, *When Corporations Rule the World* (West Hartford, Conn.: Kumarian, 1995).

## Chapter 6. Maximum Domain

Robert Kuttner, *Everything for Sale: The Virtues and Limits of Markets* (New York: Knopf, 1997).

## Chapter 7. Chosen Domain

On the ever-changing, ever-debated boundaries of the chosen domain of the market system, see Robert Kuttner, *Everything for Sale: The Virtues and Limits of Markets* (New York: Knopf, 1997).

For an analysis of arguments for allowing in, or excluding from, the market system, particular commodities like blood or body parts and particular services like counseling, see Margaret Jane Radin, *Contested Commodities* (Cambridge: Harvard University Press, 1996).

## Chapter 8. Quid Pro Quo

In his classic *The Great Transformation* (New York: Farrar & Rinehart, 1944), Karl Polanyi analyzes the causes and intolerable consequences of a historical process by which, in market systems, land, labor, and money are turned into commodities in a self-regulating market system. My analysis of the quid pro quo is in large part a restatement (excluding, for my purposes, what he says about land and money) using a terminology less troublesome, I think, than his.

On the absence of a correlation between a tight quid pro quo and high output, see studies in Thomas Byrne Edsall, *The New Politics of Inequality* (New York: W. W. Norton, 1984), 224–26.

On inequality of income and wealth, see United Nations Development Programme, *Human Development Report, 1997* (New York: Oxford University Press, 1997).

## Chapter 10. Market-System Efficiency

The reference to Carnegie is from Paul Johnson, *A History of the American People* (New York: HarperCollins, 1997), 552.

## Chapter 11. Inefficiencies

On the fears and predictions of environmental catastrophe from spillover from the World Resources Institute and other organizations, see William E. Halal and Kenneth B. Taylor, editors, *Twenty-First Century Economics: Perspectives of Economics for a Changing World* (New York: St. Martin's, 1999) 189 f.

On spillovers, Sharon Beder presents the evidence in her *Global Spin: The Corporate Assault on Environmentalism* (White River Junction, Vt.: Chelsea Green, 1998) that corporations are not simply inattentive but aggressively hostile to environmental protection. On the magnitude of the problem in China, see Lin Binyan and Perry Link, "The Great Leap Backward," *New York Review of Books,* October 8, 1998, 19–23. To see that spillovers are not a problem limited to heavy or smokestack industry, see how they appear in Silicon Valley in Aaron Sachs, "Virtual Ecology," *World Watch,* January–February 1999, 12–21.

On inequality, see United Nations Development Programme, *Human Development Report, 1997* (New York: Oxford University Press, 1997), and Cass R. Sunstein, *Free Markets and Social Justice* (Oxford: Oxford University Press, 1997).

On questionable or unacceptable entrepreneurial motivation, the references to illegal operations in the United Kingdom, France, Japan, and Germany are from David Vogel, *Kindred Strangers: The Uneasy Relationship Between Politics and Business in America* (Princeton, N.J.: Princeton University Press, 1996), 92ff and 102ff. On corruption, see Susan Rose-Ackerman, *Corruption and Government: Causes, Consequences, and Reform* (London: Cambridge University Press, 1999).

## Chapter 12. Too Little, Too Late

I recognize that many economists treat prior allocations as not having any consequences for efficiency but only for equity in distribution. Because market interchanges are voluntary, some economists see them as moving toward a situation, as in our game, in which everyone is better off for having engaged in them and in which, as at the end of the game, there are no further opportunities for mutually advantageous exchanges. That movement they see as of enormous consequence for human welfare, and they understandably wish to distinguish it from further possible interchanges, in which some participants can benefit only by taking benefits from others. So they call only the mutually advantageous moves efficient and declare the other moves, in which some people gain at the expense of others, to be neither efficient nor inefficient but only equitable or inequitable. Hence prior determinations are neither efficient nor inefficient, only equitable or not.

For many purposes theirs is an excellent distinction. But for our purposes it is regrettable that economists wish to appropriate the word "efficiency" for only the mutually advantageous interactions. The more common definition of efficiency—and the one used throughout our analysis—says that a choice or allocation is efficient if the gains warrant the losses, no matter on whom the gains or losses fall. Thus we can say of a decision on land use, for example, that we judge it to be efficient because the gains in recreational use of wilderness areas are worth the tax burdens imposed to support them, even if most taxpayers never visit the areas. Judgments of that kind are inescapable. Evaluations of the market system cannot do without them, whatever the terminology.

## Chapter 13. Freedom?

Advocates of the market system are, as I read and hear from them, more vocal on freedom than on efficiency as a market-system attribute. That may reflect their priorities, or it may simply mean that freedom is easier to argue than efficiency. In any case, two of the most conspicuous of them make freedom their dominant value. The late Austrian economist Friedrich A. von Hayek reached his largest audience with *Road to Serfdom* (Chicago: University of Chicago Press, 1944). His more scholarly works sounded the same theme, but with more sophistication. The University of Chicago economist Milton Friedman signaled his concern in his titles *Capitalism and Freedom* (Chicago: University of Chicago Press, 1962) and *Free to Choose: A Personal Statement* (New York: Harcourt Brace Jovanovich, 1980). The quality of his analysis of freedom in the market system does not match Hayek's nor the quality of Friedman's brilliant work in monetary theory.

Chapter 14. Personality and Culture

In contrast to speculation and historical interpretation, research findings on the effects of market system on personality and culture are relatively recent. They have been surveyed and analyzed in Robert E. Lane's *Market Experience* (Cambridge: Cambridge University Press, 1991); and those researches to which I refer are to be found there. It is a landmark book.

Marx deplored the effects of the market system in the *Communist Manifesto* (with Friedrich Engels in 1848). John Ruskin expressed his misgivings in *"Unto This Last," Four Essays on the First Principles of Political Economy*, edited by Lloyd J. Hubenka (Lincoln: University of Nebraska Press, 1967), 74ff. Erich Fromm in *Escape from Freedom* (New York: Rinehart, 1941); and Herbert Marcuse in *One-Dimensional Man: Studies in the Ideology of Advanced Industrial Society* (Boston: Beacon, 1964).

I think it correct to say that social-science thinking on the relation between market system and personality and culture was dominated for several decades by two excellent studies still exercising great influence: one by the polymath Max Weber, *Die Protestantische Ethik und der Geist des Kapitalismus* (1904–5), published in English as *The Protestant Ethic and the Spirit of Capitalism* (New York: Charles Scribner's Sons, 1930); and the other by the historian and social critic Richard H. Tawney, *Religion and the Rise of Capitalism* (New York: Harcourt, Brace, 1926).

Ferdinand Tönnies's distinction between *Gemeinschaft* and *Gesellschaft* appears in his book of that title in 1887 and in English under the title *Community and Society* (East Lansing: Michigan State University Press, 1957).

For current controversy, you might juxtapose Tyler Cowen, *In Praise of Commercial Culture* (Cambridge: Harvard University Press, 1998) and Robert H. Frank, *Luxury Fever: Why Money Fails to Satisfy in an Era of Excess* (New York: Free Press, 1999). And consider both in light of Richard Sennett, *The Corrosion of Character: The Personal Consequences of Work in the New Capitalism* (New York: W. W. Norton, 1998).

On the alleged decline of civic engagement, for two contrasting views, see Robert Putnam, *Bowling Alone: The Collapse and Revival of American Community* (New York: Simon & Schuster, 2000); and Everett Carll Ladd, *The Ladd Report* (New York: Free Press, 1999).

On the decline of happiness, see Robert E. Lane, *The Loss of Happiness in Market Democracies* (New Haven: Yale University Press, 2000).

For some insightful history of thought on market-system effects, see Albert O. Hirschman, "Rival Interpretations of Market Society," *Journal of Economic Literature* 20 (December 1988): 146–84.

## Chapter 15. Persuading the Masses

Some estimates of advertising expenditure, both U.S. and global, are in David C. Korten, *The Post Corporate World: Life After Capitalism* (West Hartford, Conn.: Kumarian, 1999), 32ff. A brief but highly insightful analysis of distraction and obfuscation is Neil Postman, *Amusing Ourselves to Death: Public Discourse in the Age of Show Business* (New York: Vintage, 1986).

On the public-relations content of news, see Sharon Beder, *Global Spin: The Corporate Assault on Environmentalism* (White River Junction, Vt.: Chelsea Green, 1998), 197.

For the alternative ways (idols, insinuations, manufactured will, and others) in which the concept of impairment of thought has been formulated, see Neal Wood, *The Politics of Locke's Philosophy: A Social Study of "An Essay Concerning Public Understanding"* (Berkeley: University of California Press, 1983), 95; Joseph A. Schumpeter, *Capitalism, Socialism, and Democracy* (New York: Harper & Brothers, 1942), 256–64; Jürgen Habermas, *Knowledge and Human Interest* (Boston: Beacon, 1971), chapters 3 and 9; and E. E. Schattschneider, *Semisovereign People: A Realist's Guide to Democracy in America* (New York: Holt, Rinehart and Winston, 1960).

The quotations on elite control of mass in the Renaissance are from John Hale, *The Civilization of Europe in the Renaissance* (New York: Atheneum, 1944), 464, 471.

I hardly know how to choose from a near torrent of publications that in recent years have documented the existence of massive programs of propaganda, "education," and special appeals directed at mass by elites. On corporate control and use of the mass media, see Dean Alger, *Megamedia: How Giant Corporations Dominate Mass Media, Distort Competition, and Endanger Democracy* (Lanham, Md.: Rowman and Littlefield, 1998). Don Herzog's *Poisoning the Minds of the Lower Orders* (Princeton, N.J.: Princeton University Press, 1998) looks back two hundred years. Amitai Etzioni, *Capital Corruption: The New Attack on American Democracy* (New York: Harcourt Brace Jovanovich, 1984), takes a broad view of a corruption of mind and politics from various sources. See also Beder, *Global Spin*, above. And for a long historical view of public discourse since Plato, see, by all means, Paul E. Corcoran, *Political Language and Rhetoric* (St. Lucia, Queensland: University of Queensland Press, 1979).

Charles E. Lindblom, *Inquiry and Change: The Troubled Attempt to Understand and Shape Society* (New Haven: Yale University Press, 1990), chapters 5–7, has more to say on the assault on the mind.

On class relations, Robert Perrucci and Earl Wysong explore what they see as a move from middle-class to two-class society in *The New Class Society* (Lanham, Md.: Rowman and Littlefield, 1999).

## Chapter 16. Necessary to Democracy?

The quotation from a British member of Parliament on the working classes becoming masters is from Robert McKenzie and Allan Silver, *Angels in Marble: Working Class Conservatives in Urban England* (Chicago: University of Chicago Press, 1988), 5.

A profound historical study of relations between market system and democracy is Barrington Moore, Jr., *Social Origins of Dictatorship and Democracy: Lord and Peasant in the Making of the Modern World* (Boston: Beacon, 1966).

## Chapter 17. Enterprise Obstructions to Democracy

On the corporation as a fictitious person, see William G. Roy, *Socializing Capital: The Rise of the Large Industrial Corporation in America* (Princeton, N.J.: Princeton University Press, 1996).

The striking estimate of U.S. government land gifts to railroads is from Paul Johnson, *A History of the American People* (New York: HarperCollins, 1997), 534.

A fuller development of the privileged position of business is in Charles E. Lindblom, *Politics and Markets: The World's Political-Economic Systems* (New York: Basic Books, 1977), chapter 13. See also *Time*'s series on corporate welfare (November 9, 16, and 30, 1998). The words of the Dutch minister of economic affairs are translated from *Parliamentary Proceedings* 1994–95, pp. 5085–88, 86th assembly, June 13, 1995.

For more on the relation between enterprise and democracy, see Neil J. Mitchell, *The Conspicuous Corporation: Business, Public Policy, and Representative Democracy* (Ann Arbor: University of Michigan Press, 1997); David Vogel, *Kindred Strangers: The Uneasy Relationship Between Politics and Business in America* (Princeton, N.J.: Princeton University Press, 1996); Kim McQuaid, *Uneasy Partners: Big Business in American Politics, 1945–1990* (Baltimore: Johns Hopkins University Press, 1994); and Daniel Yergin and Joseph Stanislaw, *The Commanding Heights* (New York: Touchstone/Simon and Schuster, 1998).

See also an interesting analysis of entrepreneurs turning away from hostility to democracy in Leigh A. Payne, *Brazilian Industrialists and Democratic Change: The Battle Between Government and the Marketplace That Is Remaking the Modern World* (Baltimore: Johns Hopkins University Press, 1994).

## Chapter 18. Alternative Market Choices

An informative set of studies on what lies ahead, with special attention to the Information Revolution, which is compared with the Industrial Revolution, is William E. Halal and Kenneth B. Taylor, editors, *Twenty-First Century Economics: Perspectives of Economics for a Changing World* (New York: St. Martin's, 1998).

On the difficulties of the welfare state, see Dean Baker and Mark Weisbrot, *Social Security: The Phony Crisis* (Chicago: University of Chicago Press, 1999). On its prospects, see Christopher Pierson, *Beyond the Welfare State? A New Political Economy of Welfare* (Cambridge, Eng.: Polity, 1991). On both, see Theodore R. Marmor, Jerry L. Mashaw, and Philip L. Harvey, *America's Misunderstood Welfare State: Persistent Myths, Enduring Realities* (New York: Basic Books, 1990).

The stakeholder proposal is from Bruce Ackerman and Anne Alstott, *The Stakeholder Society* (New Haven: Yale University Press, 1999).

# Index

Aristotle, 28, 200, 204
Assault on mind: by distraction, 217, 287; by obfuscation, 217–18, 287; through corporate and governmental public relations, 219–21; degradation of discourse, 219; and circularity, 221–25; on democracy-market-system connection, 232

Bacon, Francis: on "idols," 22
Barter, 54–55
Behavior pattern, market system as, 39–40
Black markets, 51, 181
Broadcasting, 213
Burdens: defined, 127; and costs, 128–29. *See also* Cost

Capital: markets for, 6; and "capitalism," 9, 57; creation of, 39, 141; corporate accumulation of, 63
Carnegie, Andrew, 140
Central planning: abandonment of conventional, 1; history, 6; with and without efficiency prices, 7, 269, 271; "indicative," 229; in both market and nonmarket systems, 267–68; scope of, 268; through subsidies and taxes, 270; market system as instrument of, 270–71; through sequential decisions, 272; in household, 272–73
Circularity: and inefficiency, 212; in market, 212, 214–16; in polity, 221–25; in history of thought, 222

Civil society, 104–6
Coincidence, first and second, 54–56
Collectives, corporations as, 57–58
Commercialism, 198–99
Communist systems: abandoning planning, 1; gangsterism, 2; markets in, 4, 48, 271; black markets in, 51; income distribution in, 122; allocative inefficiency in, 126, 138; spillovers in, 152; freedoms in, 181–82; personal relationships in, 202; degradation of work in, 204; ethics in, 204
Competition, 40, 69, 156. *See also* Monopoly
"Competition of ideas," 212, 222, 223
Compulsions: in spillovers, 186; in transaction termination, 186; to work, 186–87; in inequality, 187–88; of ignorance and irrationality, 188–90; in sales promotion, 189. *See also* Freedom; Voluntarism
Conflict: as source of coordination, 20; versus trade, 47; of classes, 48; in labor relations, 68–69. *See also* Elites
Consumer free choice: defined, 181; in communist systems, 181–82; in democratic central planning, 182; market system not required for, 182; contrasted with consumer sovereignty, 182–83; and freedom, 183–84; in all central planning, 265–66